GOR ■ Publications

Titles in the Series

H.-O. Günther and *P. v. Beek* (Eds.)
Advanced Planning and Scheduling
Solutions in Process Industry
VI, 426 pages. 2003. ISBN 3-540-00222-7

J. Schönberger
Operational Freight Carrier Planning
IX, 164 pages. 2005. ISBN 3-540-25318-1

Professor Dr. Christoph Schwindt
Institut für Wirtschaftswissenschaft
TU Clausthal
Julius-Albert-Straße 2
38678 Clausthal-Zellerfeld
E-mail: christoph.schwindt@tu-clausthal.de

Library of Congress Control Number: 2005926096

ISBN 3-540-25410-2   Springer Berlin Heidelberg New York

Springer is a part of Springer Science+Business Media
springeronline.com

© Springer-Verlag Berlin Heidelberg 2005
Printed in Germany

Cover design: Erich Kirchner
Production: Helmut Petri
Printing: Strauss Offsetdruck

SPIN 11409960   Printed on acid-free paper – 42/3153 – 5 4 3 2 1 0

Christoph Schwindt

Resource Allocation in Project Management

With 13 Figures
and 12 Tables

 Springer

Die Seele jeder Ordnung ist ein großer Papierkorb.

Kurt Tucholsky, Schnipsel

Preface

This monograph grew out of my research in the field of resource-constrained project scheduling conducted from 1995 to 2004 during my work as teaching assistant and assistant professor at the Institute for Economic Theory and Operations Research of the University of Karlsruhe. The aim of the book is to give an introduction to quantitative concepts and methods for resource allocation in project management with an emphasis on an order-theoretic framework allowing for a unifying treatment of various problem types. In order to make the work accessible for general readers, the basic concepts needed are reviewed in introductory sections of the book.

Many people have contributed to the outcome of this research. First and foremost, I would like to express my deep appreciation to my supervisor Professor Klaus Neumann, who introduced me to the field and the community of project scheduling. I have greatly benefited from his comprehensive scientific knowledge and expertise, his continuous encouragement, and his support. During all these years, his department has been a stimulating and attractive place for doing research and teaching in Operations Research.

Moreover, I would like to thank my former colleagues for many fruitful discussions on various research topics and their continuing interest in my work. A major part of my research has been done in collaboration with the colleagues of the Karlsruhe project scheduling group, Birger Franck, Cord-Ulrich Fündeling, Karsten Gentner, Steffen Hagmayer, Dr. Thomas Hartung, Dr. Roland Heilmann, Christoph Mellentien, Dr. Hartwig Nübel, Dr. Thomas Selle, PD Dr. Norbert Trautmann, and Professor Jürgen Zimmermann. Our work has been greatly influenced by the activities of a research unit on project scheduling funded by the Deutsche Forschungsgemeinschaft and involving colleagues from the universities of Berlin (Professor Rolf Möhring), Bonn (Professor Erwin Pesch), Karlsruhe (Professor Klaus Neumann), Kiel (Professor Andreas Drexl), and Osnabrück (Professor Peter Brucker). Numerous joint workshops on project scheduling and the "cooperative-competitive" spirit in this group have been a great incentive to work even harder.

Finally, I grateful acknowledge the help of several people in preparing the manuscript of this monograph: Klaus Neumann for many valuable comments on different versions of the manuscript, Gerhard Grill for carefully proof-reading and improving the English wording of the manuscript, Frederik Stork for pointing me to state-of-the-art contributions in convex programming, and Jürgen Zimmermann for making experimental results on resource levelling problems available to me. Of course the faults and deficiencies remaining are entirely my own.

Clausthal-Zellerfeld, February 2005   *Christoph Schwindt*

Contents

Introduction

Project management and resource allocation. A project is a major one-time undertaking dedicated to some well-defined objective and involving considerable money, personnel, and equipment. It is usually initiated either by some need of the parent organization or by a customer request. The life cycle of a project can be structured into five consecutive phases involving specific managerial tasks (cf. Klein 2000, Section 1.2). Starting with some proposal, several preliminary studies such as a feasibility study, an economic analysis, or a risk analysis are conducted in the *project conception phase* in order to decide whether or not a corresponding project will be performed. In the *project definition phase*, the objectives of the project are formulated, the type of project organization is selected, resources are assigned to the project, and different tasks with associated milestones are identified. Subsequently, the *project planning phase* at first decomposes each task into precedence-related activities by means of a structural analysis of the project. The time and resource estimations then provide the duration and resource requirements for each activity as well as temporal constraints between activities that are connected by precedence relationships. The result of the structural analysis and the time and resource estimations is the representation of the project as a network modelling the activities and the prescribed precedence relationships among them. Next, the temporal scheduling of the project provides the earliest and latest start times as well as the slack times of the activities, limitations with respect to resource availability yet being disregarded. The last and most complex issue of project planning consists in allocating the scarce resources over time to the execution of the activities. During the *project execution phase*, the implementation of the project is controlled by monitoring the project progress against the schedule which has been established in the project planning phase. In case of significant deviations from schedule, the resource allocation has to be performed again. The final *project termination phase* evaluates and documents the project after its completion to facilitate the management of future projects.

Each phase in the project life cycle requires specific project management techniques. Several recent textbooks on project management are devoted to the managerial and behavioral aspects of project conception, project definition, project planning, project execution, and project termination (see, e.g., Lewis 1998, Pinto 1998, Turner 1999, Keeling 2000, Meredith and Mantel 2002, or Kerzner 2003). This book is concerned with quantitative methods for the project planning phase and, more specifically, with the problem of optimally allocating resources over time.

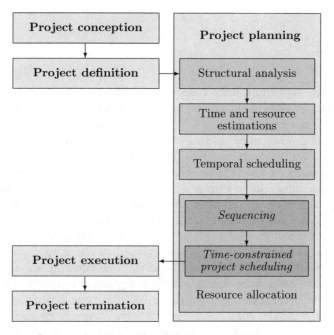

Project planning within the life cycle of a project

The complexity of resource allocation arises from the interaction between the activities of a project by explicit and implicit dependencies, which may be subject to some degree of uncertainty. Explicit dependencies are given by the precedence relationships between activities emanating from technological or organizational requirements. In the course of time estimation, those dependencies are transformed into temporal constraints between activities. The scarcity of the resources used establishes an implicit dependency between activities, which can be formulated as resource constraints referring to sets of activities competing for the same resources or in terms of an objective function penalizing excessive resource requirements. The *resource allocation* problem consists in assigning time intervals to the execution of the activities while taking into account the prescribed temporal constraints and resource scarcity. If resource constraints are given, we also speak of a resource-constrained project scheduling problem. We distinguish between two subproblems: *sequencing* and *time-constrained project scheduling*. The limited availability of resources necessitates the definition of additional precedence relationships between activities when performing the resource allocation task. Again, those precedence relationships can be expressed in the form of temporal constraints. In contrast to the structural analysis, however, the precedence relationships to be introduced are subject to decision. This sequencing problem forms the core problem of project planning. Time-constrained project scheduling is concerned with computing the project schedule such that all temporal constraints – predetermined by the structural analysis or arising from sequencing – are observed and some objective function reflecting the managerial goal of the project is optimized. In the resource allocation methods developed in this book, sequencing and time-constrained project scheduling will be performed jointly in an iterative manner.

If activities can be performed in alternative execution modes that differ in durations and resource requirements, the selection of an appropriate execution mode for each activity may be included into the resource allocation problem. In that case, the time and resource estimations provide the sets of alternative execution modes, and solving the mode assignment problem constitutes the first step of resource allocation. Depending on whether the sets of execution modes are countable or uncountable, we speak of a discrete or a continuous mode assignment problem. A resource allocation problem that comprises a mode assignment problem is termed a multi-mode resource allocation problem.

Historical perspective and state of the art. Algorithms for resource allocation in project management date back to the 1960s, see Davis (1966), Laue (1968), Herroelen (1972), and Davis (1973) for overviews. The early work was concerned with three types of resource allocation problems: the time-cost tradeoff problem, the project duration problem, and the resource levelling problem. For all three problem types it is assumed that a strict order in the set of activities specifies completion-to-start precedence constraints among activities. The *time-cost tradeoff problem* is a multi-mode resource allocation problem which arises when certain activity durations can be reduced at the expense of higher direct cost. The project budget is then regarded as the resource to be allocated. If for each activity the cost incurred is a convex function in the activity duration, the continuous mode assignment problem that consists in computing all combinations of project duration and corresponding least-cost schedule can be determined by applying network flow techniques (see Kelley 1961). A survey of multi-mode resource allocation problems including different types of tradeoffs between the durations, resource requirements, and direct costs of activity execution modes can be found in Domschke and Drexl (1991). The *project duration problem* consists in scheduling the activities of a project subject to the limited availability of renewable resources like manpower or machinery such that all activities are completed within a minimum amount of time. Early approaches to solving the project duration problem include mixed-integer linear programming formulations (see, e.g., Wiest 1963) and priority-rule methods (cf. Kelley 1963, Verhines 1963, and Moder and Phillips 1964). The objective when dealing with a *resource levelling problem* is to "smooth" the utilization of renewable resources over time as much as possible, within a prescribed maximum project duration. In some cases, a desired threshold limit on the resource availability is given, and resources are to be levelled around this target. In other cases, one strives at minimizing the variance of resource utilization over time or minimizing the absolute magnitude of fluctuation in the resource profiles. The first procedures for resource levelling offered by Burgess and Killebrew (1962) and Levy et al. (1963) were based on sequentially moving in time slack activities.

In the following years, a great deal of effort has been devoted to heuristic and exact algorithms for the project duration problem. In the 1990s, project planning methods gained increasing importance from their applicability to scheduling problems arising beyond the area of proper project management, for example, in production planning, time-tabling, or investment scheduling. Different generalizations of the basic resource allocation problems have received growing attention in recent years. Those expansions include a variety of objectives as well as the presence of different kinds of resources, general temporal constraints given by prescribed minimum and maximum time lags between the start times of activities, and uncertainty with respect to activity durations. For a review of solution procedures, we refer to the survey papers by Icmeli et al. (1993), Elmaghraby (1995), Özdamar and Ulusoy (1995), Tavares (1995), Herroelen et al. (1998), Brucker et al. (1999), Kolisch and Padman (2001), and Kolisch (2001a). A comprehensive state-of-the-art overview of the field is given by the handbook of Demeulemeester and Herroelen (2002), with an emphasis on algorithms for project scheduling problems with precedence constraints among activities instead of temporal constraints. A detailed treatment of specific project scheduling problems of the latter type can be found in the monographs by Kolisch (1995), Schirmer (1998), Hartmann (1999a), Klein (2000), and Kimms (2001a). The book by Hajdu (1997) is mainly concerned with several types of time-cost tradeoff problems. Solution procedures for several project scheduling problems with general temporal constraints have been discussed by De Reyck (1998), De Reyck et al. (1999), Neumann and Zimmermann (1999a), Zimmermann (2001a), and Neumann et al. (2003b). Models and algorithms for project scheduling with stochastic activity durations are studied in the doctoral dissertations of Stork (2001) and Uetz (2002). A review of models and algorithms for projects with stochastic evolution structure can be found in Neumann (1999b).

Contribution. In this monograph we discuss structural issues, efficient solution methods, and applications for various types of *deterministic resource allocation problems* including general temporal constraints, different types of resource requirements, and several classes of objective functions. The diversity of the models dealt with permits us to cover many features that arise in industrial scheduling problems. Each resource allocation problem gives rise to a corresponding project scheduling model, which provides a formal statement of the resource allocation task as an optimization problem. This model may or may not include explicit resource constraints. In the latter case, limitations on the availability of resources are taken into account by the objective function. Our main focus in this book is on developing a unifying algorithmic framework within which the different kinds of project scheduling models can be treated. This framework is based on the seminal work by research groups around Rolf Möhring and Franz-Josef Radermacher, who have proposed an order-theoretic approach to stochastic and deterministic resource-constrained project scheduling (see, e.g., Radermacher 1978, Möhring 1984, Radermacher 1985, or Bartusch et al. 1988). We extend the order-theoretic approach to resource allocation problems involving so-called cumulative resources, which represent a generalization of both renewable and nonrenewable resources known thus far. Based on the results of a structural analysis of resource constraints and objective functions, we discuss two general types of resource allocation procedures. By enhancing the basic models treated with supplemental kinds of constraints we bridge the gap between issues of greatly academic interest and requirements emerging in industrial contexts.

Synopsis. The book is divided into six chapters. Chapter 1 provides an introduction to three basic project scheduling models. First we address project scheduling subject to temporal constraints and review how the temporal scheduling calculations for a project can be performed efficiently by calculating longest path lengths in project networks. We then discuss resource constraints which arise from the scarcity of renewable resources required. If the availability of a resource at some point in time depends on all previous requirements, we speak of a cumulative resource. We consider the case where cumulative resources are depleted and replenished discontinuously at certain points in time. The available project funds, depleted by disbursements and replenished by progress payments, or the residual storage space for intermediate products are examples of cumulative resources. For both kinds of resource constraints, we explain how to observe the limited resource availability by introducing precedence relationships between activities.

In Chapter 2 we discuss a relation-based characterization of feasible schedules, which is based on different types of relations in the set of activities. Each relation defines a set of precedence constraints between activities. This characterization provides two representations of the feasible region of project scheduling problems as unions of finitely many relation-induced convex sets. Whereas the first representation refers to a covering of the feasible region by relation-induced polytopes, the second representation arises from partitioning the feasible region into sets of feasible schedules for which the same precedence constraints are satisfied. Those two representations are the starting point for a classification of schedules as characteristic points like minimal or extreme points of certain relation-induced subsets of the feasible region. For different types of objective functions, we show which class of schedules has to be investigated for finding optimal schedules.

Depending on the objective function under study, we propose two different basic solution approaches. Chapter 3 is dedicated to relaxation-based algorithms, which at first delete the resource constraints and solve the resulting time-constrained project scheduling problem. Excessive resource utilization is then stepwise settled by iteratively introducing appropriate precedence relationships between activities (i.e., sequencing) and re-performing the time-constrained project scheduling. For different objective functions, we discuss efficient primal and dual methods for solving the time-constrained project scheduling problem. Those methods are used within branch-and-bound algorithms based on the relaxation approach.

If we deal with objective functions for which time-constrained project scheduling cannot be performed efficiently, we apply a constructive approach. The candidate schedules from the respective class are enumerated by constructing schedule-induced preorders in the activity set and investigating appropriate vertices of the corresponding polytopes. In Chapter 4 we treat local search algorithms operating on those sets of vertices, where the schedules are represented as spanning trees of preorder-induced expansions of the underlying project network.

Chapter 5 is concerned with several expansions of the basic project scheduling models. First we discuss the case where during certain time periods given by break calendars, resources are not available for processing activities. Certain activities may be suspended at the beginning of a break, whereas other activities must not be interrupted. Suspended activities have to be resumed immediately after the break. The second expansion consists in sequence-dependent changeover times between the activities of a project. Changeover times occur, for example, if the project is executed at distributed locations and resources have to be transferred between the different sites. Next, we review methods to discrete multi-mode project scheduling, where activities can be performed in a finite number of alternative execution modes. Finally, we consider continuous cumulative resources that are depleted and replenished continuously over time.

In Chapter 6 we discuss several applications of the models treated in Chapters 1 to 5 to scheduling problems arising outside the field of proper project planning in production planning (make-to-order and small-batch production in manufacturing, batch scheduling in the process industries) and finance (evaluation of investment projects). Finally, we propose two alternative techniques for coping with uncertainty in project scheduling, which is commonly encountered when performing real-life projects.

1

Models and Basic Concepts

In this chapter we introduce three basic project scheduling problems: the time-constrained project scheduling problem, the resource-constrained project scheduling problem with renewable resources, and the resource-constrained project scheduling problem with cumulative resources. The time-constrained project scheduling problem consists in scheduling the activities of a project such that all temporal constraints are satisfied and some objective function is optimized. We review how temporal scheduling of the project can be performed by solving specific time-constrained project scheduling problems. We distinguish between two types of resources, namely renewable and cumulative resources, depending on whether or not resource availability at a given point in time is affected by the complete past project evolution. For both types of resources we show how to cope with resource constraints by establishing precedence relationships among the activities from so-called forbidden sets, whose joint resource requirements exceed the resource availability.

1.1 Temporal Constraints

1.1.1 Time-Feasible Schedules

A project can be considered to be a set of interacting tasks requiring time and resources for their completion. The structural analysis of the project provides a decomposition of the tasks into a set V of activities and a set E of precedence relationships among them. Set V consists of n activities $i = 1, \ldots, n$ to be scheduled and two auxiliary activities 0 and $n + 1$, representing the project beginning and the project termination, respectively. The precedence relationships can be represented as activity pairs (i, j) where $i \neq j$, saying that the start time of activity i affects the earliest start time of activity j. Thus, $E \subset V \times V$ is some irreflexive relation in set V. Note that this relation may not be asymmetric if there are two activities $i, j \in V$ which mutually influence their earliest start times. The time estimation associates a duration

$p_i \in \mathbb{Z}_{\geq 0}$ with each activity and a time lag $\delta_{ij} \in \mathbb{Z}$ with each pair $(i,j) \in E$. An activity $i \in V$ is referred to as *fictitious activity* or *event* if $p_i = 0$. Otherwise, we speak of a *real activity*. The project beginning and termination, the receipt of materials, or milestones are examples of events. V^a and V^e respectively denote the sets of real activities and events of the project. We assume that the real activities must not be interrupted once they have been begun. Let S_i denote the start time of activity i, which has to be determined when scheduling the project in the temporal scheduling and resource allocation steps. If i is a fictitious activity, S_i is also termed the occurrence time of event i. The time lags δ_{ij} give rise to the *temporal constraints*

$$S_j - S_i \geq \delta_{ij} \quad ((i,j) \in E) \tag{1.1}$$

If $(i,j) \in E$, activity j cannot be started earlier than δ_{ij} units of time after the start of activity i. A nonnegative value of δ_{ij} corresponds to a *minimum time lag* $d_{ij}^{min} = \delta_{ij} \geq 0$ between activities i and j, whereas a negative value of δ_{ij} can be viewed as a *maximum time lag* $d_{ji}^{max} = -\delta_{ij} > 0$ between activities j and i. If $d_{ij}^{min} = p_i$, inequality (1.1) is referred to as a *precedence constraint* between activities i and j. For what follows, we establish the following convention.

Remark 1.1. The project is started at time 0 and must be completed by a prescribed deadline $\overline{d}$, i.e., $S_0 = 0$ and $S_{n+1} \leq \overline{d}$. The deadline is represented as a maximum time lag $d_{0,n+1}^{max} = \overline{d}$ between the project beginning 0 and the project termination $n+1$.

The temporal constraints (1.1) connect the *start* times of activities i and j. Since by assumption activities must not be interrupted when being in progress,

$$C_i := S_i + p_i$$

is the completion time of activity i. Thus, start-to-start, start-to-completion, completion-to-start, and completion-to-completion relationships among activities can easily be transformed into one another (cf. e.g., Bartusch et al. 1988).

Remark 1.2. Some constraints that occur frequently in practice can be modelled by minimum and maximum time lags between activities (see Neumann and Schwindt 1997):

(a) Release date r_i for the start of activity i (head of i): $d_{0i}^{min} = r_i$.
(b) Deadline $\overline{d}_i$ for the completion of activity $i \in V$: $d_{0i}^{max} = \overline{d}_i - p_i$.
(c) Quarantine time q_i after the completion of activity i (tail of i):
   $d_{i,n+1}^{min} = p_i + q_i$.
(d) Fixed start time t_i for activity i: $d_{0i}^{min} = d_{0i}^{max} = t_i$.
(e) Simultaneous start of activities i and j: $d_{ij}^{min} = d_{ij}^{max} = 0$.
(f) Simultaneous completion of activities i and j with $p_i \geq p_j$:
   $d_{ij}^{min} = d_{ij}^{max} = p_i - p_j$.

(g) Consecutive execution of activities i and j without any delay in between:
$d_{ij}^{min} = d_{ij}^{max} = p_i$.

(h) Overlapping of activities i and j for at least $x_{ij} \leq \min(p_i, p_j)$ units of time: $d_{ij}^{max} = p_i - x_{ij}$, $d_{ji}^{max} = p_j - x_{ij}$.

From $C_i = S_i + p_i$ it follows that the schedule for executing the activities $i \in V$ of the project is uniquely given by specifying the respective start times S_i. That is why we shall always represent solutions to project scheduling problems by a vector of activity start times.

Definition 1.3 (Time-feasible schedule). *A vector $S = (S_0, S_1, \ldots, S_{n+1})$ of start times for the activities where $S_i \geq 0$ $(i \in V)$ and $S_0 = 0$ is called a schedule. Schedule S is said to be time-feasible if it satisfies the temporal constraints (1.1). The set of all time-feasible schedules is denoted by $\mathcal{S}_T$.*

Obviously, set $\mathcal{S}_T$ represents an integral polytope in $\mathbb{R}_{\geq 0}^{n+2}$. Assume that $\mathcal{S}_T \neq \emptyset$. It is well-known that the partially ordered set $(\mathcal{S}_T, \leq)$ possesses exactly one minimum ES, where $S \leq S'$ precisely if $S_i \leq S_i'$ for all $i \in V$. We refer to ES as the *earliest schedule*. Furthermore, by Remark 1.1 $(\mathcal{S}_T, \leq)$ possesses exactly one maximum LS, which is termed the *latest schedule*. This means that there is no time-feasible schedule S such that $S_i < ES_i$ or $S_i > LS_i$ for any $i \in V$. The interval $[ES_i, LS_i]$ is termed the *time window* (for the start) of activity i.

Now let $f : \mathcal{S}_T \to \mathbb{R}$ be an *objective function* assigning a value $f(S)$ to each time-feasible schedule S. Without loss of generality we assume that the objective function has to be minimized. The basic *time-constrained project scheduling problem* can then be stated as follows:

$$\boxed{\begin{array}{ll} \text{Minimize} & f(S) \\ \text{subject to} & S \in \mathcal{S}_T \end{array}} \qquad (1.2)$$

Definition 1.4 (Time-optimal schedule). *A time-feasible schedule S solving the time-constrained project scheduling problem (1.2) is called time-optimal.*

All objective functions that will be considered in this book are lower semi-continuous, i.e., any lower-level set $L_\alpha = \{S \in \mathcal{S}_T \mid f(S) \leq \alpha\}$, $\alpha \in \mathbb{R}$, is closed. Since set $\mathcal{S}_T$ is compact, this property ensures that there always exists a time-optimal schedule provided that $\mathcal{S}_T \neq \emptyset$.

1.1.2 Project Networks

In this subsection we shall show how the activities $i \in V$ and the temporal constraints $S_j - S_i \geq \delta_{ij}$ for $(i, j) \in E$ can be represented by a *project network*. Basically, there are three different types of project networks. *Activity-on-arc* or *CPM networks* associate an arc (u, v) with each activity i, where the nodes u and v represent events (see Kelley 1961). CPM stands for "Critical Path Method", a temporal scheduling method based on activity-on-arc networks. u is the first start of all activities i belonging to arcs emanating from node u, whereas v is the last completion of all activities i belonging to arcs terminating at node v. Arc (u, v) is weighted by the duration p_i of the corresponding activity i. Though only precedence constraints can be modelled by CPM networks, this type of project network is widely used in practice. In general, dummy activities have to be introduced for modelling the precedence constraints among the activities and there is no unique representation of the project as a CPM network. The problem to assign a CPM network to the project in question using a minimum number of dummy activities is known to be NP-hard (cf. Garey and Johnson 1979, problem ND44). Neumann (1999a) devises an $\mathcal{O}(n^6)$ time algorithm for the construction of a CPM network with a small number of dummy activities, which is based on a procedure by Brucker (1973).

In *activity-on-node networks*, the nodes are identified with the activities. For each time lag δ_{ij}, the network contains one arc (i, j) with initial node i and terminal node j, i.e., V is the node set and E is the arc set of the network. An arc $(i, j) \in E$ is weighted by δ_{ij}. Activity-on-node networks belong to the class of *MPM networks* (cf. Roy 1964, Sect. II.2.1). MPM is the acronym of "Metra Potential Method", the temporal scheduling method for activity-on-node networks to be discussed in Subsection 1.1.3. Similar to CPM, MPM is based on calculating longest directed paths in the project network. Obviously, activity-on-node networks can cope with general temporal constraints. In addition, due to the one-to-one correspondence between precedence relationships and arcs, there is a unique activity-on-node representation of the project (cf. Neumann and Schwindt 1997).

Elmaghraby and Kamburowki (1992) have introduced the following *event-on-node network*. Each real activity i is represented by two events i^s and i^c in node set V. i^s corresponds to the start and i^c to the completion of activity i. Both nodes are linked by two arcs (i^s, i^c) and (i^c, i^s) with weights $\delta_{i^s i^c} = p_i$ and $\delta_{i^c i^s} = -p_i$. For each time lag δ_{ij} between activities i and j, arc set E contains an arc (i^c, j^s) with weight $\delta_{i^c j^s} = \delta_{ij} - p_i$. Analogously to activity-on-node networks, the arcs of the resulting MPM network can be interpreted as minimum and maximum time lags between the incident events. The arcs (i^s, i^c) and (i^c, i^s) state that the completion of activity i must occur exactly p_i units of time after its start, i.e., activity i must not be interrupted. The arcs (i^c, j^s) represent completion-to-start time lags between activities i and j.

Example 1.5. We consider a project with four real activities $i = 1, 2, 3, 4$ for which we assume that activities 3 and 4 cannot be started before activities 1 and 2 have been completed. The project must be completed by a prescribed deadline $\bar{d}$. Figure 1.1a shows the corresponding activity-on-arc project network, where the dashed-line arcs represent dummy activities required for modelling the precedence relationships. The arcs are labelled with the durations of the respective activities. The activity-on-node network of the project is shown in Figure 1.1b, where square nodes correspond to real activities and circular nodes represent events. By splitting up each real activity into a start and a completion event, one obtains the representation of the project as an event-on-node network, which is shown in Figure 1.1c.

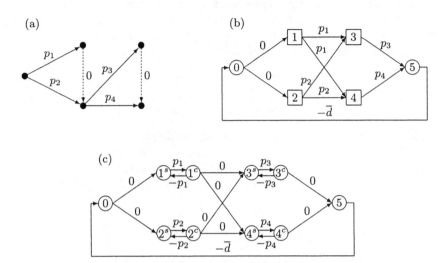

Fig. 1.1. Types of project networks: (**a**) activity-on-arc network; (**b**) activity-on-node network; (**c**) event-on-node network

Throughout this monograph, we shall represent projects by MPM networks. If not stated otherwise, the project network is an activity-on-node network. Event-on-node networks will be used when dealing with project scheduling problems where events instead of activities take up resources (the case of cumulative resources treated in Section 1.3).

1.1.3 Temporal Scheduling Computations

In this subsection we review the Metra Potential Method for the temporal scheduling of the project. Let $N = (V, E, \delta)$ be the MPM network under consideration, where $\delta = (\delta_{ij})_{(i,j)\in E}$ denotes the vector of arc weights. Temporal scheduling consists of

(a) computing earliest and latest start time of activities,
(b) finding the shortest project duration,
(c) calculating total floats, early free floats, and late free floats of activities, and
(d) identifying the critical activities with zero total float

with respect to the temporal constraints (1.1).

A vector $\pi \in \mathbb{R}^{n+2}$ is called a *potential* on project network N if the corresponding *tensions* $\pi_j - \pi_i$ are greater than or equal to the respective lower bounds δ_{ij} (cf. Berge 1970, Sect. 5.3). Let S be some schedule and assume that $S_T \neq \emptyset$. Clearly, S is a potential on N if and only if schedule S is time-feasible. The earliest schedule ES thus corresponds to the componentwise minimal potential $\pi \geq 0$, and the latest schedule LS equals the componentwise maximal potential $\pi \geq 0$ with $\pi_0 = 0$ (and thus $\pi_{n+1} \leq \overline{d}$, see Remark 1.1). In other words, ES is the unique solution to the following minimization problem:

$$\left.\begin{array}{ll} \text{Minimize} & \sum_{i \in V} \pi_i \\ \text{subject to} & \pi_j - \pi_i \geq \delta_{ij} \quad ((i,j) \in E) \\ & \pi_i \geq 0 \qquad\qquad (i \in V) \end{array}\right\} \qquad (1.3)$$

Problem (1.3) corresponds to the time-constrained optimization problem (1.2) where $f(S) = \sum_{i \in V} S_i$. The latest schedule LS is obtained by solving (1.3) with objective function $-\sum_{i \in V} \pi_i$ and additional constraint $\pi_0 = 0$.

Now let $D = (d_{ij})_{i,j \in V}$ be the matrix solving the following system of equations

$$\left.\begin{array}{ll} d_{ii} = 0 & (i \in V) \\ d_{ij} = \max\limits_{(h,j) \in E}(d_{ih} + \delta_{hj}) & (i,j \in V : i \neq j) \end{array}\right\} \qquad (1.4)$$

The values d_{ij} can be interpreted as time lags between activities i and j which are induced by the set of given time lags δ_{ij} $((i,j) \in E)$.

Remarks 1.6.

(a) Due to $\delta_{ij} \in \mathbb{Z}$ for all $(i,j) \in E$, matrix D is integral as well.

(b) For each activity $i \in V$, we assume that $d_{0i} \geq 0$ (i.e, activity i cannot be started before the project beginning) and $d_{i,n+1} \geq p_i$ (i.e., the project cannot be terminated before all activities have been completed).

(c) Each node $i \in V$ in project network N is reachable from node 0 and node $n + 1$ is reachable from each node $i \in V$. Since we always have a maximum time lag $d_{0,n+1}^{max} = -\delta_{n+1,0} = \overline{d}$ between the project beginning and the project termination and thus $(n + 1, 0) \in E$, project network N is strongly connected.

(d) Without loss of generality we assume that $\overline{d}$ is the latest project termination time, i.e., $d_{n+1,0} = \overline{d}$.

(e) The minimum time lag between the project beginning and activity i equals the earliest start time ES_i of activity i, i.e.,

$$ES_i = d_{0i} \quad (i \in V)$$

(f) Likewise, the maximum time lag between the project beginning and activity i equals the latest start time of activity i, i.e.,

$$LS_i = -d_{i0} \quad (i \in V)$$

If there is no given maximum time lag $d_{0i}^{max} = -\delta_{i0}$ between the project beginning and activity i, then $LS_i = \bar{d} - d_{i,n+1}$.

(g) The earliest and latest completion times of activity i are

$$EC_i = ES_i + p_i \text{ and } LC_i = LS_i + p_i \quad (i \in V)$$

Recall that a directed walk in network N is a sequence $(i_1, i_2, \ldots, i_\nu)$ of nodes of N such that $(i_\mu, i_{\mu+1}) \in E$ for all $\mu = 1, \ldots, \nu - 1$, where the sum $\sum_{\mu=1}^{\nu-1} \delta_{i_\mu i_{\mu+1}}$ is referred to as the length of the directed walk. A directed walk without any repetition of nodes is called a directed path. A directed cycle is a directed walk $(i_1, i_2, \ldots, i_\nu, i_1)$ such that $(i_1, i_2, \ldots, i_\nu)$ is a directed path. The lower equations in (1.4) correspond to the Bellman equations for calculating longest directed walks in MPM networks. Thus, each induced time lag d_{ij} coincides with the length of a longest directed walk from node i to node j, provided that there is such a longest directed walk. Since according to Remark 1.6c network N is strongly connected, there is always a directed walk in N from any node $i \in V$ to any node $j \in V$. In Roy (1962) it is shown that there exists a *longest* directed walk from any node $i \in V$ to any node $j \in V$ in N if and only if N does not contain any directed cycle of positive length. On the other hand, system of equations (1.4) possesses a solution precisely if there is a longest directed walk from i to j for all $i, j \in V$. In the latter case, the longest directed walks in N coincide with the longest directed paths in N, and $D = (d_{ij})_{i,j \in V}$ is called the *distance matrix* of N. Thus, we have the following proposition.

Proposition 1.7 (Roy 1962). *There is a time-feasible schedule for a project (i.e., $\mathcal{S}_T \neq \emptyset$) if and only if project network N does not contain any directed cycle of positive length.*

Let $m := |E|$ denote the number of arcs in project network N. Problem (1.3) can be solved in $\mathcal{O}(mn)$ time by the label-correcting procedure shown in Algorithm 1.1 (cf. Bellman 1958), where Q is a queue. Although this algorithm has been devised more than four decades ago, it is still the most efficient algorithm for solving longest-path problems in cyclic networks with arbitrary arc weights. The procedure may be terminated if some node i has been examined $n+2$ times (see, e.g., Ahuja et al. 1993, Sect. 5.5). In that case, (1.3) is unsolvable and thus $\mathcal{S}_T = \emptyset$, which means that contradictory temporal constraints have been specified.

The solution D to equations (1.4) is the elementwise minimal matrix satisfying

$$\left. \begin{array}{ll} d_{ii} = 0 & (i \in V) \\ d_{ij} \geq \delta_{ij} & ((i,j) \in E) \\ d_{ij} \geq d_{ih} + d_{hj} & (h, i, j \in V) \end{array} \right\} \quad (1.5)$$

This formulation gives rise to the following Algorithm 1.2 by Floyd and Warshall (cf. Floyd 1962) for computing distances d_{ij} for all $i, j \in V$. After having

---

Algorithm 1.1. Earliest schedule

Input: MPM project network $N = (V, E, \delta)$.
Output: Earliest schedule ES.

> set $d_{00} := 0$, $Q := \{0\}$, and $d_{0i} := -\infty$ for all $i \in V \setminus Q$;
> **while** $Q \neq \emptyset$ **do**
>   dequeue i from Q;
>   **for all** $(i, j) \in E$ with $d_{0j} < d_{0i} + \delta_{ij}$ **do**
>   set $d_{0j} := d_{0i} + \delta_{ij}$;
>   **if** $j \notin Q$ **then** enqueue j to Q;
> **return** earliest schedule $ES = (d_{0i})_{i \in V}$;

---

initialized the values d_{ij} according to the prescribed time lags δ_{ij}, the algorithm computes the transitive closure of those time lags by iteratively putting into force the *triangle inequalities*

$$d_{ij} \geq d_{ih} + d_{hj} \tag{1.6}$$

(1.5) and thus (1.4) is solvable exactly if the matrix D calculated by the Floyd-Warshall algorithm satisfies $d_{ii} = 0$ for all $i \in V$. The number of computations performed is $\mathcal{O}(n^3)$, which is the best possible time complexity for this problem (note that for checking whether or not distances d_{ij} satisfy (1.5), $\mathcal{O}(n^3)$ triangle inequalities must be evaluated).

Algorithm 1.2. Distance matrix

Input: MPM project network $N = (V, E, \delta)$.
Output: Distance matrix D.

> **for all** $i, j \in V$ **do**
>   **if** $(i, j) \in E$ **then** set $d_{ij} := \delta_{ij}$; **elsif** $i = j$ set $d_{ij} := 0$; **else** set $d_{ij} := -\infty$;
> **for all** $h, i, j \in V$ with $d_{ih} > -\infty$ and $d_{hj} > -\infty$ **do**
>   **if** $d_{ij} < d_{ih} + d_{hj}$ **then** set $d_{ij} := d_{ih} + d_{hj}$;
> **return** distance matrix $D = (d_{ij})_{i,j \in V}$;

The next algorithm, which is due to Bartusch et al. (1988), achieves the update of the distance matrix D in $\mathcal{O}(n^2)$ time when adding some arc (i, j) to the project network (see Algorithm 1.3). The calculation of the distance matrix D from scratch by initializing the values d_{ij} as in the Floyd-Warshall algorithm and then applying the algorithm for all arcs $(i, j) \in E$ would require $\mathcal{O}(mn^2)$ time, which is more expensive than using the Floyd-Warshall algorithm. The former procedure, however, will prove useful later on when dealing with resource constraints and the resolution of so-called resource conflicts, where individual arcs are added to N.

Algorithm 1.3. Addition of arc (i, j) with weight δ_{ij}

Input: Distance matrix D, an arc (i, j) with weight δ_{ij}.
Output: Updated distance matrix D.

> **for all** $g, h \in V$ **do**
>   **if** $d_{gh} < d_{gi} + \delta_{ij} + d_{jh}$ **then** set $d_{gh} := d_{gi} + \delta_{ij} + d_{jh}$;
> **return** distance matrix $D = (d_{ij})_{i,j \in V}$;

Remark 1.8. The update of distances d_{0h} (or, equivalently, earliest start times ES_h) after the addition of some arc (i, j) to project network N can be performed in $\mathcal{O}(n)$ time by putting $d_{0h} := \max(d_{0h}, d_{0i} + \delta_{ij} + d_{jh})$ for all $h \in V$. This can easily be seen by using the fact that the correctness of Algorithm 1.3 does not depend on the sequence in which pairs (g, h) are iterated. Symmetrically, distances d_{g0} (which coincide with the negative latest start times $-LS_g$) can be updated by putting $d_{g0} := \max(d_{g0}, d_{gi} + \delta_{ij} + d_{j0})$ for all $g \in V$. Moreover, adding some arc $(0, j)$ to N does not affect distances d_{i0} $(i \in V)$ and adding some arc $(i, 0)$ to N does not affect distances d_{0j} $(j \in V)$.

Proposition 1.9 shows that the creation of a directed cycle of positive length when adding arc (i, j) to N can be tested before calling Algorithm 1.3.

Proposition 1.9. *Let N be a project network with distance matrix D. The addition of arc (i, j) with weight δ_{ij} to N generates a directed cycle of positive length if and only if $\delta_{ij} > -d_{ji}$.*

Proof. Sufficiency: After the addition of arc (i, j) with $\delta_{ij} > -d_{ji}$ to N it holds that $d_{ij} \geq \delta_{ij}$. Thus, we have $d_{ij} + d_{ji} \geq \delta_{ij} + d_{ji} > 0$, which means that there is a directed cycle of positive length containing nodes i and j.

Necessity: Now assume that $\delta_{ij} \leq -d_{ji}$ and consider an iteration of Algorithm 1.3 for some pair (g, h) such that distance d_{gh} is increased. Then the updated distance is $d_{gh} = d_{gi} + \delta_{ij} + d_{jh} \leq d_{gi} - d_{ji} + d_{jh}$. The triangle inequalities (1.6) say that $d_{ji} \geq d_{jh} + d_{hg} + d_{gi}$ and thus $d_{gh} + d_{hg} \leq d_{gi} - (d_{jh} + d_{hg} + d_{gi}) + d_{jh} + d_{hg} = 0$. This means that after applying Algorithm 1.3 it holds that $d_{gh} + d_{hg} \leq 0$ for all $g, h \in V$, i.e., N contains no directed cycle of positive length. $\qquad\square$

Next, we consider three different floats or slack times of an activity $i \in V$. The *total float* TF_i is the maximum amount of time by which the start of activity i can be delayed beyond its earliest start time ES_i such that the project is terminated on time, i.e., $S_{n+1} \leq \overline{d}$. In other words,

$$TF_i = LS_i - ES_i = -d_{i0} - d_{0i} \quad (i \in V)$$

Activity $i \in V$ is called *critical* if i cannot be delayed, i.e., if the maximum time lag $-d_{i0}$ equals the minimum time lag d_{0i} between the project beginning and activity i and thus fixes the start time S_i of i to $ES_i = LS_i$. Activity i is critical exactly if $TF_i = 0$.

The *early free float* EFF_i is the maximum amount of time by which the earliest start of activity i at time ES_i can increase given that any other activity j can be begun at its earliest start time ES_j. Hence,

$$EFF_i = \min_{(i,j)\in E}(ES_j - \delta_{ij}) - ES_i = \min_{j\in V:i\neq j}(d_{0j} - d_{ij}) - d_{0i} \quad (i \in V)$$

The *late free float* LFF_i is the maximum amount of time by which the latest start of activity i at time LS_i can decrease given that any other activity j can be begun at its latest start times LS_j. Thus,

$$LFF_i = LS_i - \max_{(j,i)\in E}(LS_j + \delta_{ji}) = \min_{j\in V:i\neq j}(d_{j0} - d_{ji}) - d_{i0} \quad (i \in V)$$

1.2 Renewable-Resource Constraints

To perform the activities of a project, different types of resources are required. Basically, we may distinguish between resources whose availability solely depends on the activities being in progress (like manpower or machinery) and resources for which the availability results from the entire project history (such as the project budget, materials, or storage space). In this section we deal with *renewable resources*, which belong to the former type and to which the overwhelming part of research in the field of resource-constrained project scheduling has been dedicated. The case of *cumulative resources*, corresponding to the second type, will be discussed in Section 1.3. In the present section, we suppose that no cumulative resources need to be considered. At first, we provide a formal statement of the constraints arising from the scarcity of renewable resources. We are then concerned with conditions on the start times of activities whose joint requirements for renewable resources exceed the resource capacities and which thus cannot be in progress simultaneously. Finally, we discuss consistency tests for detecting temporal constraints that are implied by the limited availability of renewable resources.

1.2.1 Resource-Feasible Schedules

Let $\mathcal{R}^\rho$ be the set of renewable resources k with *capacity* $R_k \in \mathbb{N} \cup \{\infty\}$ that have been assigned to the project during the project definition phase. $R_k = \infty$ means that the availability of resource k is not explicitly bounded from above but can be adapted, at a certain cost, to any usage over time. The resource estimation yields (resource) *requirements* $r_{ik} \in \mathbb{Z}_{\geq 0}$ for each real activity $i \in V^a$ and each resource $k \in \mathcal{R}^\rho$. r_{ik} corresponds to the number of capacity units of resource k which are taken up for processing activity i from start time S_i (inclusively) to completion time $C_i = S_i + p_i$ (exclusively).

$r_{ik} = 0$ means that activity i does not use resource k. Furthermore, we assume that

$$r_{ik} \leq R_k \quad (i \in V^a,\ k \in \mathcal{R}^\rho)$$

which ensures that sufficient resource capacity is available for processing each activity individually. For simplicity, we may omit resource index k when there is only one renewable resource available.

Now let S be some schedule and let t be some point in time. Then

$$\mathcal{A}(S,t) := \{i \in V^a \mid S_i \leq t < S_i + p_i\}$$

is the *active set* of activities being in progress at time t. The corresponding requirement for resource $k \in \mathcal{R}^\rho$ at time t is given by

$$r_k(S,t) := \sum_{i \in \mathcal{A}(S,t)} r_{ik}$$

For given schedule S, function $r_k(S,\cdot) : \mathbb{R} \to \mathbb{Z}_{\geq 0}$ is termed the *loading profile* for renewable resource k. $r_k(S,\cdot)$ is a right-continuous step function with at most $2n$ jump discontinuities. Obviously, we have $r_k(S,t) = 0$ for all $t < 0$.

The *renewable-resource constraints* can be stated as follows:

$$r_k(S,t) \leq R_k \quad (k \in \mathcal{R}^\rho,\ 0 \leq t \leq \overline{d}) \tag{1.7}$$

Definition 1.10 (Resource-feasible and feasible schedules). *A schedule S satisfying the renewable-resource constraints (1.7) is called resource-feasible with respect to renewable resources $k \in \mathcal{R}^\rho$. The set of all resource-feasible schedules is denoted by $\mathcal{S}_R$. $\mathcal{S} := \mathcal{S}_T \cap \mathcal{S}_R$ is the set of all feasible schedules.*

As we shall see later on, unlike the polytope of time-feasible schedules $\mathcal{S}_T$, set $\mathcal{S}_R$ represents a finite union of polytopes which is generally not connected. As an intersection of a polytope and a finite union of polytopes, $\mathcal{S}$ is the union of finitely many polytopes as well. Resource allocation consists in assigning start times S_i (and thus execution time intervals $[S_i, C_i[$) to the activities of the project such that the corresponding schedule $S = (S_i)_{i \in V}$ is feasible and minimizes the objective function on set $\mathcal{S}$.

The basic *resource-constrained project scheduling problem with renewable resources* reads as follows:

$$\boxed{\begin{array}{ll} \text{Minimize} & f(S) \\ \text{subject to} & S \in \mathcal{S}_T \cap \mathcal{S}_R \end{array}} \tag{1.8}$$

Recall that we have assumed objective function f to be lower semicontinuous. The compactness of $\mathcal{S}$ then implies that there exists an optimal solution to problem (1.8) precisely if $\mathcal{S} \neq \emptyset$. Note, however, that due to the presence of maximum time lags it may happen that $\mathcal{S}_T \neq \emptyset$ and $\mathcal{S}_R \neq \emptyset$ but $\mathcal{S} = \emptyset$.

Definition 1.11 (Optimal schedule). *A feasible schedule S solving the resource-constrained project scheduling problem (1.8) is called optimal.*

By replacing the set $\mathcal{S} = \mathcal{S}_T \cap \mathcal{S}_R$ of feasible schedules with the set of resource-feasible schedules $\mathcal{S}_R$ we obtain the *temporal relaxation* of the resource-constrained project scheduling problem (1.8). Since we have assumed that $r_{ik} \leq R_k$ for all $i \in V^a$ and all $k \in \mathcal{R}^\rho$, each schedule carrying out the activities one after another is resource-feasible. The *resource relaxation* of (1.8) arises from deleting the resource constraints (1.7) or, equivalently, setting $R_k := \infty$ for all $k \in \mathcal{R}^\rho$. The resource relaxation coincides with the basic time-constrained project scheduling problem (1.2). As we noticed in Subsection 1.1.3, the existence of a time-feasible schedule can be checked in $\mathcal{O}(mn)$ time by applying Algorithm 1.1 to project network N. The following theorem, however, shows that it cannot be decided in polynomial time whether or not there exists a feasible schedule.

Theorem 1.12 (Bartusch et al. 1988). *The following decision problem is NP-complete.*

Instance: A project with one renewable resource and requirements $r_i = 1$ for all $i \in V^a$.

Question: Does there exist a feasible schedule?

Proof. The feasibility of a given schedule S can be checked by computing $S_j - S_i$ for all arcs $(i, j) \in E$ of project network N as well as the resource requirements $r_k(S, t)$ for all resources $k \in \mathcal{R}^\rho$ and all start times $t = S_i$ of real activities $i \in V^a$. Thus, verification of schedule feasibility can be done in polynomial time, and the problem to decide upon the existence of a feasible schedule belongs to *NP*. In Bartusch et al. (1988) it is shown by transformation from problem PRECEDENCE CONSTRAINED SCHEDULING with m processors and strict order $\prec$ that the decision problem whether or not $\mathcal{S} \neq \emptyset$ is NP-hard. An equivalent instance of the latter problem is obtained by considering one renewable resource with capacity $R = m$ and choosing $r_i = 1$, $p_i = 1$, $d_{0i}^{min} = 0$, $d_{i,n+1}^{min} = 1$ for all $i \in V^a$, as well as $d_{ij}^{min} = 1$ if $i \prec j$ and $d_{0,n+1}^{max} = 3$. $\square$

When dealing with the project duration problem, we may drop the assumption that there is a deadline $\overline{d}$ on the project termination because the objective is to maximize the slack $\overline{d} - S_{n+1}$ of the deadline constraint. The construction of a feasible schedule then turns into an easy problem if there are no maximum time lags given. In that case, project network N is acyclic, and the activities can be scheduled consecutively according to any topological ordering of the nodes $i \in V$ of N.

1.2.2 Forbidden Sets and Delaying Alternatives

The resource-feasibility of schedules is closely related to the concept of forbidden sets introduced by Radermacher (1978). The forbidden-set perspective of resource constraints is useful for investigating the set S of feasible schedules.

Definition 1.13 (Forbidden and feasible sets). *A set of real activities* $F \subseteq V^a$ *is called a forbidden set if there is some resource* $k \in \mathcal{R}^\rho$ *such that*

$$\sum_{i \in F} r_{ik} > R_k$$

If F is $\subseteq$-minimal in the set of all forbidden sets, we speak of a minimal forbidden set. By $\mathcal{F}$ we denote the set of all minimal forbidden sets. A set $A \subseteq V^a$ that is not forbidden is termed a feasible set. A is said to be a maximal feasible set if it is $\subseteq$-maximal in the set of all feasible sets.

When solving the resource-constrained project scheduling problem (1.8), the activities from a forbidden set F must be scheduled in such a way that they do not all overlap in time. In other terms, each forbidden set F has to be partitioned into a feasible set A and some nonempty set B, no activity from set B being executed simultaneously with all activities from set A. In literature, such a set B is called a delaying alternative (cf. e.g., Christofides et al. 1987 or Demeulemeester and Herroelen 1992, 1997).

Definition 1.14 (Delaying alternative). *Let F be a forbidden set. $B \subseteq F$ is called a delaying alternative for F if $F \setminus B$ is a feasible set. If additionally B is $\subseteq$-minimal in the set of all delaying alternatives for F (i.e., $F \setminus B$ is a maximal feasible set), we speak of a minimal delaying alternative for F.*

The number of minimal delaying alternatives for a forbidden set F grows exponentially in the cardinality of set F. Given some forbidden set F and a subset $B \subseteq F$, it can be decided in polynomial time whether or not B is a minimal delaying alternative for F by evaluating the following two conditions (1.9) and (1.10). This can be achieved in $\mathcal{O}(|\mathcal{R}^\rho||F|)$ time.

$$\sum_{i \in F \setminus B} r_{ik} \leq R_k \text{ for all } k \in \mathcal{R}^\rho \tag{1.9}$$

$$\sum_{i \in F \setminus B} r_{ik} + \min_{j \in B} r_{jk} > R_k \text{ for some } k \in \mathcal{R}^\rho \tag{1.10}$$

Nevertheless, Neumann et al. (2003b) have shown that a minimal delaying alternative B cannot be generated efficiently by iteratively transferring activities from set F to set B.

Proposition 1.15 (Neumann et al. 2003b, Sect. 2.5). *The following decision problem is NP-complete.*

> *Instance: A project with one renewable resource, a forbidden set F, and an activity $h \in F$.*

> *Question: Does there exist a minimal delaying alternative B for F containing h?*

Proof. Since conditions (1.9) and (1.10) can be verified in polynomial time, the problem is contained in *NP*. Let B with $h \in B$ be an arbitrary set of activities using the single resource. Then B is a minimal delaying alternative if and only if $R - \min_{j \in B} r_j < \sum_{i \in F \setminus B} r_i \leq R$. For $r_h = 1$, we then have $r_h = \min_{j \in B} r_j$ and thus $R - 1 < \sum_{i \in F \setminus B} r_i \leq R$, i.e., $\sum_{i \in F \setminus B} r_i = R$. Hence, there is a minimal delaying alternative B containing h exactly if there is a set $A \subseteq F \setminus \{h\}$ with $\sum_{i \in A} r_i = R$. Now let I be an instance of problem SUBSET SUM with index set $\mathcal{I}$, sizes $s(i) \in \mathbb{N}$ for $i \in \mathcal{I}$, and threshold $M \in \mathbb{N}$ (cf. Garey and Johnson 1979, problem SP13). We obtain an equivalent instance of our decision problem by choosing $F = \mathcal{I} \cup \{h\}$, $r_i = s(i)$ for all $i \in \mathcal{I}$, $r_h = 1$, and $R = M$.   □

Similarly it can be shown that it is also NP-complete to decide whether a given activity h is contained in some minimal forbidden set $F \in \mathcal{F}$ (cf. Stork and Uetz 2005, who devise a polynomial transformation from PARTITION).

In what follows, we describe a recursion for computing minimal delaying alternatives for a forbidden set F (see Neumann et al. 2003b, Sect. 2.5). Given a delaying alternative B, the set $\mathcal{B}$ of all minimal delaying alternatives $B' \subseteq B$ for F is either equal to $\{B\}$ if B is a minimal delaying alternative for F or equal to the set of all minimal delaying alternatives $B' \subseteq B \setminus \{i\}$ for F with $i \in B$. To avoid the multiple generation of one and the same minimal delaying alternative B' (as subset of two different sets $B \setminus \{i_1\}$ and $B \setminus \{i_2\}$), we restrict the recursion to subsets B' of $B \setminus \{i\}$ for which $j > i$ holds for all $j \in (B \setminus \{i\}) \setminus B'$. Since F itself is a delaying alternative, which includes all minimal delaying alternatives for F, we start the recursion with $B = F$. Algorithm 1.4 shows the corresponding recursive procedure, where $i = 0$ if $B = F$ at recursion level 0 and i is the number of the activity removed in the preceding call to the recursion, otherwise. A call to *MinimalDelayingAlternatives*$(F, 0)$ determines the set $\mathcal{B}$ of all minimal delaying alternatives for forbidden set F.

An alternative approach to calculating all feasible subsets $A \subset F$ (and thus all delaying alternatives $B = F \setminus A$) has been proposed by Brucker et al. (1998). Assume that $F = \{i_1, i_2, \ldots, i_\nu\}$. Brucker's procedure constructs a binary decision tree, where each node at level $\mu = 1, \ldots, \nu$ corresponds to some feasible set $A' \subseteq \{i_1, i_2, \ldots, i_\mu\}$ and branching from a node at level $\mu - 1$ corresponds to the decision whether or not activity i_μ is contained in the respective child node at level μ. Each leaf of the decision tree belongs to one feasible set A.

Algorithm 1.4. *MinimalDelayingAlternatives*(B, i)

Input: A project, a forbidden set B, an index i.
Ensure: $\mathcal{B}$ contains all minimal delaying alternatives $B' \subseteq B$ for F with $\min(B \setminus B') > i$.

    if B satisfies (1.9) **then** $(* B$ is delaying alternative $*)$
        if B satisfies (1.10) **then** $(* B$ is minimal delaying alternative $*)$
        $\mathcal{B} := \mathcal{B} \cup \{B\}$;
    else
        for all $j \in B$ with $j > i$ **do** *MinimalDelayingAlternatives*$(B \setminus \{j\}, j)$;

The following proposition establishes the relationship between minimal delaying alternatives and minimal forbidden sets.

Proposition 1.16 (Schwindt 1998c). *A minimal delaying alternative B for a forbidden set F is an $\subseteq$-minimal set containing an activity j of each minimal forbidden set $F' \subseteq F$.*

Proof. We assume that there is a minimal delaying alternative B for F and a forbidden subset $F' \subseteq F$ with $B \cap F' = \emptyset$. Then set $F \setminus B \supseteq F'$ is feasible. Since every superset of a forbidden set is forbidden, this contradicts the fact that F' is forbidden. $\qquad\square$

1.2.3 Breaking up Forbidden Sets

When scheduling the activities of a project, *resource conflicts* caused by the simultaneous execution of the activities of some forbidden set have to be resolved. The following theorem by Bartusch et al. (1988) shows how resource conflicts can be settled by introducing precedence constraints between activities of minimal forbidden sets.

Theorem 1.17 (Bartusch et al. 1988). *A schedule S is resource-feasible if and only if for each minimal forbidden set $F \in \mathcal{F}$, there are two activities $i, j \in F$ such that $S_j \geq S_i + p_i$.*

Proof. Sufficiency: We consider the active set $\mathcal{A}(S, t)$ for a resource-infeasible schedule S at some time $t \geq 0$ such that $\mathcal{A}(S, t)$ is forbidden. Since $\mathcal{A}(S, t)$ is forbidden, there is a subset F of $\mathcal{A}(S, t)$ that is minimally forbidden. By definition of $\mathcal{A}(S, t)$, all activities of F overlap at time t, which implies that there are no two activities $i, j \in F$ with $S_j \geq S_i + p_i$.

Necessity: Assume that there is some minimal forbidden set F for which no two activities $i, j \in F$ satisfy $S_j \geq S_i + p_i$. Then $[S_i, S_i + p_i[\cap [S_j, S_j + p_j[\neq \emptyset$ for any two activities $i, j \in F$. The Helly property of intervals (cf. e.g., Golumbic 2004, Sect. 4.5) then implies that $\cap_{i \in F}[S_i, S_i + p_i[\neq \emptyset$, and thus there is some point in time t at which all activities i from set F overlap. Since F is a forbidden set, $r_k(S, t) = \sum_{i \in F} r_{ik} > R_k$ for some $k \in \mathcal{R}^\rho$. $\qquad\square$

As a direct consequence of Theorem 1.17 we obtain the following Corollary.

Corollary 1.18 (Bartusch et al. 1988). *The set S of all feasible schedules represents the union of finitely many integral polytopes.*

We say that a constraint C *breaks up* minimal forbidden set F if for each schedule satisfying C, there are two activities $i, j \in F$ such that $S_j \geq S_i + p_i$. Minimal forbidden sets can be broken up in different ways. According to Theorem 1.17, the first possibility consists in choosing two activities $i, j \in F$ and introducing an (ordinary) precedence constraint

$$S_j \geq S_i + p_i \tag{1.11}$$

between i and j. Alternatively one may define a *disjunctive precedence constraint*

$$S_j \geq \min_{i \in F : i \neq j} (S_i + p_i) \tag{1.12}$$

between set $F \setminus \{j\}$ and activity j saying that j must not be started before the earliest completion of some other activity i from set F. Disjunctive precedence constraint (1.12) is equivalent to the disjunction of the precedence constraints (1.11) for all $i \in F$, $i \neq j$ and represents a so-called linear reverse-convex constraint (see, e.g., Tuy 1995, Sect. 7). Whereas the number of alternatives for breaking up F by precedence constraints is $\mathcal{O}(|F|^2)$, this number is of linear order $\mathcal{O}(|F|)$ when using disjunctive precedence constraints. The set of all schedules satisfying a disjunctive precedence constraint is generally disconnected and thus in particular nonconvex. As will be shown in Subsection 3.1.2, the minimization of regular (i.e., componentwise nondecreasing) objective functions can nevertheless be done with a time complexity that is linear in the maximum project duration $\bar{d}$. In literature, disjunctive precedence constraints are also referred to as *AND/OR precedence constraints* or *waiting conditions* (cf. Möhring et al. 2004). They have been introduced by Igelmund and Radermacher (1983) in the form of preselective strategies for resource-constrained project scheduling with stochastic activity durations.

An arbitrary forbidden set F is said to be broken up if all minimal forbidden subsets of F are broken up. Let B be some minimal delaying alternative for F. From Proposition 1.16 it then follows that breaking up F can be achieved by imposing a set of precedence constraints

$$S_j \geq S_i + p_i \quad (j \in B)$$

between some activity i from the maximal feasible set $A = F \setminus B$ and all activities $j \in B$ or by a disjunctive precedence constraint

$$\min_{j \in B} S_j \geq \min_{i \in A}(S_i + p_i)$$

between set A and set B. Note that in the case of precedence constraints, one and the same activity $i \in F \setminus B$ can be chosen for all $j \in B$ because any conjunction of precedence constraints (1.11) for the activities j from delaying alternative B implies shifting all $j \in B$ behind the earliest finishing activity $i \in F \setminus B$, which breaks up forbidden set F.

1.2.4 Consistency Tests

The NP-hardness of finding feasible schedules implies that resource allocation can only be performed by enumerating alternative sets of precedence relationships among activities using common resources. *Consistency tests* designate algorithms for detecting constraints that must be satisfied by any feasible schedule and that can be evaluated without enumeration to rule out in advance certain inadmissible alternatives from further consideration. A consistency test is described through a condition and a constraint that can be established whenever the condition is satisfied. From a geometric point of view, applying consistency tests provides a convex set containing all feasible schedules. In the best case, this convex set coincides with the convex hull $\text{conv}(\mathcal{S})$ of the feasible region. From Theorem 1.12, however, it immediately follows that $\text{conv}(\mathcal{S})$ cannot be computed in polynomial time (otherwise, problem (1.8) with linear objective function f could be efficiently solved by finding some optimal vertex of $\text{conv}(\mathcal{S})$). Since $\mathcal{S}$ is the union of finitely many integral polytopes, the convex hull $\text{conv}(\mathcal{S})$ is integral as well.

In enumeration procedures, consistency tests are often applied dynamically to the search space of any enumeration node. The tests then refer to search spaces rather than to the feasible region. In scheduling literature, consistency tests are also known under the names preprocessing (if they are applied to the root node before starting the enumeration), immediate selection algorithms, edge finding rules, constraint propagation techniques, or satisfiability tests. Instead of directly checking given conditions, consistency tests may also try to refute additional, hypothetical constraints. If the test rejects the hypothesis, the alternative hypothesis has been shown to be true and thus can be used to reduce the search space. Consistency tests have been applied with great success in machine scheduling and for the resource-constrained project duration problem (see Brucker et al. 1998, Dorndorf et al. 2000*a*, or Dorndorf et al. 2000*c*). The algorithm of Carlier and Pinson (1989) that solved the famous Fisher and Thompson (1963) job shop scheduling problem with 10 jobs and 10 machines for the first time has become a classical reference in the field.

We review some consistency tests that have been proposed in literature for project scheduling with renewable resources (see, e.g., Dorndorf et al. 1999). All procedures to be discussed provide additional temporal constraints that can be added in the form of arcs to project network N. Let d_{ij} again denote the length of a longest directed path from node i to node j in project network N, where we assume that $\mathcal{S}_T \neq \emptyset$. Consistency tests are usually used in an iterative fashion as long as new temporal constraints can be identified and thus distance matrix D is modified (see Algorithm 1.5, where Γ denotes the set of consistency tests to be applied). The reason for this is that due to updating distance matrix D, certain tests that in previous iterations failed may possibly deduce additional constraints. In general, the distance matrix yielded depends on the sequence in which the different tests are applied. For the consistency tests to be discussed below, however, it can be shown that the resulting matrix is unique (cf. Dorndorf et al. 2000b). More precisely, any consistency test can be interpreted as a function γ mapping distance matrices D to updated distance matrices $\gamma(D)$. If for all consistency tests $\gamma \in \Gamma$, $D \leq D'$ implies $\gamma(D) \leq \gamma(D')$, then there exists only one fixed-point matrix D with $D = \gamma(D)$.

Algorithm 1.5. Search space reduction by consistency tests $\gamma \in \Gamma$

Input: A project, a set Γ of consistency tests.
Output: Updated distance matrix D.

   compute distance matrix D; ($*$ Algorithm 1.2 $*$)
   repeat
     for all consistency tests $\gamma \in \Gamma$ **do**
       apply γ;
       if new temporal constraint $S_j - S_i \geq \delta_{ij}$ has been established **then**
          update distance matrix D, i.e., set $D := \gamma(D)$; ($*$ Algorithm 1.3 $*$)
   until distance matrix D has not been changed during last iteration;
   return distance matrix D;

Disjunctive activities tests try to establish precedence constraints between activities which cannot be processed at the same time. Let $i, j \in V^a$ be two different real activities that, with respect to the temporal constraints, can be executed in parallel and for which j cannot be completed before i is started, i.e.,

$$-p_j < d_{ij} < p_i \text{ and } d_{ji} < p_j$$

We say that i and j are *in disjunction* if due to the resource constraints they cannot be processed at the same time. In that case, we can introduce a new precedence constraint $S_j \geq S_i + p_i$ between i and j that will be satisfied by any feasible schedule S.

Obviously, the activities of two-element forbidden sets are in disjunction. However, i and j may also be in disjunction if $r_{ik} + r_{jk} \leq R_k$ for all $k \in \mathcal{R}^\rho$. Brucker et al. (1998) have used the concept of *symmetric triples* for finding such activities. We call (h, i, j) a symmetric triple if $\{h, i, j\}$ is a forbidden set and activity h must be executed simultaneously with activity i (i.e., $d_{hi} > -p_i$ and $d_{ih} > -p_h$) and with activity j (i.e., $d_{hj} > -p_j$ and $d_{jh} > -p_h$). For a symmetric triple (h, i, j), activities i and j cannot be in progress at the same time because this would imply that h, i, and j were carried out in parallel, which is impossible because $\{h, i, j\}$ is a forbidden set. Obviously, detecting all symmetric triples takes $\mathcal{O}(n^3)$ time. After having established a new precedence constraint, distance matrix D must be updated, which can be done in $\mathcal{O}(n^2)$ time by using Algorithm 1.3.

Many consistency tests are based on lower bounds on the work that must be performed in certain time intervals $[a, b[$ with $0 \leq a < b \leq \bar{d}$. Those tests are referred to as *energetic reasoning* ("raisonnement énergétique", see Lopez et al. 1992) or interval capacity tests (Dorndorf et al. 1999). If $b - a = 1$, we speak of *unit-interval capacity tests*. Given some schedule S, $\int_a^b r_k(S, t)dt$ is the *workload* to be processed by resource $k \in \mathcal{R}^\rho$ in time interval $[a, b[$. $R_k(b - a)$ is termed the *interval capacity* of resource k in interval $[a, b[$. The execution time of activity i in interval $[a, b[$ equals $(\min(b - a, p_i, C_i - a, b - S_i))^+$, where $(x)^+ := \max(0, x)$. It follows that the workload of resource k in interval $[a, b[$ can be written as $\sum_{i \in V^a} r_{ik}(\min(b - a, p_i, C_i - a, b - S_i))^+$. Now let

$$p_i(a, b) := (\min(b - a, p_i, EC_i - a, b - LS_i))^+ \qquad (1.13)$$

denote the minimum time activity i has to be processed in interval $[a, b[$. For any time-feasible schedule $S \in \mathcal{S}_T$,

$$w_k(a, b) := \sum_{i \in V^a} r_{ik} p_i(a, b) \qquad (1.14)$$

then represents a lower bound on the workload of resource $k \in \mathcal{R}^\rho$ in $[a, b[$.

Dorndorf et al. (2000c) have used energetic reasoning for finding further activities i, j being in disjunction. i and j are in disjunction if for all times t at which the temporal constraints allow both activities to be in progress, the combined resource requirements of i and j for some resource $k \in \mathcal{R}^\rho$ exceed the maximum residual capacity of k at time t. This condition can be formulated as follows. Activities i and j may be executed in parallel at time t if $t_1 \leq t < t_2$ where $t_1 = \max[\max(ES_i, ES_j), \min(EC_i, EC_j) - 1]$ and $t_2 = \min[\min(LC_i, LC_j), \max(LS_i, LS_j) + 1]$. The minimum workload in interval $[t, t + 1[$ (or, equivalently, the minimum requirement at time t) that is due to the execution of activities from set $V^a \setminus \{i, j\}$ equals $w_k(t, t + 1) - r_{ik} p_i(t, t + 1) - r_{jk} p_j(t, t + 1)$. Accordingly, activities i and j cannot overlap in time if there exists a resource $k \in \mathcal{R}^\rho$ such that for all $t \in [t_1, t_2[$

$$r_{ik} + r_{jk} > R_k - [w_k(t, t + 1) - r_{ik} p_i(t, t + 1) - r_{jk} p_j(t, t + 1)] \qquad (1.15)$$

For given resource $k \in \mathcal{R}^\rho$, the *core loading profile* $r_k^c : \mathbb{R} \to \mathbb{Z}_{\geq 0}$ where $r_k^c(t) = w_k(t, t + 1)$ represents a lower approximation to the loading profiles $r_k(S, \cdot)$ of all time-feasible schedules $S \in \mathcal{S}_T$. By using a support-point representation of step function r_k^c, all disjunctive activities $i, j \in V^a$ satisfying (1.15) can be identified in $\mathcal{O}(|\mathcal{R}^\rho| n^2)$ time (cf. Dorndorf et al. 2000c). Each time a new precedence constraint has been established, we have to recalculate the earliest and latest start times of activities and to update the core loading profiles of renewable resources, which, for given distance matrix D, requires $\mathcal{O}(|\mathcal{R}^\rho| n \log n)$ time. Recall that after the addition of an arc (i, j) to project network N, the earliest and latest start times can be updated in linear time (see Remark 1.8).

The **shaving** technique is intended to tighten the time windows $[ES_i, LS_i]$ of activities $i \in V^a$ by falsifying hypothetical earliest or latest start times. We first consider the case of a hypothetical earliest start time t_i. Assume that after the addition of the respective arc $(0, i)$ with weight t_i to project network N it holds that

$$w_k(t, t+1) > R_k \qquad (1.16)$$

for some resource $k \in \mathcal{R}^\rho$ and some time t. Then the capacity of resource k is not sufficient to match the requirements for resource k at time t, i.e., we have shown that any feasible schedule S satisfies $S_i \leq t_i - 1$ (recall that conv(S) is integral). For each activity i, the values for t_i can be tested according to a binary search in set $[ES_i, LS_i] \cap \mathbb{Z}$, where t_i is decreased if the test fails in refuting the hypothesis, and increased, otherwise. Testing hypothetical latest start times can be performed analogously. When we apply the test to a given activity $i \in V^a$, we have to update the core loading profiles r_k^c at each iteration of the binary search, which again takes $\mathcal{O}(|\mathcal{R}^\rho| n \log n)$ time. Obviously, inequality (1.16) needs only to be evaluated at jump-up discontinuities of the core loading profiles, i.e., at points $t = LS_j$ ($j \in V$). Thus, the time complexity of applying shaving to activity i is $\mathcal{O}(\log \bar{d} |\mathcal{R}^\rho| n \log n)$. Since updating the core loading profiles is included in the shaving procedure, establishing a new earliest or latest start time does not incur any additional effort.

The following **unit-interval capacity test** determines points in time at which certain activities cannot be executed. Consider some real activity $i \in V^a$ that, at a given time t, is not necessarily in progress (i.e., $ES_i \leq t - p_i$ or $LS_i \geq t+1$). In this case, activity i cannot be carried out at time t if for some resource $k \in \mathcal{R}^\rho$

$$w_k(t, t+1) + r_{ik} > R_k$$

which implies $S_i \in [ES_i, t - p_i] \cup [t+1, LS_i]$ for any feasible schedule S (note that due to $p_i(t, t+1) = 0$, requirement r_{ik} does not enter into workload $w_k(t, t+1)$). Two particular cases allow the introduction of additional temporal constraints. If t is less than the earliest completion time EC_i of activity i, we obtain $S_i \geq t+1$, and if t is greater than or equal to the latest start time LS_i of i, it follows that $S_i \leq t - p_i$. Again, it suffices to consider points in time t coinciding with the latest start time LS_j of some $j \in V^a$. Accordingly, applying the unit-interval capacity test to activity i requires $\mathcal{O}(|\mathcal{R}^\rho| n)$ time. The update of core loading profiles after having established a new earliest or latest start time can again be performed in $\mathcal{O}(|\mathcal{R}^\rho| n \log n)$ time.

The **activity-interval capacity test** generalizes several consistency tests that have been devised for machine scheduling (see Dorndorf et al. 1999). Let $U \subseteq V^a$ be a nonempty set of real activities and let $U', U'' \subset U$ be two subsets of U. If for some resource $k \in \mathcal{R}^\rho$, the interval capacity in the interval from the earliest start of an activity from set $U \setminus U'$ to the latest completion of an activity from set $U \setminus U''$ is less than the workload of the activities from set U, i.e.,

$$\sum_{h \in U} r_{hk} p_h > R_k \max_{\substack{g \in U \setminus U', \\ h \in U \setminus U''}} (LC_h - ES_g) \qquad (1.17)$$

then there is some activity from set U' that is started first or some activity from set U'' that is completed last among the activities from set U:

$$\min_{g \in U'} S_g < \min_{h \in U \setminus U'} S_h \quad \text{or} \quad \max_{h \in U''} C_h > \max_{g \in U \setminus U''} C_g \tag{1.18}$$

For certain choices of sets U' and U'', the disjunction (1.18) results in temporal constraints (cf. Table 1.1). The corresponding consistency tests are known as input, output, input negation, and output negation tests. The computational effort associated with the different activity-interval consistency tests will arise from the analysis of the next consistency test.

Table 1.1. Specific implementations of the activity-interval capacity test

Test	(U', U'')	Temporal constraint(s)
Input	$(\{i\}, \emptyset)$	$S_j - S_i \geq 1$ for all $j \in U, j \neq i$
Output	$(\emptyset, \{j\})$	$S_j - S_i \geq p_i - p_j + 1$ for all $i \in U, i \neq j$
Input negation	$(U \setminus \{j\}, \{j\})$	$S_j \geq \min(\min\limits_{i \in U \setminus \{j\}} ES_i, \max\limits_{i \in U \setminus \{j\}} EC_i - p_j) + 1$
Output negation	$(\{i\}, U \setminus \{i\})$	$S_i \leq \max(\min\limits_{j \in U \setminus \{i\}} LS_j, \max\limits_{j \in U \setminus \{i\}} LC_j - p_i) - 1$

The **general interval capacity test** refers to time intervals $[a, b[$ for which the residual interval capacity $R_k(b - a) - w_k(a, b)$ for given resource $k \in \mathcal{R}^\rho$ is minimum. In Schwindt (1998c), Sect. 3.3, and, independently, in Baptiste et al. (1999) it has been shown that intervals $[a, b[$ with minimum residual interval capacity can be determined by investigating $\mathcal{O}(n^2)$ critical intervals (where interestingly it is not sufficient to consider only intervals whose endpoints coincide with earliest or latest start or completion times). Similarly to the shaving technique, we may establish a hypothesis on the consistency of some temporal constraint $S_i - S_j \geq t_{ji}$. If under this assumption there is a resource k with

$$\max_{0 \leq a < b \leq \overline{d}} w_k(a, b) > R_k(b - a)$$

the hypothesis has been refuted and thus we can introduce the reverse temporal constraint $S_j - S_i \geq -t_{ji} + 1$. For each pair $(i, j) \in V^a \times V^a$ where $i \neq j$, a binary search in set $[d_{ji}, -d_{ij}] \cap \mathbb{Z}$ provides, within $\mathcal{O}(\log \overline{d})$ iterations, the minimum t_{ji} for which $S_i - S_j \geq t_{ji}$ can be disproved. Since for given resource k, an interval $[a, b[$ with minimum residual interval capacity can be found in $\mathcal{O}(n^2 \log n)$ time (cf. Schwindt 1998c, Sect. 3.3), the time required for applying the general interval capacity test to a given pair (i, j) is of order $\mathcal{O}(\log \overline{d} |\mathcal{R}^\rho| n^2 \log n)$.

The general interval capacity test represents a generalization of all activity-interval consistency tests listed in Table 1.1. This can be seen as follows. Consider, for given sets U, U', U'', the time interval $[a, b[$ where $a := \min_{g \in U \setminus U'} ES_g$ and $b := \max_{h \in U \setminus U''} LC_h$. Then the right-hand side of inequality (1.17) coincides with the interval capacity $R_k(b - a)$ of interval $[a, b[$. We first show that the general interval capacity test generalizes the input test. Let $U \subseteq V^a$

be a set containing two different activities i, j. According to Table 1.1, we choose $U' = \{i\}$ and $U'' = \emptyset$, i.e., $a = \min_{g \in U \setminus \{i\}} ES_g$ and $b = \max_{h \in U} LC_h$. Now assume that $S_i - S_j \geq 0$. Then $\min_{g \in U \setminus \{i\}} ES_g = \min_{g \in U} ES_g$ and thus $[ES_h, LC_h[\subseteq [a, b[$ for all $h \in U$, which implies $\sum_{h \in U} r_{hk} p_h \leq w_k(a, b)$. This means that any temporal constraint that can be deduced by using the input test also arises from applying the general interval capacity test where for each pair (i, j), time lag t_{ji} is chosen to be equal to 0. We now turn to the input negation test with $U' = U \setminus \{j\}$ and $U'' = \{j\}$, i.e., $a = ES_j$ and $b = \max_{h \in U \setminus \{j\}} LC_h$. We apply the general interval capacity test with hypothesis $S_0 - S_j \geq -\min(\min_{g \in U \setminus \{j\}} ES_g, \max_{h \in U \setminus \{j\}} EC_h - p_j)$. From $S_j \leq \min_{g \in U \setminus \{j\}} ES_g$ it follows that $ES_g \geq ES_j = a$ for all $g \in U \setminus \{j\}$, and $S_j + p_j \leq \max_{h \in U \setminus \{j\}} EC_h$ implies $LC_j \leq \max_{h \in U \setminus \{j\}} LC_h = b$. We then again have $[ES_h, LC_h[\subseteq [a, b[$ for all $h \in U$. For reasons of symmetry, the output and output negation tests can be dealt with analogously.

The **energy precedence test** has been devised by Laborie (2003). If there is an (implied) minimum time lag $d_{ij} \geq p_i$ between the starts of activities i and j, then a workload of $r_{ik} p_i$ units has to be processed on each resource $k \in \mathcal{R}^\rho$ between S_i and S_j, which takes at least $\max_{k \in \mathcal{R}^\rho} r_{ik} p_i / R_k$ units of time. Thus, for each feasible schedule S we have

$$S_j \geq \min_{i \in V^a : d_{ij} \geq p_i} ES_i + \max_{k \in \mathcal{R}^\rho} \left\lceil \sum_{i \in V^a : d_{ij} \geq p_i} r_{ik} p_i / R_k \right\rceil$$

Note that in contrast to the preceding interval capacity tests, the effectiveness of the energy precedence test is independent of the tightness of time windows $[ES_i, LS_i]$. Applying the energy precedence test to activity j requires $\mathcal{O}(|\mathcal{R}^\rho| n)$ time. If the energy precedence test is applied to all activities, the amortized computational effort per activity can be decreased to $\mathcal{O}(|\mathcal{R}^\rho| + n)$.

1.3 Cumulative-Resource Constraints

Cumulative resources represent a generalization of *nonrenewable resources* like money or raw materials, which have been studied in the context of project scheduling problems where activities can be performed in one out of several alternative execution modes differing with respect to duration and resource requirements (cf. e.g., Węglarz 1980 or Słowiński 1981). Unlike renewable resources, which are *used* during the execution time of activities and released after completion, nonrenewable resources are *consumed*. Since the availability of nonrenewable resources is nonincreasing over time, the feasibility of a resource allocation and the respective cost incurred is independent of the schedule S established and solely depends on the assignment of execution modes to activities. Thus, nonrenewable resources can be disregarded if each activity can only be performed in one mode. How to solve the mode assignment problem in case of multiple execution modes will be discussed in Section 5.3.

In practice, resources that are consumed are generally renewed later on. If the replenishment occurs during the project execution, the availability of the resource increases at certain points in time. In that case, the feasibility of a schedule generally depends on the sequence of depletions and replenishments. For example, in many real-life projects certain project activities are associated with disbursements for materials or staff leasing, and progress payments arise for completed subprojects. It may then be necessary to delay certain disbursements behind payments in order to avoid a negative cash balance. Resources that are depleted and replenished over time are called *cumulative resources*. The concept of cumulative resources has been introduced by Schwindt (1998c). A cumulative resource can be regarded as the inventory level in some storage facility of finite capacity. The inventory level is bounded from below by some safety stock and bounded from above by the capacity of the storage facility.

Carlier and Rinnooy Kan (1982) and Carlier (1989) have dealt with the special case where activities consume nonrenewable resources that become available at given points in time. The authors provide a polynomial-time algorithm for minimizing regular and max-separable objective functions f. In addition they show that in presence of replenishing activities the optimization problem becomes NP-hard.

Shewchuk and Chang (1995) have considered scheduling problems with *recyclable resources*, i.e., renewable resources whose availability expires after a given lifespan and which may be reused after a certain repair time (like cutters that have to be re-ground from time to time). Such a recyclable resource can be viewed as the combination of a classical renewable resource and a cumulative resource keeping the residual time before recycling becomes necessary.

Of course, cumulative resources can also be used to formulate part availability constraints arising, e.g., in construction projects or assembly manufacturing (see, e.g., Kolisch 2000, who has devised a mixed-integer linear program for scheduling in assembly environments). If certain intermediate products represent *common parts*, which are components of different subassemblies or final products, one has to decide on the sequence in which completed items of those common parts are allotted to the respective products into which they are installed (assignment-sequence problem, cf. Neumann and Schwindt 1997). The concept of cumulative resources permits to integrate the assignment-sequence problem into the resource allocation problem (see Section 6.1). A further application of cumulative resources in the context of assembly management is the modelling of spatial capacity constraints, which are due to the limited assembly area. Kolisch and Heß (2000) have developed schedule-improvement methods for assembly scheduling problems including the latter type of constraints (see also Kolisch 2001b, Ch. 10).

The case of general cumulative resources has been considered by Neumann and Schwindt (2002), who have discussed structural issues and have proposed a branch-and-bound algorithm for project scheduling subject to inventory constraints. Constraint-based methods for solving scheduling problems with cumulative resources have been developed by Beck (2002) and Laborie (2003).

For what follows, we assume that cumulative resources are depleted and replenished discontinuously at the occurrence of certain events like the starts and completions of real activities. Accordingly, we associate the resource requirements with events instead of real activities, and we represent the project under study by an event-on-node network (see Subsection 1.1.2). The case where cumulative resources are replenished and depleted continuously over the processing time of activities is treated in Section 5.4.

1.3.1 Resource-Feasible Schedules

Let $\mathcal{R}^\gamma$ be the set of cumulative resources. For each resource $k \in \mathcal{R}^\gamma$ a minimum inventory level or *safety stock* $\underline{R}_k \in \mathbb{Z} \cup \{-\infty\}$ and a maximum inventory level or *storage capacity* $\overline{R}_k \in \mathbb{Z} \cup \{\infty\}$ is given, where $\overline{R}_k \geq \underline{R}_k$. The (storage) *requirement* $r_{ik} \in \mathbb{Z}$ of event $i \in V^e$ for resource k equals the increase in the inventory level of resource k at the occurrence of i. r_{ik} is positive if i replenishes k and negative if i depletes k. For example, a replenishing event may represent the completion of some real activity producing an intermediate product that is stocked in resource k, whereas a depleting event may coincide with the start of some real activity consuming the intermediate product. Another example of replenishing and depleting events are progress payments received and disbursements for materials and subcontractors. Resource requirement r_{0k} can be regarded as the *initial inventory level* in resource k. We assume that

$$\underline{R}_k \leq \sum_{i \in V^e} r_{ik} \leq \overline{R}_k \quad (k \in \mathcal{R}^\gamma) \tag{1.19}$$

which ensures that the inventories $\sum_{i \in V^e} r_{ik}$ of resources $k \in \mathcal{R}^\gamma$ at the project termination neither fall below the safety stocks $\underline{R}_k$ nor exceed the storage capacities $\overline{R}_k$.

Now let $V_k^{e^-} := \{i \in V^e \mid r_{ik} < 0\}$ and $V_k^{e^+} := \{i \in V^e \mid r_{ik} > 0\}$ denote the sets of events depleting and replenishing, respectively, resource $k \in \mathcal{R}^\gamma$. Given a schedule S,

$$\mathcal{A}(S, t) := \{i \in V^e \mid S_i \leq t\}$$

is the *active set* of events that have taken place by time t and thus determine the inventory level in resource $k \in \mathcal{R}^\gamma$ at time t. By

$$r_k(S, t) := \sum_{i \in \mathcal{A}(S,t)} r_{ik}$$

we denote the inventory level of resource $k \in \mathcal{R}^\gamma$ at time t given schedule S. $r_k(S, t)$ corresponds to the cumulative resource demands for resource k in time interval $[0, t]$. The right-continuous step function $r_k(S, \cdot)$ is again called the *loading profile* of resource k. The *cumulative-resource constraints* can be written as

$$\underline{R}_k \leq r_k(S, t) \leq \overline{R}_k \quad (k \in \mathcal{R}^\gamma, \ 0 \leq t \leq \overline{d}) \tag{1.20}$$

Definition 1.19 (Resource-feasible and feasible schedules). *A schedule S satisfying the cumulative-resource constraints (1.20) is called resource-feasible with respect to cumulative resources $k \in \mathcal{R}^\gamma$. The set of all resource-feasible schedules is denoted by $\mathcal{S}_C$. $\mathcal{S} := \mathcal{S}_T \cap \mathcal{S}_C$ is the set of all feasible schedules.*

Notice that conditions (1.19) are necessary and sufficient for the existence of a resource-feasible schedule. Under conditions (1.19), a resource-feasible schedule is obtained by scheduling all events at time 0.

The basic *resource-constrained project scheduling problem with cumulative resources* can be stated as follows:

$$
\boxed{
\begin{array}{ll}
\text{Minimize} & f(S) \\
\text{subject to} & S \in \mathcal{S}_T \cap \mathcal{S}_C
\end{array}
}
\tag{1.21}
$$

Definition 1.20 (Optimal schedule). *A feasible schedule S solving the resource-constrained project scheduling problem (1.21) is called optimal.*

Remarks 1.21.

(a) Without loss of generality we may assume that $\overline{R}_k = \infty$ for all $k \in \mathcal{R}^\gamma$ because the storage capacity of resource k can be taken into account by introducing a fictitious resource k' with $\underline{R}_{k'} = -\overline{R}_k$, $\overline{R}_{k'} = \infty$, and $r_{ik'} = -r_{ik}$ for all $i \in V^e$. Since $\mathcal{S}_R$ remains unchanged when adding some integer $r \in \mathbb{Z}$ to r_{0k}, $\underline{R}_k$, and $\overline{R}_k$, we may in addition assume that $\underline{R}_k = 0$ for all $k \in \mathcal{R}^\gamma$.

(b) The resource-constrained project scheduling problem (1.8) with renewable resources is a special case of problem (1.21). To formulate the renewable-resource constraints in terms of temporal and cumulative-resource constraints, we replace each real activity i by two events activities i^s and i^c with $d_{i^s i^c}^{min} = d_{i^s i^c}^{max} = p_i$. For each renewable resource $k \in \mathcal{R}^\rho$, we introduce a cumulative resource k' with safety stock $\underline{R}_{k'} = 0$, storage capacity $\overline{R}_{k'} = \infty$, as well as requirements $r_{0k'} = R_k$, $r_{n+1,k'} = 0$ and $r_{i^s k'} = -r_{ik}$, $r_{i^c k'} = r_{ik}$ for all real activities $i \in V^a$.

In analogy to Section 1.2, the problem without temporal constraints is termed *temporal relaxation*. The *resource relaxation* again coincides with time-constrained project scheduling problem (1.2).

The NP-hardness of finding some feasible schedule follows from the fact that first, the respective problem for the case of renewable resources is NP-hard (cf. Theorem 1.12) and that second, renewable-resource constraints can be expressed by temporal and cumulative-resource constraints without changing the order of magnitude of the problem size. The following theorem shows that, unlike the case of renewable resources, the problem remains NP-hard even if all maximum time lags are deleted.

Theorem 1.22 (Neumann and Schwindt 2002). *The following decision problem is NP-complete.*

> *Instance: A project with one cumulative resource of infinite storage capacity, with $\delta_{ij} \geq 0$ for all $(i,j) \in E$, $(i,j) \neq (n+1,0)$, and with an arbitrarily large project deadline $\overline{d}$.*
>
> *Question: Does there exist a feasible schedule?*

Proof. Clearly, the resource-feasibility of a schedule S can be verified in polynomial time by evaluating the resource constraints for all $k \in \mathcal{R}^\gamma$ and all occurrence times $t = S_i$ of events $i \in V^e$. Hence, the decision problem is contained in NP.

Consider an instance of the NP-complete decision problem 3-PARTITION (cf. Garey and Johnson 1979, problem SP15). Given a set $\mathcal{I}$ of 3ν indices $i = 1,\ldots,3\nu$ with sizes $s(i) \in \mathbb{N}$ and given a bound $M \in \mathbb{N}$ such that $M/4 < s(i) < M/2$ for all $i \in \mathcal{I}$ and $\sum_{i \in \mathcal{I}} s(i) = \nu M$. The question is whether or not $\mathcal{I}$ can be partitioned into ν sets $\mathcal{I}_1,\ldots,\mathcal{I}_\nu$ such that $\sum_{i \in \mathcal{I}_\mu} s(i) = M$ for all $\mu = 1,\ldots,\nu$. An equivalent instance of our decision problem can be constructed as follows. Besides the project beginning 0 and the project termination $n+1$, set V^e contains $n = 4\nu$ events $i = 1,\ldots,4\nu$. There is one cumulative resource with safety stock $\underline{R} = 0$ and infinite storage capacity $\overline{R} = \infty$. The requirements for the cumulative resource are $r_0 = r_{n+1} = 0$, $r_i = s(i)$ for $i = 1,\ldots,3\nu$, and $r_i = -M$ for $i = 3\nu + 1,\ldots,4\nu$. In addition, we define $\nu - 1$ minimum time lags $d^{min}_{i,i+1} = 1$ for $i = 3\nu + 1,\ldots 4\nu - 1$, which prevent the simultaneous occurrence of any two depleting events. Due to $\underline{R} = 0$, each unit consumed must immediately be replenished, which can be achieved precisely if the replenishing events can be assigned to the depleting events such that at each depletion time t, the total replenishment by those events $i = 1,\ldots,3\nu$ with $S_i = t$ equals M. $\square$

1.3.2 Forbidden Sets and Delaying Alternatives

In the case of cumulative resources, we have to consider depletions and replenishments of resources. Moreover, in addition to upper bounds $\overline{R}_k$, there are lower bounds $\underline{R}_k$ on the inventories ($k \in \mathcal{R}^\gamma$). This results in two different types of forbidden sets: so-called surplus sets if the storage capacity is exceeded and shortage sets if the inventory falls below the safety stock.

Definition 1.23 (Surplus and shortage sets). *For a resource $k \in \mathcal{R}^\gamma$, a set of events $F \subseteq V^e$ is called a k-surplus set if*

$$\sum_{i \in F} r_{ik} > \overline{R}_k$$

F is termed a minimal k-surplus set if F is a k-surplus set and there is no k-surplus set $F' \subset F$ with $F \setminus F' \subseteq V_k^{e^+}$ and no k-surplus set $F'' \supset F$ with $F'' \setminus F \subseteq V_k^{e^-}$. Likewise, a set of events $F \subseteq V^e$ is called a k-shortage set if

$$\sum_{i \in F} r_{ik} < \underline{R}_k$$

F is termed a *minimal k-shortage set* if F is a k-shortage set and there is no k-shortage set $F' \subset F$ with $F \setminus F' \subseteq V_k^{e^+}$ and no k-shortage set $F'' \supset F$ with $F'' \setminus F \subseteq V_k^{e^-}$. By $\mathcal{F}_k^+$ and $\mathcal{F}_k^-$ we denote the sets of all minimal k-surplus and all minimal k-shortage sets, respectively.

Note that one and the same set F can be a surplus set with respect to a resource $k \in \mathcal{R}^\gamma$ and a shortage set with respect to a different resource $k' \in \mathcal{R}^\gamma$. In the following, we refer to sets F being k-surplus or k-shortage sets for some resource $k \in \mathcal{R}^\gamma$ as *forbidden sets*. A *minimal forbidden set* is a minimal k-surplus or a minimal k-shortage set for some resource $k \in \mathcal{R}^\gamma$.

Remark 1.24. We assume that $\underline{R}_k \leq 0$ and $\overline{R}_k \geq 0$ for all $k \in \mathcal{R}^\gamma$, which ensures that $F = \emptyset$ is not a forbidden set. It follows from Remark 1.21a that this convention does not mean any loss of generality.

Similarly to the case of renewable resources, the concept of minimal delaying alternatives can be used for breaking up several minimal forbidden sets at once.

Definition 1.25 (Delaying alternative). *Let F be a k-surplus set (a k-shortage set). $B \subseteq F$ is called a delaying alternative for F and k if $F \setminus B$ is not a k-surplus set (not a k-shortage set). If additionally B is $\subseteq$-minimal in the set of all delaying alternatives for F and k, we speak of a minimal delaying alternative for F and k.*

The following two conditions (1.22) and (1.23) are necessary and sufficient for a set $B \subseteq V^e$ to be a minimal delaying alternative for F and k.

$$\sum_{i \in F \setminus B} r_{ik} \leq \overline{R}_k \quad \left(\sum_{i \in F \setminus B} r_{ik} \geq \underline{R}_k \right) \tag{1.22}$$

$$\sum_{i \in F \setminus B} r_{ik} + \min_{j \in B} r_{jk} > \overline{R}_k \quad \left(\sum_{i \in F \setminus B} r_{ik} + \max_{j \in B} r_{jk} < \underline{R}_k \right) \tag{1.23}$$

From (1.23) it immediately follows that minimal delaying alternatives for surplus sets only contain replenishing events and that conversely, minimal delaying alternatives for shortage sets only contain depleting events.

To prove the basic theorem that will show how to resolve resource conflicts in a systematic way, we need the following preliminary lemma.

Lemma 1.26 (Neumann and Schwindt 2002).

(a) *For each k-surplus set F, there exists some set $F' \in \mathcal{F}_k^+$ satisfying the conditions $\emptyset \neq F' \cap V_k^{e^+} \subseteq F \cap V_k^{e^+}$ and $F' \cap V_k^{e^-} \supseteq F \cap V_k^{e^-}$.*
(b) *For each k-shortage set F, there exists some set $F' \in \mathcal{F}_k^+$ satisfying the conditions $\emptyset \neq F' \cap V_k^{e^-} \subseteq F \cap V_k^{e^-}$ and $F' \cap V_k^{e^+} \supseteq F \cap V_k^{e^+}$.*

Proof. Let F be a k-surplus set. We construct a minimal k-surplus set F' satisfying the condition of (a) as follows. We set $F' := F$ and scan the events $j \in F' \cap V_k^{e^+}$. Event j is removed from set F' if $F' \setminus \{j\}$ is still a k-surplus set. Remark 1.24 implies that the resulting set F' contains a replenishing event. Then, we scan the events $j \in V_k^{e^-} \setminus F$ and add j to set F' if $F' \cup \{j\}$ is still a k-surplus set. Consequently, for all events $j \in F'$ replenishing resource k, $F' \setminus \{j\}$ is no longer a k-surplus set and for all events $j \notin F'$ depleting resource k, $F' \cup \{j\}$ is not a k-surplus set, either. Thus, F' represents a minimal k-surplus set meeting the condition of (a). The reasoning for a k-shortage set F is analogous. $\qquad\square$

Proposition 1.27 (Neumann and Schwindt 2002). *Let F be a k-surplus set (resp. k-shortage set). Set B represents a minimal delaying alternative for F and k if and only if B is an $\subseteq$-minimal set containing one event $j \in V_k^{e^+}$ of each minimal k-surplus set $F' \in \mathcal{F}_k^+$ with $F' \cap V_k^{e^+} \subseteq F \cap V_k^{e^+}$ and $F' \cap V_k^{e^-} \supseteq F \cap V_k^{e^-}$ (resp. one event $j \in V_k^{e^-}$ of each minimal k-shortage set $F' \in \mathcal{F}_k^-$ with $F' \cap V_k^{e^-} \subseteq F \cap V_k^{e^-}$ and $F' \cap V_k^{e^+} \supseteq F \cap V_k^{e^+}$).*

Proof. Let F be a k-surplus set for some $k \in \mathcal{R}^\gamma$.

Sufficiency: We consider a set B satisfying

$$\left. \begin{array}{l} F' \cap V_k^{e^+} \cap B \neq \emptyset \text{ for all } F' \in \mathcal{F}_k^+ \text{ with} \\ F' \cap V_k^{e^+} \subseteq F \cap V_k^{e^+} \text{ and } F' \cap V_k^{e^-} \supseteq F \cap V_k^{e^-} \end{array} \right\} \qquad (1.24)$$

Now assume that $\sum_{j \in F \setminus B} r_{jk} > \overline{R}_k$. Then $F \setminus B$ is a k-surplus set, and Lemma 1.26 implies the existence of a set $F' \in \mathcal{F}_k^+$ with $F' \cap V_k^{e^+} \subseteq (F \setminus B) \cap V_k^{e^+}$ and $F' \cap V_k^{e^-} \supseteq (F \setminus B) \cap V_k^{e^-}$. From $F' \cap V_k^{e^+} \subseteq (F \setminus B) \cap V_k^{e^+}$ it then follows that $F' \cap V_k^{e^+} \cap B = \emptyset$, which contradicts the assumption. Consequently, we have $\sum_{j \in F \setminus B} r_{jk} \leq \overline{R}_k$ for any set B with property (1.24), and thus each $\subseteq$-minimal set B meeting condition (1.24) is a minimal delaying alternative.

Necessity: Now let B be a minimal delaying alternative. We assume the existence of a set $F' \in \mathcal{F}_k^+$ with $F' \cap V_k^{e^+} \subseteq F \cap V_k^{e^+}$, $F' \cap V_k^{e^-} \supseteq F \cap V_k^{e^-}$, and $F' \cap V_k^{e^+} \cap B = \emptyset$. Clearly, we have $r_{jk} > 0$ for all $j \in B$, which then implies $B \cap V_k^{e^+} = B$, i.e., $F' \cap B = \emptyset$ and $F' = F' \setminus B$. Thus, $\sum_{j \in F'} r_{jk} = \sum_{j \in F' \setminus B} r_{jk} \leq \sum_{j \in F \setminus B} r_{jk} \leq \overline{R}_k$, i.e., F' is not a k-surplus set, which contradicts the assumption. Moreover, we have $\sum_{j \in F \setminus B'} r_{jk} > \overline{R}_k$ for all subsets $B' \subset B$, which implies that for each $B' \subset B$, there is a set $F' \in \mathcal{F}_k^+$ with $F' \cap V_k^{e^+} \subseteq F \cap V_k^{e^+}$ and $F' \cap V_k^{e^+} \cap B' = \emptyset$ (see the proof of sufficiency). Thus, B is $\subseteq$-minimal in the set of all sets satisfying (1.24).

The proofs for the case of a shortage set F are analogous. $\qquad\square$

Algorithm 1.6, which is a variant of Algorithm 1.4, shows the corresponding recursive procedure used for computing the set $\mathcal{B}$ of all minimal delaying alternatives for a forbidden set F and a resource k. Since the project beginning 0 may be contained in minimal delaying alternatives, the procedure is invoked by *MinimalDelayingAlternatives*$(F, k, -1)$.

Algorithm 1.6. *MinimalDelayingAlternatives*(B, k, i)

Input: A project, a forbidden set B, a resource k, an index i.
Ensure: $\mathcal{B}$ contains all minimal delaying alternatives $B' \subseteq B$ for F and k with $\min(B \setminus B') > i$.

    if B satisfies (1.22) **then** (∗ B is delaying alternative ∗)
      if B satisfies (1.23) **then** (∗ B is minimal delaying alternative ∗)
        $\mathcal{B} := \mathcal{B} \cup \{B\}$;
      else
        for all $j \in B$ with $j > i$ **do** *MinimalDelayingAlternatives*$(B \setminus \{j\}, k, j)$;

1.3.3 Breaking up Forbidden Sets

The following theorem provides a sufficient and necessary condition on the resource-feasibility of schedules with respect to cumulative resources.

Theorem 1.28 (Neumann and Schwindt 2002). *A schedule S is resource-feasible if and only if*

(a) *for each $F \in \mathcal{F}_k^+$ with $k \in \mathcal{R}^\gamma$, there exist two events $j \in F \cap V_k^{e^+}$ and $i \in V_k^{e^-} \setminus F$ such that $S_j \geq S_i$, and*
(b) *for each $F \in \mathcal{F}_k^-$ with $k \in \mathcal{R}^\gamma$, there exist two events $j \in F \cap V_k^{e^-}$ and $i \in V_k^{e^+} \setminus F$ such that $S_j \geq S_i$.*

Proof. Sufficiency: Let S be a schedule with $r_k(S,t) > \overline{R}_k$ for some resource $k \in \mathcal{R}^\gamma$ and some point in time $t \geq 0$. Lemma 1.26 then provides the existence of a minimal k-surplus set $F \in \mathcal{F}_k^+$ for which $\emptyset \neq F \cap V_k^{e^+} \subseteq \mathcal{A}(S,t) \cap V_k^{e^+}$ and $F \cap V_k^{e^-} \supseteq \mathcal{A}(S,t) \cap V_k^{e^-}$. Moreover, (1.19) ensures that $V_k^{e^-} \setminus F \neq \emptyset$. Due to $F \cap V_k^{e^+} \subseteq \mathcal{A}(S,t)$ we have $S_j \leq t$ for all $j \in F \cap V_k^{e^+}$. In addition, $V_k^{e^-} \setminus F \subseteq V^e \setminus \mathcal{A}(S,t)$ implies $S_i > t$ for all $i \in V_k^{e^-} \setminus F$. Thus, $S_j < S_i$ holds for all $j \in F \cap V_k^{e^+}$ and all $i \in V_k^{e^-} \setminus F$, which contradicts condition (a). Similarly it can be shown that from a shortage in some resource k at a time $t \geq 0$ it follows that condition (b) is not met.

Necessity: Let $F \in \mathcal{F}_k^+$ be a minimal k-surplus set violating (a), i.e., for all $j \in F \cap V_k^{e^+}$ and all $i \in V_k^{e^-} \setminus F$, we have $S_j < S_i$. From Remark 1.24 it follows that F contains an event replenishing resource k. Let $t := \max_{j \in F \cap V_k^{e^+}} S_j$ be the point in time at which the last replenishing event $j \in F$ occurs. Due to $F \cap V_k^{e^+} \subseteq \mathcal{A}(S,t)$ and $(V_k^{e^-} \setminus F) \cap \mathcal{A}(S,t) = \emptyset$, we obtain $r_k(S,t) \geq \sum_{j \in F} r_{jk} > \overline{R}_k$, i.e., S is not resource-feasible. The case of $F \in \mathcal{F}_k^-$ can be dealt with analogously. $\square$

Theorem 1.28 states that any *resource conflict* caused by the occurrence of the events of some forbidden set can be resolved by adding precedence constraints $S_j \geq S_i$ to the original temporal constraints. As a consequence, the set $\mathcal{S}_C$ of all resource-feasible schedules represents a union of polyhedral cones, and the set $\mathcal{S}$ of all feasible schedules again is a finite union of integral polytopes. Since each project scheduling problem with renewable-resource constraints can be represented as an equivalent project scheduling problem with cumulative-resource constraints, this union is generally disconnected.

Similarly to the case of renewable resources, forbidden sets F can be broken up by introducing (ordinary) precedence constraints or disjunctive precedence constraints. Let F be a k-surplus set for some resource k and let B be some minimal delaying alternative for F and k. Then we may either impose a set of precedence constraints

$$S_j \geq S_i \quad (j \in B)$$

between some depleting event i from set $A = V_k^{e^-} \setminus F$ and all replenishing events j from set B or, alternatively, a disjunctive precedence constraint

$$\min_{j \in B} S_j \geq \min_{i \in A} S_i$$

between sets A and B. For breaking up a k-shortage set F, we may introduce a set of precedence constraints

$$S_j \geq S_i \quad (j \in B)$$

between some replenishing event i from set $A = V_k^{e^+} \setminus F$ and all events j from a corresponding minimal delaying alternative B or by a disjunctive precedence constraint

$$\min_{j \in B} S_j \geq \min_{i \in A} S_i$$

between sets A and B. Since compared to project scheduling with renewable-resource constraints, set A typically contains a large number of elements, the use of disjunctive precedence constraints instead of ordinary precedence constraints generally leads to a tremendous decrease in the size of the enumeration tree of branch-and-bound methods.

1.3.4 Consistency Tests

As for project scheduling problems with renewable-resource constraints, consistency tests can be used to draw conclusions about temporal constraints that must necessarily be satisfied by resource-feasible schedules.

Neumann and Schwindt (2002) have used the **profile test** for calculating lower bounds on the minimum project duration. Assume that some event i cannot take place before a hypothetical earliest occurrence time t_i. We add the corresponding arc $(0, i)$ with weight t_i to project network N. Let S^k with $k \in \mathcal{R}^\gamma$ be the (generally not time-feasible) schedule where replenishments arise as early as possible and depletions occur late as possible, i.e.,

$$\left. \begin{array}{l} S_i^k = ES_i, \text{ if } r_{ik} > 0 \\ S_i^k = LS_i, \text{ otherwise} \end{array} \right\} \quad (i \in V^e)$$

The corresponding loading profile $r_k(S^k, \cdot)$ then provides an upper approximation to the loading profile of any resource-feasible schedule. If $r_k(S^k, t) < \underline{R}_k$ for some time t, it has thus been shown that event i must arise before time t_i, i.e., $S_i \leq t_i - 1$ (notice that $\mathrm{conv}(\mathcal{S})$ is again an integral polytope). The contradiction may also be derived from comparing the storage capacity $\overline{R}_k$ of resources k with lower approximations to resource-feasible loading profiles obtained by scheduling depletions at earliest and replenishments at latest occurrence times. Similarly to the shaving technique for project scheduling with renewable resources, the tentative values for t_i can be tested according to a binary search in set $[ES_i, LS_i] \cap \mathbb{Z}$. Hence, the profile test can be implemented to run in $\mathcal{O}(\log \overline{d} |\mathcal{R}^\gamma| n \log n)$ time per event i. Recalculating the earliest occurrence times after having applied the test takes $\mathcal{O}(n)$ time (cf. Remark 1.8). Instead of earliest occurrence times we can also establish hypotheses on latest occurrence times, which may then be falsified by the same techniques.

The following **balance test** has been devised by Laborie (2003). Event $h \in V^e$ *must* occur before event $j \in V^e$ precisely if $d_{hj} > 0$, and h *may* occur before j exactly if $d_{jh} < 0$. Now let $d_{0j} > 0$. By considering all depleting events that must occur before j and all replenishing events that may occur before j, we obtain the upper bound

$$\overline{r}_k^<(j) = \sum_{h \in V_k^{e^-} : d_{hj} > 0} r_{hk} + \sum_{h \in V_k^{e^+} : d_{jh} < 0} r_{hk}$$

on the inventory level in resource k just before the occurrence of j. By rearranging the terms, $\overline{r}^<(j)$ can also be written as

$$\overline{r}_k^<(j) = \sum_{h \in V^e : d_{hj} > 0} r_{hk} + \sum_{\substack{h \in V_k^{e^+} : \\ d_{jh} < 0, d_{hj} \leq 0}} r_{hk}$$

i.e., as the sum of all requirements that must take place before j and all replenishments that possibly but not necessarily occur before j. Now assume that $\sum_{h \in V^e : d_{hj} > 0} r_{hk} < \underline{R}_k$, which implies that some of the latter replenishments must arise before j. Let $h_1, \ldots, h_\nu$ be a numbering of the events from set $V_k^{e^+}(j) := \{h \in V_k^{e^+} \mid d_{jh} < 0, d_{hj} \leq 0\}$ according to nondecreasing earliest occurrence times ES_h, and let μ be the smallest index such that

$$\sum_{h \in V^e : d_{hj} > 0} r_{hk} + \sum_{\lambda=1}^{\mu} r_{h_\lambda k} \geq \underline{R}_k$$

Then j must occur after time ES_{h_μ}, and we obtain the temporal constraint $S_j \geq ES_{h_\mu} + 1$. If distance matrix D is given, the time needed for applying the balance test to activity j is of order $\mathcal{O}(|\mathcal{R}^\gamma| n \log n)$. Updating matrix D after having increased ES_j takes $\mathcal{O}(n^2)$ time.

The balance test can be strengthened as follows. We consider one event $i \in V_k^{e^+}(j)$ and we assume that $S_i \geq S_j$. Then upper bound $\overline{r}_k^<(j)$ on the inventory level in resource k at time S_j-1 can be reduced by all replenishments from set $V_k^{e^+}(j)$ which cannot occur strictly before i (and due to $S_i \geq S_j$ thus cannot occur strictly before j). This means that if

$$\overline{r}_k^{\leq}(j) - \sum_{\substack{h \in V_k^{e^+}: \\ d_{jh}<0, d_{hj}\leq 0, d_{ih}\geq 0}} r_{hk} < \underline{R}_k$$

for some $k \in \mathcal{R}^\gamma$, then it must hold that $S_j \geq S_i + 1$. This variant of the test takes $\mathcal{O}(|\mathcal{R}^\gamma|n)$ time per pair (i,j) of events.

Similar consistency tests can be performed based on the upper bound

$$\overline{r}_k^{\leq}(j) = \sum_{i \in V_k^{e^-}:d_{ij}\geq 0} r_{ik} + \sum_{i \in V_k^{e^+}:d_{ji}\leq 0} r_{ik}$$

on the inventory level at the occurrence of event j and the corresponding lower bounds $\underline{r}_k^{\leq}(j)$ and $\underline{r}_k^{\leq}(j)$.

Relations, Schedules, and Objective Functions

When allocating scarce resources over time we have to define precedence relationships among the activities of the project. Those precedence relationships establish a binary relation in the activity set of the project. Together with the original temporal constraints, the binary relation gives rise to a preorder in the activity set. Depending on the type of basic project scheduling problem given and the specific objective function to be minimized, different types of preorders have to be investigated. In this chapter we review and extend a classification of schedules and objective functions that has been proposed by Neumann et al. (2000). The classification is based on two basic representations of the feasible region of project scheduling problems as unions of relation-induced polytopes. The purpose of the classification is to provide, for each class of objective functions, a finite set of candidates for optimal schedules that are characterized as specific points of the relation-induced polytopes such as minimal points, local minimizers of the objective function, or vertices.

2.1 Resource Constraints and Feasible Relations

Before we discuss the relationship between resource constraints and certain relations in the set of real activities or events, respectively, we first review some basic terminology.

Definition 2.1 (Binary relation, preorder, and strict order). *A binary relation ρ in (ground) set X is a set of pairs $(x, y) \in X \times X$. Relation ρ' in X with $\rho' \supseteq \rho$ is termed an extension of ρ. $tr(\rho)$ denotes the transitive hull of relation ρ, i.e., the $\subseteq$-minimal transitive extension of ρ in X. A transitive binary relation θ in set X is termed a preorder in X. Two elements $x, y \in X$ are referred to as comparable in preorder θ if $(x, y) \in \theta$ or $(y, x) \in \theta$, and incomparable, otherwise. θ is a complete preorder if $(i, j) \in \theta$ or $(j, i) \in \theta$ for all $i, j \in X$, $i \neq j$. A set $U \subseteq X$ of pairwise incomparable elements is called an antichain in θ. $\mathrm{Pred}^\theta(x) = \{y \in X \mid (y, x) \in \theta\}$ is the set of predecessors of*

x in θ. $x \in Y \subseteq X$ is called a *maximal element of* Y in θ if $(y, x) \in \theta$ implies $(x, y) \in \theta$ for all $y \in Y$, $y \neq x$. An irreflexive preorder is asymmetric and thus represents a strict order. The covering relation $cr(\theta)$ of strict order θ is the $\subseteq$-minimal binary relation ρ in X with $tr(\rho) = \theta$. The precedence graph of strict order θ is the directed graph $G(\theta)$ with node set X and arc set $cr(\theta)$.

When we deal with renewable resources, forbidden sets F are broken up by introducing precedence constraints $S_j \geq S_i + p_i$ between real activities $i, j \in F$. In other words, we construct a strict order θ in the set V^a of real activities where $(i, j) \in \theta$ means that activity j cannot be started before activity i has been completed. In case of cumulative resources, surplus and shortage sets F are broken up by introducing precedence constraints $S_j \geq S_i$ between events $i \in V^e \setminus F$ and events $j \in F$. Thus, by resolving cumulative-resource conflicts we establish a reflexive preorder θ in event set V^e whose elements (i, j) say that event j cannot take place before the occurrence of event i.

The following two types of preorders will be needed when studying precedence relationships between real activities or events that are induced by a given schedule.

Definition 2.2 (Interval order and weak order). *An interval order in set X is a strict order θ in X for which $(w, x), (y, z) \in \theta$ implies $(w, z) \in \theta$ or $(y, x) \in \theta$ for all $w, x, y, z \in X$. A (reflexive) weak order in set X is a complete and reflexive preorder in X.*

2.1.1 Renewable-Resource Constraints

In this subsection we consider irreflexive relations in the set V^a of real activities for the scheduling of projects with renewable resources. We first define the concepts of time-feasible and feasible relations, which go back to the work of Radermacher (1978) and Bartusch et al. (1988). In difference to the treatment of the material by Neumann et al. (2000) and Neumann et al. (2003b), Sect. 2.3, we use relations instead of strict orders, which allows of a unifying view on renewable-resource and cumulative-resource constraints.

Definition 2.3 (Time-feasible and feasible relations). *Let ρ be an irreflexive relation in set V^a and let $\mathcal{S}_T(\rho) := \{S \in \mathcal{S}_T \mid S_j \geq S_i + p_i$ for all $(i, j) \in \rho\}$ be the set of all time-feasible schedules satisfying the precedence constraints given by ρ. $\mathcal{S}_T(\rho)$ is called the relation polytope of ρ. Relation ρ is termed time-feasible if $\mathcal{S}_T(\rho) \neq \emptyset$. A time-feasible relation ρ with $\mathcal{S}_T(\rho) \subseteq \mathcal{S}$ is called feasible.*

Condition $\mathcal{S}_T(\rho) \neq \emptyset$ means that the precedence constraints from relation ρ do not contradict the prescribed temporal constraints. If $\mathcal{S}_T(\rho) \subseteq \mathcal{S}$, all schedules satisfying those precedence constraints are feasible. If ρ is a feasible relation, then all time-feasible extensions $\rho' \supseteq \rho$ are feasible as well. A feasible relation ρ represents a solution to the *sequencing problem* of resource allocation, which consists in determining a (partial) order in which competing activities are processed on the resources. The subsequent *time-constrained project scheduling* of the activities is achieved by finding some (necessarily feasible) schedule $S \in \mathcal{S}_T(\rho)$ minimizing objective function f on $\mathcal{S}_T(\rho)$.

Let $\mathcal{M} \subseteq \mathcal{S}_T$ be a nonempty set of time-feasible schedules. We say that S is a *minimal point* of $\mathcal{M}$ if there is no $S' \in \mathcal{M}$ with $S' < S$, where $S' < S$ means $S' \leq S$ and $S' \neq S$. Relation polytope $\mathcal{S}_T(\rho)$ is the set of all time-feasible schedules belonging to the following "expanded" project network $N(\rho)$. As a consequence, the corresponding earliest schedule represents the *unique* minimal point of polytope $\mathcal{S}_T(\rho)$ (see Subsection 1.1.3).

Definition 2.4 (Relation network). *Given relation ρ in set V^a, the relation network $N(\rho)$ results from project network N by adding, for each pair $(i,j) \in \rho$, the arc (i,j) with weight p_i. By $D(\rho) = (d_{ij}^{\rho})_{i,j \in V^a}$ we denote the distance matrix belonging to relation network $N(\rho)$.*

Bartusch et al. (1988) consider time-feasible strict orders θ that are extensions of the strict order

$$\Theta(D) := \{(i,j) \in V^a \times V^a \mid d_{ij} \geq p_i\}$$

in V^a induced by distance matrix D. We shall call such a strict order θ *BMR-feasible* if no antichain U in θ is forbidden. As we shall prove later on, the antichains in θ are exactly the sets of real activities which, subject to the precedence constraints from θ, can be in progress simultaneously. That is why any BMR-feasible strict order is feasible as well. On the other hand, there may be feasible strict orders $\theta \supseteq \Theta(D)$ which are not BMR-feasible, as will be illustrated in Example 2.10. The reason for this is that in general $\Theta(D(\theta)) \supset tr(\theta \cup \Theta(D))$. In the case where $\delta_{ij} \geq p_i$ for all $(i,j) \in E$, strict order θ is feasible precisely if $tr(\theta \cup \Theta(D)) = \Theta(D(\theta))$ is feasible.

By applying Theorem 1.17 we obtain the first basic representation of the set $\mathcal{S}$ of all feasible schedules.

Proposition 2.5 (Bartusch et al. 1988). *Let $\mathcal{MFR}$ be the set of all $\subseteq$-minimal feasible relations in activity set V^a. Then $\{\mathcal{S}_T(\rho) \mid \rho \in \mathcal{MFR}\}$ is a covering of $\mathcal{S}$.*

Notice that in general the above covering is not a partition of $\mathcal{S}$ because two different time-feasible relations ρ and ρ' may not be contradicting each other (i.e., $\mathcal{S}_T(\rho \cup \rho') = \mathcal{S}_T(\rho) \cap \mathcal{S}_T(\rho') \neq \emptyset$). Proposition 2.5 will be useful when dealing with objective functions that can efficiently be minimized on convex polytopes like regular or convex functions. In this case, the basic resource-constrained project scheduling problem (1.8) can be solved by enumerating (subsets of) relations $\rho \in \mathcal{MFR}$.

In the following we develop characterizations of time-feasible and feasible relations that allow for efficiently checking the feasibility of a given relation.

The latter technique will be used when dealing with the case of uncertain input data in Section 6.5, where solving a resource allocation problem requires the generation of appropriate feasible relations in the activity set. We shall apply a similar approach in Section 5.2 for deciding on the feasibility of schedules when resource units are occupied during a sequence-dependent changeover time between the execution of consecutive activities.

Proposition 2.6 (Neumann et al. 2000). *Relation ρ in V^a is time-feasible if and only if relation network $N(\rho)$ does not contain any directed cycle of positive length.*

Proof. By definition, relation ρ is time-feasible exactly if $\mathcal{S}_T(\rho) \neq \emptyset$. Polytope $\mathcal{S}_T(\rho)$ corresponds to the set of time-feasible schedules belonging to network $N(\rho)$. From Proposition 1.7 it follows that there is a time-feasible schedule for $N(\rho)$ precisely if $N(\rho)$ does not contain any directed cycle of positive length. $\qquad\square$

As a consequence of Proposition 2.6, checking the time-feasibility of ρ can be done in $\mathcal{O}(n[m + |\rho|])$ time by applying Algorithm 1.1 to relation network $N(\rho)$ for computing distances d_{0i}^ρ for all $i \in V^a$. The next proposition shows how the feasibility of ρ can be established on the basis of distance matrix $D(\rho)$. We need the following preliminary lemma.

Lemma 2.7. *Let $\mathcal{S}_T \neq \emptyset$ and let $U \subseteq V^a$ be a set of real activities such that $d_{ij} < p_i$ for all $i, j \in U$. Then there exists a time-feasible schedule S with $\mathcal{A}(S, t) \supseteq U$ for some $t \geq 0$.*

Proof. Two activities $i, j \in U$ necessarily overlap in time if $d_{ij}^{max} < p_i$ and $d_{ji}^{max} < p_j$. Now assume that we add, for all $i, j \in U$ with $i \neq j$, a corresponding arc (j, i) weighted by $\delta_{ji} = -p_i + 1$ to project network N. We consider the addition of one of those arcs (j, i). $d_{ij} < p_i$ or, equivalently, $d_{ij} \leq p_i - 1$ implies $d_{ij} + \delta_{ji} \leq p_i - 1 - p_i + 1 = 0$. Proposition 1.9 then says that there is no directed cycle of positive length in the resulting (expanded) network. Moreover, for all modified distances d_{gh} with $g, h \in U$ we have $d_{gh} = d_{gj} + \delta_{ji} + d_{ih} = d_{gj} - p_i + 1 + d_{ih} \leq p_g - 1 - p_i + 1 + p_i - 1 = p_g - 1$ so that property $d_{gh} < p_g$ is preserved for all $g, h \in U$. Thus, after the addition of all arcs $(j, i) \in U \times U$ with $i \neq j$ there is no directed cycle of positive length in the resulting network N'. Proposition 1.7 then yields $\mathcal{S}_T' \neq \emptyset$ for the set $\mathcal{S}_T'$ of time-feasible schedules belonging to network N'. Due to the added maximum time lags, any two activities $i, j \in U$ overlap in time for each schedule $S \in \mathcal{S}_T'$, i.e., $[S_i, S_i + p_i[\cap [S_j, S_j + p_j[\neq \emptyset$ for all $i, j \in U$. The Helly property of intervals then implies that the interval $\cap_{i \in U} [S_i, S_i + p_i[$ during which all activities from set U overlap is nonempty for each $S \in \mathcal{S}_T'$. $\qquad\square$

A constructive proof of Lemma 2.7 for the case where no deadline $\overline{d}$ for the latest termination of the project is prescribed can be found in Bartusch et al. (1988).

Proposition 2.8 (Neumann et al. 2003b, Sect. 2.3). *Time-feasible relation ρ in V^a is feasible if and only if for each minimal forbidden set $F \in \mathcal{F}$, relation network $N(\rho)$ contains a directed path of length $d_{ij}^\rho \geq p_i$ from some node $i \in F$ to some node $j \in F$.*

Proof. Sufficiency: Let ρ be a time-feasible relation such that for all minimal forbidden sets $F \in \mathcal{F}$, there is a pair (i, j) of activities $i, j \in F$ with $d_{ij}^\rho \geq p_i$. Each schedule $S \in \mathcal{S}_T(\rho)$ satisfies precedence constraint $S_j \geq S_i + p_i$ for all those pairs $(i, j) \in \Theta(D(\rho))$. From Theorem 1.17 it then follows that all schedules $S \in \mathcal{S}_T(\rho)$ are resource-feasible. Thus, with $\mathcal{S}_T(\rho) \subseteq \mathcal{S}_T$ we have $\emptyset \neq \mathcal{S}_T(\rho) \subseteq \mathcal{S}_R \cap \mathcal{S}_T = \mathcal{S}$.

Necessity: We assume that there is a forbidden set F with $d_{ij}^\rho < p_i$ for all $i, j \in F$. Then from Lemma 2.7 it follows that there exists a schedule $S \in \mathcal{S}_T(\rho)$ for which all activities $i \in F$ overlap in time. Thus, S is not resource-feasible and $\mathcal{S}_T(\rho) \not\subseteq \mathcal{S}$, which contradicts the feasibility of relation ρ. $\qquad\square$

The following theorem is a direct consequence of Proposition 2.8.

Theorem 2.9. *Time-feasible relation ρ in V^a is feasible if and only if no antichain in strict order $\Theta(D(\rho))$ is forbidden.*

Proof. U is an antichain in $\Theta(D(\rho))$ exactly if $d_{ij}^\rho < p_i$ for all $i, j \in U$. Proposition 2.8 says that ρ is feasible if and only if no antichain in $\Theta(D(\rho))$ is a minimal forbidden set. Obviously, this is true exactly if no antichain is an (arbitrary) forbidden set because any forbidden antichain U would embed some minimal forbidden subchain $U' \subseteq U$. $\qquad\square$

Theorem 2.9 implies that the feasibility of a time-feasible relation ρ can be verified by finding, for each $k \in \mathcal{R}^\rho$, a maximum-weight stable set U_k in the precedence graph $G(\theta)$ of strict order $\theta = \Theta(D(\rho))$ with weights r_{ik} for nodes $i \in V^a$. Since $G(\theta)$ is a transitive directed graph (see, e.g., Bang-Jensen and Gutin 2002, Sect. 1.8), such a set U_k can be determined efficiently by computing a minimum (s, t)-flow u^k in a flow network $\overline{G}_k(\theta)$ arising from $G(\theta)$ by adding two nodes s and t and arcs (s, i) and (j, t) for sources i and sinks j of $G(\theta)$ and where lower node capacities r_{ik} for nodes $i \in V^a$ have to be observed (cf. Kaerkes and Leipholz 1977 and Möhring 1985). This can be done in $\mathcal{O}(n^3)$ time by two applications of the FIFO preflow push algorithm for the maximum-flow problem with upper arc capacities (see, e.g., Ahuja et al. 1993, Sect. 7.7, or Bang-Jensen and Gutin 2002, Sect. 3.9). ρ is feasible precisely if for each $k \in \mathcal{R}^\rho$, the minimum-flow value $\phi(u^k)$ and thus the weight $\sum_{i \in U_k} r_{ik}$ of stable set U_k is less than or equal to resource capacity R_k.

Example 2.10. We consider a project with four real activities and one renewable resource. Figure 2.1a shows the relation network $N(\rho)$ belonging to strict order $\rho = \{(1, 2), (3, 4)\}$, where nodes $i \in V^a$ are labelled with durations p_i on the top and resource requirements r_i in boldface on the bottom. The resource capacity is $R = 2$. There are five minimal forbidden sets $\{1,2\}$, $\{1,3\}$, $\{1,4\}$, $\{2,4\}$, and $\{3,4\}$. ρ is *not* BMR-feasible because antichains $\{1,3\}$, $\{1,4\}$, and $\{2,4\}$ are forbidden sets. The strict order $\theta = \Theta(D(\rho))$ induced by distance matrix $D(\rho)$ equals $\{(1,2),(1,3),(1,4),(2,4),(3,4)\}$. The corresponding flow network $\overline{G}(\theta)$ is shown in Figure 2.1b. Each node i is labelled with lower node capacity r_i and each arc (i,j) is labelled with minimum flow u_{ij} on (i,j). A maximum-weight antichain in θ is $U = \{2,3\}$ whose weight $r_2 + r_3 = 2 \le R$ equals the minimum flow value $\phi(u)$. Thus, strict order ρ is feasible.

(a)

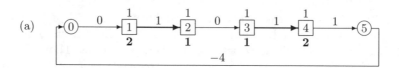

(b)

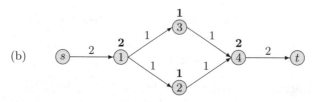

Fig. 2.1. Difference between feasibility and BMR-feasibility of strict orders: **(a)** relation network $N(\rho)$; **(b)** minimum (s,t)-flow in network $\overline{G}(\theta)$

We now turn to strict orders θ in V^a that are given by the precedence relationships induced by some schedule S.

Definition 2.11 (Schedule-induced strict order). *Given a schedule S, strict order $\theta(S) := \{(i,j) \in V^a \times V^a \mid S_j \ge S_i + p_i\}$ is the schedule-induced strict order which corresponds to the precedence relationships established by S. The relation polytope $\mathcal{S}_T(\theta(S))$ of $\theta(S)$ is called the schedule polytope of S, and the relation network $N(\theta(S))$ is called the schedule network of S.*

Schedule-induced strict orders $\theta(S)$ belong to the class of interval orders. This can be seen as follows. Let S be some schedule and let $(g,h),(i,j) \in \theta(S)$. If $(i,h) \notin \theta(S)$, then $S_j \ge S_i + p_i > S_h \ge S_g + p_g$, i.e., $(g,j) \in \theta(S)$.
By Definition 2.3 we have

$$\mathcal{S}_T(\rho) = \{S \in \mathcal{S}_T \mid \theta(S) \supseteq \rho\} \tag{2.1}$$

If schedule S is time-feasible, $\mathcal{S}_T(\theta(S))$ contains S. If schedule S is feasible, we have $\mathcal{S}_T(\theta(S)) \subseteq S$. The reason for this is that all schedules $S' \in \mathcal{S}_T(\theta(S))$ satisfy $\theta(S') \supseteq \theta(S)$ (compare (2.1)) and thus each active set $\mathcal{A}(S',t')$ with

$0 \le t' < \overline{d}$ is a subset of some active set $\mathcal{A}(S, t)$ where $0 \le t < \overline{d}$. This proves the following proposition.

Proposition 2.12 (Neumann et al. 2000). *Strict order $\theta(S)$ induced by a time-feasible schedule S is feasible if and only if schedule S is feasible.*

Notice that for a time-feasible schedule S, strict order $\theta(S)$ represents *the* $\subseteq$-maximal relation whose relation polytope contains S. This can easily be shown by assuming the existence of some relation $\rho \supset \theta(S)$ with $S \in \mathcal{S}_T(\rho)$. Then relation ρ contains a pair $(i, j) \notin \theta(S)$. That is, we have $S_j < S_i + p_i$, which contradicts the assumption $S \in \mathcal{S}_T(\rho)$. The latter observation implies the following statement.

Proposition 2.13. *Each $\subseteq$-maximal feasible relation is induced by some feasible schedule.*

The relation polytope $\mathcal{S}_T(\theta)$ of some strict order θ is the set of all time-feasible schedules inducing an extension of θ. The set of all schedules inducing θ is termed the equal-order set of θ.

Definition 2.14 (Equal-order set). *Let θ be some schedule-induced strict order in set V^a. Equal-order set $\mathcal{S}_T^{\overline{=}}(\theta) := \{S \in \mathcal{S}_T \mid \theta(S) = \theta\}$ is the set of all time-feasible schedules inducing strict order θ.*

Equal-order sets represent differences of schedule polytopes and thus are generally not closed. If θ is an $\subseteq$-maximal time-feasible strict order, we have $\mathcal{S}_T^{\overline{=}}(\theta) = \mathcal{S}_T(\theta)$, and $\mathcal{S}_T^{\overline{=}}(\theta) \subset \mathcal{S}_T(\theta)$, otherwise. Equal-order sets are convex because every schedule S on a line segment joining two schedules $S', S'' \in \mathcal{S}_T^{\overline{=}}(\theta)$ induces strict order θ. The concept of equal-order sets leads to the second basic representation of the set $\mathcal{S}$ of all feasible schedules.

Proposition 2.15. *Let $\mathcal{SIO}$ be the set of all feasible schedule-induced strict orders. Then $\{\mathcal{S}_T^{\overline{=}}(\theta) \mid \theta \in \mathcal{SIO}\}$ is a partition of $\mathcal{S}$.*

We will refer to this representation of $\mathcal{S}$ when dealing with resource levelling problems, where the objective function is regular or concave on equal-order sets and thus can be minimized by investigating minimal points or vertices, respectively, of equal-order sets. The following proposition shows that this corresponds to enumerating minimal points or vertices of schedule polytopes.

Proposition 2.16. *For a given project, the set of all minimal points (resp. vertices) of equal-order sets coincides with the set of all minimal points (resp. vertices) of schedule polytopes.*

Proof. We show the coincidence of the vertex sets. The same reasoning can be applied to minimal points. Let S be a vertex of some schedule polytope $\mathcal{S}_T(\theta)$. Then S is a vertex of equal-order set $\mathcal{S}_T^{\overline{=}}(\theta(S))$ as well because $S \in \mathcal{S}_T^{\overline{=}}(\theta(S))$ and $\mathcal{S}_T^{\overline{=}}(\theta(S)) \subseteq \mathcal{S}_T(\theta)$. Now let S be a vertex of some equal-order set $\mathcal{S}_T^{\overline{=}}(\theta)$. Then $\mathcal{S}_T^{\overline{=}}(\theta) = \mathcal{S}_T(\theta(S)) \setminus (\cup_{\rho \supset \theta} \mathcal{S}_T(\rho))$. Since set $\cup_{\rho \supset \theta} \mathcal{S}_T(\rho)$ is closed, S must be a vertex of $\mathcal{S}_T(\theta(S))$. $\qquad\square$

2.1.2 Cumulative-Resource Constraints

In this subsection we are concerned with relations establishing precedence relationships between the events of a project with cumulative resources. The concepts of time-feasible and feasible relations are defined in analogy to (time-) feasible relations for the case of renewable resources.

Definition 2.17 (Time-feasible and feasible relations). *Let ρ be a relation in event set V^e and let $\mathcal{S}_T(\rho) := \{S \in \mathcal{S}_T \mid S_j \geq S_i \text{ for all } (i,j) \in \rho\}$ be the relation polytope of ρ. Relation ρ is termed time-feasible if $\mathcal{S}_T(\rho) \neq \emptyset$. A time-feasible relation ρ is called feasible if $\mathcal{S}_T(\rho) \subseteq \mathcal{S}$.*

A feasible relation in set V^e defines precedence constraints between the events from set V^e which are consistent with the temporal constraints and which ensure that all schedules $S \in \mathcal{S}_T(\rho)$ are feasible. The concepts of relation network $N(\rho)$ and corresponding distance matrix $D(\rho)$ are defined as for strict orders.

$$\Theta(D) := \{(i,j) \in V^e \times V^e \mid d_{ij} \geq 0\}$$

denotes the reflexive preorder in set V^e induced by distance matrix D.

Theorem 1.28 provides the first relation-based representation of the $\mathcal{S}$ of all feasible schedules.

Proposition 2.18. *Let $\mathcal{MFR}$ be the set of all $\subseteq$-minimal feasible relations in event set V^e. Then $\{\mathcal{S}_T(\rho) \mid \rho \in \mathcal{MFR}\}$ is a covering of $\mathcal{S}$.*

Again, the covering of $\mathcal{S}$ by relation polytopes is generally not a partition.

As for relations in set V^a, we investigate how the feasibility of a given relation in the event set can be checked efficiently. We need two preliminary lemmas. The first lemma shows that any event set $U \subseteq V^e$ arising from the union of predecessor sets in reflexive preorder $\Theta(D)$ can be an active set. The second lemma states that if not all minimal forbidden sets are broken up by precedence constraints induced by distance matrix D, then there exists a forbidden set satisfying the conditions of Lemma 2.19, which implies that there are time-feasible schedules which are not resource-feasible.

Lemma 2.19. *Let $\mathcal{S}_T \neq \emptyset$ and let $U \subseteq V^e$ be a set of events such that for all $i, j \in V^e$ with $d_{ij} \geq 0$, $j \in U$ implies $i \in U$. Then there exists a time-feasible schedule S with $\mathcal{A}(S, t) = U$ for some $t \geq 0$.*

Proof. We select some $j \in U$ with $d_{ji} \leq 0$ for all $i \in U$, e.g., a maximal element of U in reflexive preorder $\Theta(D)$. Since set U is finite, such a maximal element always exists. Event $i \in U$ necessarily occurs no later than j if $d_{ij}^{min} \geq 0$, and event $i \notin U$ must occur after j if $d_{ij}^{min} > 0$. Suppose that project network N is expanded by adding an arc (i,j) with weight $\delta_{ij} = 0$ for each $i \in U$, $i \neq j$ and by adding an arc (j,i) with weight $\delta_{ji} = 1$ for each $i \notin U$. In what follows we prove that the resulting network N' does not contain directed cycles of positive length. Event j has been chosen such that (1) $d_{jh} \leq 0$ for all $h \in U$.

Moreover, from the definition of set U it follows that (2) $d_{gh} \leq -1$ for all $g \notin U$, $h \in U$. We first consider the addition of one arc (i, j) with $i \in U$. Since (1) provides $d_{ji} \leq 0$, it follows from Proposition 1.9 that no directed cycle of positive length is created. Next we show that the updated distance matrix D still satisfies inequalities (1) and (2). Obviously, adding (i, j) does not change any distance d_{jh} with $h \in U$ since from (1) we have $d_{ji} + \delta_{ij} + d_{jh} \leq 0 + 0 + d_{jh} = d_{jh}$. For distances d_{gh} with $g \notin U$ and $h \in U$ that are modified when calling Algorithm 1.3 we have $d_{gh} = d_{gi} + \delta_{ij} + d_{jh} \leq -1 + 0 + 0 = -1$ because of (1) and (2). Now consider the addition of one arc (j, i) where $i \notin U$. (2) provides $d_{ji} + d_{ij} \leq 1 + (-1) = 0$, and thus none of the created directed cycles has positive length. By applying (2) we obtain the inequality $d_{jh} = d_{jj} + \delta_{ji} + d_{ih} \leq 0 + 1 + (-1) = 0$ for the modified distances d_{jh} with $h \in U$. From (2) is also follows that $d_{gh} = d_{gj} + \delta_{ji} + d_{ih} \leq -1 + 1 - 1 = -1$ for the modified distances d_{gh} with $g \notin U$ and $h \in U$.

Thus, we can introduce a minimum time lag $d_{ij}^{min} = 0$ for all $i \in U$, $i \neq j$ and a minimum time lag $d_{ji}^{min} = 1$ for all $i \notin U$ such that the reduced set $\mathcal{S}_T'$ of time-feasible schedules belonging to expanded project network N' is nonempty. Since all events $i \in U$ occur before or at the same time as j and all events $i \notin U$ must be scheduled (strictly) later than j, the active set $\mathcal{A}(S, S_j)$ at time S_j coincides with set U for all schedules $S \in \mathcal{S}_T'$. □

Lemma 2.20. *If there is a minimal k-surplus set $F \in \mathcal{F}_k^+$ with $d_{ij} < 0$ for all $i \in V_k^{e^-} \setminus F$, $j \in F \cap V_k^{e^+}$ or a minimal k-shortage set $F \in \mathcal{F}_k^-$ with $d_{ij} < 0$ for all $i \in V_k^{e^+} \setminus F$, $j \in F \cap V_k^{e^-}$, then there exists a forbidden set F' for which $j \in F'$ implies $i \in F'$ for all $i, j \in V_k^{e^+} \cup V_k^{e^-}$ with $d_{ij} \geq 0$.*

Proof. Let F be a minimal k-surplus set with $d_{ij} < 0$ for all $i \in V_k^{e^-} \setminus F$, $j \in F \cap V_k^{e^+}$. We construct surplus set F' as follows. We first delete all $i \in V_k^{e^-} \cap F$ from F for which $d_{ij} < 0$ for all $j \in F \cap V_k^{e^+}$. Since for none of the deleted events i there is some $j \in F' \cap V_k^{e^+}$ with $d_{ij} \geq 0$, it holds that (1) $d_{ij} < 0$ for all $i \in V_k^{e^-} \setminus F'$, $j \in F' \cap V_k^{e^+}$. After the deletion of events i it holds that for any $h \in F'$ there is some $j \in F' \cap V_k^{e^+}$ with $d_{hj} \geq 0$. Now consider distances d_{ih} for $i \in V_k^{e^-} \setminus F'$ and $h \in V_k^{e^-} \cap F'$. For given $h \in V_k^{e^-} \cap F'$, let $j \in F' \cap V_k^{e^+}$ be an event such that $d_{hj} \geq 0$. (1) provides $0 < d_{ij} \leq d_{ih} + d_{hj}$ for all $i \in V_k^{e^-} \setminus F$, which together with $d_{hj} \geq 0$ implies $d_{ih} < 0$. Thus, we have (2) $d_{ih} < 0$ for all $i \in V_k^{e^-} \setminus F'$, $h \in F' \cap V_k^{e^-}$.

Next, we add all $j \in V_k^{e^+} \setminus F'$ to F' for which $d_{jj'} \geq 0$ for some $j' \in F' \cap V_k^{e^+}$, so that (3) $d_{gj} < 0$ for all $g \in V_k^{e^+} \setminus F'$, $j \in F' \cap V_k^{e^+}$. Let j be one of the added events and let $j' \in F' \cap V_k^{e^+}$ be an event such that $d_{jj'} \geq 0$. From (1) it follows that $0 > d_{ij'} \geq d_{ij} + d_{jj'}$ for all $i \in V_k^{e^-} \setminus F'$. Due to $d_{jj'} \geq 0$, this implies $d_{ij} < 0$ for all $i \in V_k^{e^-} \setminus F'$, and thus property (1) is preserved. The validity of property (2) is not affected by adding events $j \in V_k^{e^+} \setminus F'$ to F' either. Finally, consider distances d_{gh} for $g \in V_k^{e^+} \setminus F'$ and $h \in F' \cap V_k^{e^-}$. For given $h \in F' \cap V_k^{e^-}$, let $j \in F' \cap V_k^{e^+}$ be an event such that $d_{hj} \geq 0$. Using (1) we have $0 > d_{gj} \geq d_{gh} + d_{hj}$, which then implies $d_{gh} < 0$. Thus, it holds that (4) $d_{gh} < 0$ for all $g \in V_k^{e^+} \setminus F'$, $h \in F' \cap V_k^{e^-}$.

The resulting set F' is a surplus set because it arises from F by deleting events $i \in V_k^{e^-}$ and adding events $j \in V_k^{e^+}$. Moreover, from (1) to (4) we have $d_{ij} < 0$ for all $i \notin F'$ and all $j \in F'$, which proves the assertion. The case of a minimal k-shortage set F can be dealt with analogously. $\square$

The next proposition, which translates the statement of Proposition 2.8 to the case of cumulative resources, characterizes the feasibility of relations on the basis of relation network $N(\rho)$.

Proposition 2.21. *Time-feasible relation ρ in V^e is feasible if and only if for each minimal k-surplus set $F \in \mathcal{F}_k^+$, relation network $N(\rho)$ contains a directed path of length $d_{ij}^\rho \geq 0$ from some node $i \in V_k^{e^-} \setminus F$ to some node $j \in F \cap V_k^{e^+}$ and for each minimal k-shortage set $F \in \mathcal{F}_k^-$, relation network $N(\rho)$ contains a directed path of length $d_{ij}^\rho \geq 0$ from some node $i \in V_k^{e^+} \setminus F$ to some node $j \in F \cap V_k^{e^-}$.*

Proof. Sufficiency: Let ρ be a time-feasible relation satisfying the conditions of Proposition 2.21. Since for each schedule $S \in \mathcal{S}_T(\rho)$ it holds that $S_j \geq S_i$ for all $(i,j) \in \Theta(D(\rho))$, Theorem 1.28 implies the resource-feasibility of all schedules $S \in \mathcal{S}_T(\rho)$. This means that $\mathcal{S}_T(\rho) \subseteq \mathcal{S}_C$ and thus $\mathcal{S}_T(\rho) \subseteq \mathcal{S}$.

Necessity: We assume that for some resource $k \in \mathcal{R}^\gamma$, there is a k-surplus set F such that $d_{ij}^\rho < 0$ for all $i \in V_k^{e^-} \setminus F$, $j \in F \cap V_k^{e^+}$. Lemma 2.20 then provides some surplus set F' for which Lemma 2.19 establishes the existence of a time-feasible schedule S such that $\mathcal{A}(S,t) = F'$ for some $t \geq 0$, i.e., $\mathcal{S}_T(\rho) \not\subseteq \mathcal{S}$. $\square$

Now we are ready to prove the counterpart of Theorem 2.9.

Theorem 2.22. *Time-feasible relation ρ in V^e is feasible if and only if no union of predecessor sets in $\Theta(D(\rho))$ is forbidden.*

Proof. Sufficiency: Let ρ be a time-feasible relation for which no union of predecessor sets in $\Theta(D(\rho))$ is forbidden. U is a union of predecessor sets in $\Theta(D(\rho))$ precisely if for all $i,j \in V^e$ with $d_{ij}^\rho \geq 0$, $j \in U$ implies $i \in U$. Since there does not exist any surplus set U with the latter property, Lemma 2.20 implies that for each minimal surplus set $F \in \mathcal{F}_k^+$, there are two events $i \in V_k^{e^-} \setminus F$ and $j \in F \cap V_k^{e^+}$ such that $d_{ij}^\rho \geq 0$. Symmetrically it holds that for each minimal shortage set $F \in \mathcal{F}_k^-$, there are two events $i \in V_k^{e^+} \setminus F$ and $j \in F \cap V_k^{e^-}$ with $d_{ij}^\rho \geq 0$. Proposition 2.21 then establishes the feasibility of ρ.

Necessity: For any union U of predecessor sets in $\Theta(D(\rho))$, it follows from Lemma 2.19 that there exists a schedule $S \in \mathcal{S}_T(\rho)$ with $\mathcal{A}(S,t) = U$ for some $t \geq 0$. If U is a forbidden set, schedule S is not resource-feasible, which means that $\mathcal{S}_T(\rho) \not\subseteq \mathcal{S}$. $\square$

Next we discuss how the feasibility of a time-feasible relation ρ can be checked in polynomial time by using Theorem 2.22. The statement of the theorem can be reformulated in the following way: Time-feasible relation ρ in V^e is feasible precisely if for no $j \in V^e$ there is a forbidden union U of predecessor sets in $\theta = \Theta(D(\rho))$ containing j as maximal element of U in θ (compare proof of Lemma 2.19). For given $j \in V^e$, such a set U is defined by properties (1) $i \in U$ implies $h \in U$ for all $(h, i) \in \theta$, (2) $j \in U$, and (3) j is a maximal element of U in θ, i.e., for all $i \in U$, $(j, i) \in \theta$ implies $(i, j) \in \theta$. The latter condition is equivalent to $i \notin U$ for all $i \in V^e$ with $(j, i) \in \theta$ and $(i, j) \notin \theta$. Now let x_i be a binary decision variable indicating whether or not event $i \in V^e$ is contained in U. Then we have (1) $x_h \geq x_i$ for all $(h, i) \in \theta$, (2) $x_j = 1$, and (3) $x_i = 0$ for all $i \in V^e$ with $(j, i) \in \theta$ and $(i, j) \notin \theta$. The set U belonging to incidence vector $x = (x_i)_{i \in V^e}$ is forbidden exactly if for some $k \in \mathcal{R}^\gamma$, $\sum_{i \in U} r_{ik} < \underline{R}_k$ or $\sum_{i \in U} r_{ik} > \overline{R}_k$. Thus, the problem of testing the feasibility of ρ can be solved by verifying, for each event $j \in V^e$ and each resource $k \in \mathcal{R}^\gamma$, whether or not there exists a binary vector x satisfying constraints (1) to (3) such that $\sum_{i \in V^e} r_{ik} x_i$ is less than safety stock $\underline{R}_k$ or greater than storage capacity $\overline{R}_k$. For given event j and resource k, checking whether the storage capacity of k might be violated at the occurrence of j can be achieved by solving the following binary program.

$$
\begin{aligned}
\text{Maximize} \quad & \sum_{i \in V^e} r_{ik} x_i \\
\text{subject to} \quad & x_h - x_i \geq 0 \quad ((h, i) \in \theta : h \neq i) && (1) \\
& x_j = 1 && (2) \\
& x_i = 0 \quad (i \in V^e : (j, i) \in \theta, (i, j) \notin \theta) && (3) \\
& x_i \in \{0, 1\} \quad (i \in V^e) && (4)
\end{aligned}
\right\} \quad (2.2)
$$

The coefficient matrix of constraints (1) coincides with the negative transposed incidence matrix of the directed graph G_{jk} with node set V^e and arc set $\theta \setminus \{(i, i) \mid i \in V^e\}$. That is why the coefficient matrix of constraints (1) to (3) is totally unimodular, and the integrality condition (4) for variables x_i can be replaced with $0 \leq x_i \leq 1$ $(i \in V^e)$. As a consequence, problem (2.2) can be formulated as a linear program. In the sequel, we show that the dual of this linear program represents a minimum-flow problem.

Let $i \in V^e$ be some predecessor of j in θ. Then it follows from (1) and (2) that $x_i = 1$. Conversely, let j be predecessor of some $i \in V^e$ in θ with $(i, j) \notin \theta$. Then (3) implies that $x_i = 0$. The variables x_i with fixed value 1 or 0 can be eliminated as follows. If $x_i = 1$ because $(i, j) \in \theta$, the transitivity of reflexive preorder θ provides $(h, j) \in \theta$ and thus $x_h = 1$ for all $(h, i) \in \theta$. Symmetrically, assume that $x_h = 0$ because $(j, h) \in \theta$ and $(h, j) \notin \theta$. Then the transitivity of θ implies that $(j, i) \in \theta$ and $(i, j) \notin \theta$ and thus by (3) $x_i = 0$ for all $(h, i) \in \theta$. Hence, constraint (1) can be restricted to variables x_i for which $(i, j) \notin \theta$ and variables x_h for which $(j, h) \notin \theta$ or $(h, j) \in \theta$. Otherwise we would have $x_h = 1$ or $x_i = 0$, which implies (1). For those variables x_i

and x_h we can furthermore assume that $(j, i) \notin \theta$ and $(h, j) \notin \theta$ because else again $x_i = 0$ or $x_h = 1$. Now let $V_j^e := \{i \in V^e \mid (i, j), (j, i) \notin \theta\}$ be the set of all events i for which the value of x_i is not fixed in advance. Then constraint (1) needs only be considered for pairs $(h, i) \in \theta$ with $h \neq i$ and $h, i \in V_j^e$. V_j^e is the set of all $i \in V^e$ that are incomparable with j in θ. We note that due to Remark 1.6b, $\{0, n + 1\} \cap V_j^e = \emptyset$ for all $j \in V_j^e$, and in particular $V_0^e = V_{n+1}^e = \emptyset$. By $\theta_j := \theta \cap (V_j^e \times V_j^e)$ we denote the sub-preorder of θ induced by set V_j^e. We obtain the following statement of problem (2.2) as a linear program, where the additive constant $\sum_{(i,j) \in \theta} r_{ik}$ is omitted in the objective function.

$$\left. \begin{aligned} \text{Maximize} \quad & \sum_{i \in V_j^e} r_{ik} x_i \\ \text{subject to} \quad & x_h - x_i \geq 0 \quad ((h, i) \in \theta_j : h \neq i) \\ & 0 \leq x_i \leq 1 \quad (i \in V_j^e) \end{aligned} \right\} \quad (2.3)$$

Now let s and t be a source and a sink to be added to directed graph G_{jk}. By $\overline{G}_{jk} = (\overline{V}_j, \overline{\theta}_j)$ where $\overline{V}_j := V_j^e \cup \{s, t\}$ and $\overline{\theta}_j := \theta_j \cup (\{s\} \times V_j^e) \cup (V_j^e \times \{t\})$ we denote the directed graph that results from G_{jk} by adding arcs (s, i) and (i, t) for all nodes $i \in V_j^e$. The dual of (2.3) can be formulated as the following minimum-flow problem in $\overline{G}_{jk}$ with supplies r_{ik} at nodes $i \in V_j^e$, where $\phi^j(u)$ denotes the value of flow u:

$$\left. \begin{aligned} \text{Minimize} \quad & \phi^j(u) = \sum_{i \in V_j^e} u_{it} \\ \text{subject to} \quad & \sum_{(i,h) \in \overline{\theta}_j : h \neq i} u_{ih} - \sum_{(h,i) \in \overline{\theta}_j : h \neq i} u_{hi} = r_{ik} \quad (i \in V_j^e) \\ & u_{hi} \geq 0 \quad ((h, i) \in \overline{\theta}_j : h \neq i) \end{aligned} \right\} \quad (2.4)$$

Problem (2.4) can be solved in $\mathcal{O}(n^3)$ time by first substituting supplies r_{ik} at nodes i into appropriate upper arc capacities (see, e.g., Bang-Jensen and Gutin 2002, Section 3.2) and then solving the minimum-flow problem with vanishing supplies (cf. Subsection 2.1.1). Let $\overline{u}^{jk}$ be some flow solving minimum-flow problem (2.4). Then the optimal objective function value for problem (2.2) equals $\sum_{(i,j) \in \theta} r_{ik} + \phi^j(\overline{u}^{jk})$, which is equal to the maximum inventory level in resource k at the occurrence of event j.

For testing whether the inventory might fall below the safety stock, we solve the minimum-flow problem where supplies r_{ik} at nodes $i \in V_j^e$ are replaced with $-r_{ik}$. With $\underline{u}^{jk}$ designating a corresponding minimum (s, t)-flow, the optimal objective function value for (2.2) with "Minimize" instead of "Maximize" equals $\sum_{(i,j) \in \theta} r_{ik} - \phi^j(\underline{u}^{jk})$, which coincides with the minimum inventory level in resource k at the occurrence of event j. ρ is feasible if for all events $j \in V^e$ and all resources $k \in \mathcal{R}^\gamma$,

$$\underline{R}_k + \phi^j(\underline{u}^{jk}) \leq \sum_{(i,j) \in \theta} r_{ik} \leq \overline{R}_k - \phi^j(\overline{u}^{jk})$$

In sum, checking the feasibility of a relation ρ takes $\mathcal{O}(|\mathcal{R}^\gamma|n^4)$ time (recall that the time-feasibility of ρ can be verified in $\mathcal{O}(n[m + |\rho|])$ time).

We illustrate the verification of feasibility for a relation by considering an example.

Example 2.23. Figure 2.2a shows a project network with five events and one cumulative resource for which we assume a safety stock of $\underline{R} = 0$ and a storage capacity of $\overline{R} = 2$. The node labels provide the respective resource requirements. We consider the empty relation $\rho = \emptyset$. The reflexive preorder induced by $D(\rho) = D$ is $\theta = \{(0, 1), (0, 2), (0, 3), (0, 4), (1, 4), (2, 3), (2, 4), (3, 2), (3, 4)\}$ $\cup \{(i, i) \mid i \in V^e\}$. When checking against the storage capacity for event $j = 1$, we obtain the flow network $\overline{G}_1$ depicted in Figure 2.2b, where nodes $i \in V^e$ are labelled with supplies r_i. In the minimum (s, t)-flow $\overline{u}^1$, one unit is shipped from node 3 to node 2, and thus the minimum flow value $\phi^1(\overline{u}^1)$ equals 0 and $\sum_{(i,1)\in\theta} r_i + \phi^1(\overline{u}^1) = r_0 + r_1 + 0 = 2$. Figure 2.2c shows the flow network $\overline{G}_2 = \overline{G}_3$ belonging to events $j = 2$ and $j = 3$ with a minimum flow $\overline{u}^2 = \overline{u}^3$ of value $\phi^2(\overline{u}^2) = \phi^3(\overline{u}^3) = 2$ and $\sum_{(i,2)\in\theta} r_i + \phi^2(\overline{u}^2) = \sum_{(i,3)\in\theta} r_i + \phi^3(\overline{u}^3) = r_0 + r_2 + r_3 + 2 = 2$. By inverting the signs of the supplies, we obtain the minimum-flow problems for testing against the safety stock. The corresponding flow values are $\phi^1(\underline{u}^1) = 0$ and $\phi^2(\underline{u}^2) = \phi^3(\underline{u}^3) = 0$. Accordingly, we have $\sum_{(i,1)\in\theta} r_i - \phi^1(\underline{u}^1) = r_0 + r_1 - 0 = 2$ and $\sum_{(i,2)\in\theta} r_i - \phi^2(\underline{u}^2) = \sum_{(i,3)\in\theta} r_i - \phi^3(\underline{u}^3) = r_0 + r_2 + r_3 - 0 = 0$, which shows the feasibility of relation ρ.

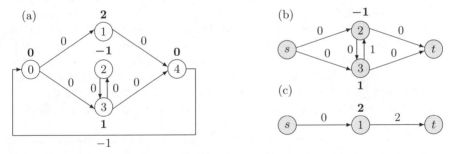

Fig. 2.2. Verification of feasibility: **(a)** project network; **(b)** minimum (s, t)-flow in network $\overline{G}_1$; **(c)** minimum (s, t)-flow in network $\overline{G}_2 = \overline{G}_3$

We close this subsection by considering reflexive preorders in set V^e that are induced by some schedule. As we shall see, the results for schedule-induced strict orders in set V^a carry over to schedule-induced reflexive preorders in set V^e.

Definition 2.24 (Schedule-induced reflexive preorder). *Given a schedule S, reflexive preorder $\theta(S) := \{(i, j) \in V^e \times V^e \mid S_j \geq S_i\}$ is the schedule-induced reflexive preorder which corresponds to the precedence relationships* established by S. $\mathcal{S}_T(\theta(S))$ is again called the schedule polytope of schedule S, and $N(\theta(S))$ is the schedule network of S.

Due to their completeness, schedule-induced reflexive preorders $\theta(S)$ are reflexive weak orders. Proposition 2.12 saying that $\theta(S)$ is feasible precisely if S is feasible also applies to schedule-induced reflexive preorders. Analogously to Proposition 2.13 it can also be shown that the $\subseteq$-maximal feasible relations in set V^e are induced by feasible schedules. Let θ be some schedule-induced reflexive preorder in V^e and let equal-preorder set $\mathcal{S}_T^{=}(\theta) := \{S \in \mathcal{S}_T \mid \theta(S) = \theta\}$ again denote the set of all time-feasible schedules inducing θ. Similarly to the case of renewable resources, set $\mathcal{S}$ of all feasible schedules can again be represented as the union of nonintersecting equal-preorder sets.

Proposition 2.25. *Let $\mathcal{SIP}$ be the set of all feasible schedule-induced reflexive preorders. Then $\{\mathcal{S}_T^{=}(\theta) \mid \theta \in \mathcal{SIP}\}$ is a partition of $\mathcal{S}$.*

Again, it can be shown that each minimal point (resp. vertex) of an equal-preorder set is a minimal point (resp. vertex) of some schedule polytope and vice versa (see Proposition 2.16).

2.2 A Classification of Schedules

In machine and project scheduling without maximum time lags, different finite sets of minimal-point schedules have been used for the optimization of regular objective functions (see, e.g., Baker 1974, Sect. 7.2, for a study of nondelay, active, and semiactive schedules in machine scheduling and Sprecher et al. 1995 for the generalization of those concepts to project scheduling with renewable resources). Based on the feasible relations discussed in Subsection 2.1.1, the classification of Sprecher et al. (1995) has been extended by Neumann et al. (2000) to project scheduling problems with general temporal constraints and nonregular objective functions. This section refers to the latter classification of schedules.

All resource allocation methods discussed in this book are based on one of the two basic representations of set $\mathcal{S}$, either as a covering by relation polytopes or as partition by equal-preorder sets (where the term equal-preorder set may also designate an equal-order set). The schedules to be dealt with in Subsections 2.2.1 and 2.2.2 refer to the first and to the second representations, respectively.

2.2.1 Global and Local Extreme Points of the Feasible Region

Let $\mathcal{M} \subseteq \mathcal{S}_T$ be a nonempty set of time-feasible schedules. $S \in \mathcal{M}$ is a *(global) extreme point* of $\mathcal{M}$ if there are no two schedules $S', S'' \in \mathcal{M}$ such that $S = \alpha S' + (1 - \alpha)S''$ for some $0 < \alpha < 1$. If $\mathcal{M}$ is a polytope, each extreme point is a *vertex* of $\mathcal{M}$ and vice versa. We say that $S \in \mathcal{M}$ is a *local extreme point* of $\mathcal{M}$ if S is an extreme point of $\mathcal{M} \cap B_\varepsilon(S)$ for some $\varepsilon > 0$, where $B_\varepsilon(S) = \{S' \in \mathbb{R}^{n+2} \mid \|S - S'\|_2 < \varepsilon\}$ is the ball of radius ε around S in $\mathbb{R}^{n+2}$. Recall that $S \in \mathcal{M}$ is a *minimal point* of $\mathcal{M}$ if there is no schedule $S' \in \mathcal{M}$ with $S' < S$. We notice that a minimal point of $\mathcal{M}$ need not represent a local extreme point of $\mathcal{M}$. As we will see later on, each minimal point of a relation polytope $\mathcal{M} = \mathcal{S}_T(\rho)$, however, is a local extreme point of $\mathcal{M}$.

Definition 2.26 (Active, stable, and pseudostable schedules). *A (feasible) schedule S is called active, stable, or pseudostable if S is a minimal point, an extreme point, or a local extreme point, respectively, of S. $\mathcal{AS}$, $\mathcal{SS}$, and $\mathcal{PSS}$ denote the sets of all active, all stable, and all pseudostable schedules.*

Active schedules have been introduced by Giffler and Thompson (1960) for solving open-shop problems with precedence constraints among operations and regular objective functions. In shop-floor scheduling, there is a one-to-one correspondence between job sequences on the machines and *semiactive schedules*, for which no operation can be processed earlier without changing the job sequences. Those semiactive schedules (as well as their analogues in project scheduling) are precisely the minimal points of components of $\mathcal{S}$, and every active schedule is semiactive.

Since each active, stable, or pseudostable schedule is a vertex of some relation polytope, the sets $\mathcal{AS}$, $\mathcal{SS}$, and $\mathcal{PSS}$ are finite. Neumann et al. (2000) provide an example of a project for which there is an active schedule that is not stable. However, each active schedule is pseudostable, which can be seen as follows. Assume that there exists some schedule $S \in \mathcal{AS} \setminus \mathcal{PSS}$. Since S is not pseudostable, we can find an open line segment ℓ passing through S that totally belongs to $\mathcal{S}$. The representation of $\mathcal{S}$ as a union of finitely many polytopes implies that ℓ can be chosen such that all points on ℓ are boundary points of $\mathcal{S}$, i.e., $\ell \subseteq \partial \mathcal{S}$. With $z \in [-1, 1]^{n+2}$ being the direction of $\ell \subset S + \mathbb{R}z$, the minimality of S in $\mathcal{S}$ implies that $z \notin [0, 1]^{n+2}$. It then follows from $\ell \subseteq \partial \mathcal{S}$ that all schedules on ℓ are minimal points, which contradicts the finiteness of $\mathcal{AS}$. Figure 2.3 summarizes the relationships between the schedule sets introduced.

In Neumann et al. (2000) it is shown by transformation from PARTITION that for the case of renewable resources, it is NP-hard to decide whether or not a given schedule is active, stable, or pseudostable. Since renewable-resource constraints can be expressed by temporal and cumulative-resource constraints without changing the order of magnitude of the problem size, this result also applies to project scheduling with cumulative resources.

2.2.2 Vertices of Relation Polytopes

All schedules considered in Subsection 2.2.1 represent vertices of $\subseteq$-*maximal* relation polytopes. We now turn to vertices of arbitrary relation polytopes.

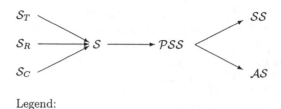

Legend:

$\mathcal{A} \to \mathcal{B}$ means $\mathcal{A} \supseteq \mathcal{B}$

Fig. 2.3. Relationship between sets of schedules

Since each vertex of a relation polytope corresponds to some time-feasible schedule that is a vertex of its schedule polytope, we may restrict ourselves to (arbitrary) schedule polytopes.

Definition 2.27 (Quasiactive and quasistable schedules). *A feasible schedule S is called quasiactive or quasistable if S is the minimal point or a vertex, respectively, of its schedule polytope $\mathcal{S}_T(\theta(S))$. $\mathcal{QAS}$ and $\mathcal{QSS}$ denote the sets of all quasiactive and all quasistable schedules.*

Since the minimal point of a relation polytope is always a vertex, any quasiactive schedule is quasistable as well.

A schedule S is quasiactive precisely if no nonempty set of activities can be scheduled earlier without deleting at least one precedence relationship $(i, j) \in \theta(S)$ or violating some temporal constraint. Schedule S is quasistable exactly if there is no nonempty set of activities which can be scheduled both earlier and later such that all precedence relationships $(i, j) \in \theta(S)$ and all temporal constraints are observed. The next proposition provides an equivalent formulation of the latter observation, which will be useful when dealing with algorithms operating on the sets $\mathcal{QAS}$ and $\mathcal{QSS}$ of all quasiactive and all quasistable schedules in Chapter 4.

Proposition 2.28 (Neumann et al. 2000). *A feasible schedule S is*

(a) *quasiactive if and only if there exists a spanning outtree $G = (V, E_G)$ of its schedule network $N(\theta(S))$ rooted at node 0 such that $S_j - S_i = d_{ij}^{\theta(S)}$ for all arcs $(i, j) \in E_G$,*

(b) *quasistable if and only if there exists a spanning tree $G = (V, E_G)$ of its schedule network $N(\theta(S))$ such that $S_j - S_i = d_{ij}^{\theta(S)}$ for all arcs $(i, j) \in E_G$.*

From Proposition 2.28 it follows that the quasiactiveness and the quasistableness of a given schedule can be checked in polynomial time. A further implication of Proposition 2.28 is that any quasistable schedule (and thus any quasiactive schedule as well) is integral and that any quasiactive schedule S satisfies

$$S_{n+1} \leq \min \left(\overline{d}, \sum_{i \in V} \max(\max_{(i,j) \in E} \delta_{ij}, p_i), \sum_{i \in V} \max(\max_{(h,i) \in E} \delta_{hi}, p_i) \right)$$

Obviously, active schedules are quasiactive, and pseudostable schedules are quasistable. Figure 2.4 locates the quasiactive and quasistable schedules within the framework of the schedule sets introduced before.

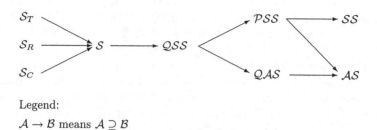

Legend:

$\mathcal{A} \to \mathcal{B}$ means $\mathcal{A} \supseteq \mathcal{B}$

Fig. 2.4. Relationship between sets of schedules, revisited

2.3 Objective Functions

An objective function $f : \mathcal{S}_T \to \mathbb{R}$ associates each time-feasible schedule S with a numerical assessment $f(S)$. Recall that we have assumed f to be lower semicontinuous and thus f takes its minimum on compact set $\mathcal{S}$ if $\mathcal{S} \neq \emptyset$. Whereas *regular* objective functions f, which are componentwise nondecreasing, refer to temporal objectives of project planning like minimizing the project duration, *nonregular* objective functions typically translate some monetary goals such as minimizing inventory holding or capacity adjustment costs or maximizing the net present value of the project. In this section we are going to study several classes of objective functions, which cover a large variety of resource allocation problems in project management. Based on the results of Sections 2.1 and 2.2 we provide for each class a finite set of schedules containing at least one optimal schedule if $\mathcal{S} \neq \emptyset$. In Subsection 2.3.1 we consider objective functions that can be minimized efficiently on relation polytopes. Subsection 2.3.2 is concerned with objective functions for which in general already the time-constrained project scheduling problem is NP-hard. The latter objective functions are typically encountered when solving resource levelling problems, where the problem amounts to minimizing the variability in resource loading profiles of renewable resources (expressed in terms of range, variance, or total variation). Whereas resource allocation problems with objective functions from Subsection 2.3.1 can be solved by enumerating $\subseteq$-minimal feasible relations, minimizing objective functions from Subsection 2.3.2 requires the investigation of arbitrary schedule-induced preorders. For certain of the latter objective functions, however, the search for an optimal schedule can be limited to schedule polytopes belonging to $\subseteq$-maximal schedule-induced pre-orders. The latter objective functions will be studied in Subsection 2.3.3.

2.3.1 Regular and Convexifiable Objective Functions

Consider some nonempty relation polytope $\mathcal{S}_T(\rho)$. Any regular objective function is minimized by the unique minimal point $\min \mathcal{S}_T(\rho)$ of $\mathcal{S}_T(\rho)$, which coincides with the earliest schedule belonging to relation network $N(\rho)$. Now let f be some convex (and due to our lower semicontinuity assumption) continuous objective function. Then finding a minimizer of f on $\mathcal{S}_T(\rho)$ can, under some mild technical assumptions, be achieved in polynomial time, e.g., by the ellipsoid method (cf. Grötschel et al. 1998, Sect. 4.1) or, more efficiently on the average, by interior-point methods based on self-concordant barriers for $\mathcal{S}_T(\rho)$. Self-concordant barriers are available for different classes of convex functions (see the book by Nesterov and Nemirovskii 1994 for details). The next definition provides a class of objective functions which admits a smooth coordinate transformation such that the resulting time-constrained project scheduling problem is a convex programming problem. Recall that a bijection φ is called a C^1-diffeomorphism if both φ and φ^{-1} are continuously differentiable.

Definition 2.29 (Convexifiable and linearizable objective functions).
Let $f : \mathcal{S}_T \to \mathbb{R}$ be some objective function. We call f convexifiable if there exists a C^1-diffeomorphism $\varphi : \mathcal{S}_T \to X$ from $\mathcal{S}_T$ onto some Euclidean space X such that $f \circ \varphi^{-1}$ is a convex function and the images $\varphi(\mathcal{S}_T(\rho)) = \{\varphi(S) \mid S \in \mathcal{S}_T(\rho)\}$ of all relation polytopes under φ are convex sets. If $f \circ \varphi^{-1}$ is linear, we speak of a linearizable objective function f.

Trivially, each convex objective function is convexifiable and each linear objective function is linearizable. In addition, we notice that due to the continuity of φ^{-1}, all images $\varphi(\mathcal{S}_T(\rho))$ are compact sets and because $\mathcal{S}_T$ is a relation polytope, set $X = \varphi(\mathcal{S}_T)$ is convex.

A time-feasible schedule $S \in \mathcal{M} \subseteq \mathcal{S}_T$ is called a *local minimizer* of f on $\mathcal{M}$ if for some $\varepsilon > 0$, S is a minimizer of f on the relative ball $\mathcal{M} \cap B_\varepsilon(S)$ around S in $\mathcal{M}$ (for the basic concepts of relative topology in Euclidean space needed for what follows we refer to Sydsæter et al. 1999, Ch. 12). Roughly speaking, the reason for the tractability of time-constrained project scheduling with convex objective functions is that each local minimizer of f on a relation polytope $\mathcal{S}_T(\rho)$ minimizes f on $\mathcal{S}_T(\rho)$. The next proposition relates the schedule sets introduced in Subsection 2.2.1 to regular and convexifiable objective functions. It also shows that, as for convex objective functions, any convexifiable objective function f can be minimized on relation polytopes $\mathcal{S}_T(\rho)$ by computing a local minimizer of f on $\mathcal{S}_T(\rho)$.

Proposition 2.30. *Let f be some lower semicontinuous objective function and assume that $S \neq \emptyset$.*

(a) *If f is regular, the set of active schedules contains an optimal schedule.*
(b) *If f is linear, the set of stable schedules contains an optimal schedule.*
(c) *If f is linearizable, the set of pseudostable schedules contains an optimal schedule.*
(d) *If f is convexifiable, any set containing a local minimizer of f for each ($\subseteq$-maximal) relation polytope contains an optimal schedule.*

Proof. (a) and (b) are obvious. We first show (d). Let S be a local minimizer of f on some relation polytope $\mathcal{S}_T(\rho)$. Then there exists some $\varepsilon > 0$ such that $f(S) \leq f(S')$ for all $S' \in \mathcal{S}_T(\rho) \cap B_\varepsilon(S)$. With $x = \varphi(S)$ and $x' = \varphi(S')$ this means that $(f \circ \varphi^{-1})(x) = f(S) \leq f(S') = (f \circ \varphi^{-1})(x')$ for all $x' \in \varphi(\mathcal{S}_T(\rho) \cap B_\varepsilon(S))$. From the injectivity of φ we can infer that $\varphi(\mathcal{S}_T(\rho) \cap B_\varepsilon(S)) = \varphi(\mathcal{S}_T(\rho)) \cap \varphi(B_\varepsilon(S))$, where it follows from the continuity of φ^{-1} that $\varphi(B_\varepsilon(S))$ is open. As a consequence, there exists some $\varepsilon' > 0$ such that the ball $B'_{\varepsilon'}(x)$ with radius ε' around x in X is included in $\varphi(B_\varepsilon(S))$. This implies that x is a minimizer of $f \circ \varphi^{-1}$ on set $\varphi(\mathcal{S}_T(\rho)) \cap B'_{\varepsilon'}(x)$, i.e., a local minimizer of $f \circ \varphi^{-1}$ on $\varphi(\mathcal{S}_T(\rho))$. Since by assumption $f \circ \varphi^{-1}$ is a convex function and $\varphi(\mathcal{S}_T(\rho))$ is a convex set, x is also a (global) minimizer of $f \circ \varphi^{-1}$ on $\varphi(\mathcal{S}_T(\rho))$, i.e., $f(S) = (f \circ \varphi^{-1})(x) \leq (f \circ \varphi^{-1})(x')$ for all $x' \in \varphi(\mathcal{S}_T(\rho))$. Thus, we have $f(S) \leq f(S')$ for all S' with $x' = \varphi(S') \in \varphi(\mathcal{S}_T(\rho))$, or, equivalently, $f(S) \leq f(S')$ for all $S' \in \mathcal{S}_T(\rho)$. As a consequence, any local minimizer of f on some relation polytope $\mathcal{S}_T(\rho)$ minimizes f on the total polytope $\mathcal{S}_T(\rho)$. From Propositions 2.5 and 2.18 it follows that $\varphi(\mathcal{S}) = \varphi(\cup_{\rho \in \mathcal{MFR}} \mathcal{S}_T(\rho)) = \cup_{\rho \in \mathcal{MFR}} \varphi(\mathcal{S}_T(\rho)))$, which proves the assertion.

We now show statement (c). Since $f \circ \varphi^{-1}$ is linear on X, there exists some extreme point x of $\varphi(\mathcal{S}) \subseteq X$ that minimizes $f \circ \varphi^{-1}$ on $\varphi(\mathcal{S})$. Now assume that $S = \varphi^{-1}(x)$ is not a local extreme point of $\mathcal{S}$. Then there is an open line segment $\ell \subset \mathcal{S}$ containing S. Since φ^{-1} is continuous and φ is injective, this means that x is a relative interior point of $\varphi(\ell) \subset \varphi(\mathcal{S})$, which contradicts the fact that x is an extreme point of $\varphi(\mathcal{S})$. $\qquad\square$

Neumann et al. (2000) have considered *quasiconcave* objective functions and so-called *binary-monotone* objective functions. An objective function f is said to be quasiconcave if its upper-level sets $U_\alpha = \{S \in \mathcal{S}_T \mid f(S) \geq \alpha\}$ are convex for every $\alpha \in \mathbb{R}$ (see, e.g., Avriel et al. 1988, Sect. 3.1). f is termed binary-monotone if f is nondecreasing or nonincreasing on each line segment in binary direction $z \in \{0, 1\}^{n+2}$. A quasiconcave function attains its minimum on a compact set $\mathcal{M}$ at an extreme point of $\mathcal{M}$ because on closed line segments, the function is minimized at one of the two endpoints. That is why there always exists a stable schedule that minimizes f on set $\mathcal{S}$ if f is quasiconcave and $\mathcal{S} \neq \emptyset$. Since each relation polytope $\mathcal{S}_T(\rho)$ arises from the intersection of finitely many half spaces $\{S \in \mathbb{R}^{n+2}_{\geq 0} \mid S_0 = 0, \ S_j - S_i \geq d^\rho_{ij}\}$ where $(i, j) \in E \cup \rho$, binary-monotone objective functions, like the linearizable objective functions, always possess a vertex of $\mathcal{S}_T(\rho)$ among their minimizers on $\mathcal{S}_T(\rho)$. Thus, binary-monotone objective functions are minimized by pseudostable schedules. Unlike the case of convexifiable objective functions, however, a local minimizer of a quasiconcave or binary-monotone objective function f on some relation polytope is generally not a global minimizer of f on $\mathcal{S}_T(\rho)$.

We proceed by providing examples of regular and convexifiable objective functions that are of interest in project scheduling. The simplest and most frequently used regular objective function is the *makespan* or *project duration*

$$f(S) = S_{n+1}$$

The project duration problem with renewable resources has been extensively studied in the literature during the four last decades (see Subsection 3.1.4 for an overview). Minimizing the project duration is a suitable objective if the majority of income payments occur at or after the end of the project, if the project deadline is tight and thus finishing the implementation of the project as early as possibly lowers the danger of exceeding the deadline, or if resource capacity is needed for future projects (cf. Kolisch 1995, Sect. 2.1).

A second regular objective function is the *total tardiness cost*

$$f(S) = \sum_{i \in V} w_i^t (S_i + p_i - d_i)^+$$

where $d_i \in \mathbb{Z}_{\geq 0}$ denotes a given due date for the completion of activity i and $w_i^t \in \mathbb{Z}_{\geq 0}$ is the cost arising from a late completion of activity i per unit time. This objective function is of particular interest for applications of resource allocation methods in make-to-order production scheduling, which will be discussed in Section 6.1. In that case, each real activity corresponds to the processing of a job on a machine, and violations of the delivery dates for the completed jobs incur conventional penalty per unit time.

We now turn to convexifiable objective functions. Of course, any linear and any convex objective function is convexifiable. A nonregular linear objective function is the *total inventory holding cost*

$$f(S) = \sum_{k \in \mathcal{R}^\gamma} c_k \int_0^{\overline{d}} r_k(S, t) dt$$

where we assume that each cumulative resource k stands for the inventory in a storage facility keeping one intermediate or final product with unit holding cost rate $c_k \in \mathbb{Z}_{\geq 0}$. Then $f(S)$ represents the cost arising from the stock in planning interval $[0, \overline{d}]$. The linearity of f can be seen as follows. A replenishment of resource k by r_{ik} units at time S_i incurs a holding cost of $c_k r_{ik}(\overline{d} - S_i)$. A depletion of k by $-r_{ik}$ units at time S_i saves a holding cost of $c_k(-r_{ik})(\overline{d} - S_i)$. Thus, the total inventory holding cost $f(S)$ can also be written as $\overline{d} \sum_{k \in \mathcal{R}^\gamma} c_k \sum_{i \in V^e} r_{ik} - \sum_{k \in \mathcal{R}^\gamma} c_k \sum_{i \in V^e} r_{ik} S_i$.

In general, certain activities and events i of a project are associated with a cash flow $c_i^f \in \mathbb{Z}$, which may be a paying out for raw materials or workforce or a paying in arising at the completion of a task when reaching a milestone.

When evaluating the profitability of a long-term project, the cash flows have to be discounted by some interest rate α, which can, e.g., be chosen to be the minimum attractive rate of return. The sum of all cash flows discounted to time 0 is called the *net present value* of the project. For the sake of simplicity, we suppose that all cash flows are discounted continuously and that each cash flow c_i^f arises at time S_i. The factor by which cash flow c_i^f is discounted then equals $e^{-\alpha S_i}$, and thus the net present value depends on the schedule S according to which the project is performed. By minimizing the negative net present value

$$f(S) = -\sum_{i \in V} c_i^f e^{-\alpha S_i}$$

we obtain a schedule that maximizes the financial benefit of the project in terms of its net present value. Grinold (1972) has shown that the (negative) net present value is a linearizable objective function. Let $\varphi : \mathcal{S}_T \to X \subseteq \mathbb{R}^{n+2}$ be defined as $\varphi(S) = (\varphi_i(S))_{i \in V}$ where $\varphi_i(S) = e^{-\alpha S_i}$. With $x_i = \varphi_i(S)$, the temporal constraints $S_j - S_i \geq \delta_{ij}$ can be stated as $x_j - e^{-\alpha \delta_{ij}} x_i \leq 0$ and $S_0 = 0$ becomes $x_0 = 1$. The linearized objective function is $(f \circ \varphi^{-1})(x) = -\sum_{i \in V} c_i^f x_i$. In addition, the net present value function f is binary-monotone because f is differentiable and for any time-feasible schedule S and any binary direction $z \in \{0, 1\}^{n+2}$, the directional derivative of f at a point $S + \sigma z \in \mathcal{S}_T$ in direction z is $df|_{S+\sigma z}(z) = e^{-\alpha \sigma} df|_S(z)$ (see Subsection 3.2.2 and Neumann et al. 2003b, Sect. 3.3).

A convex objective function considered in project management is the *total earliness-tardiness cost*

$$f(S) = \sum_{i \in V} (w_i^e [d_i - S_i - p_i]^+ + w_i^t [S_i + p_i - d_i]^+)$$

where w_i^e and w_i^t respectively denote the cost per unit time incurred by an early or a late completion of activity $i \in V$ with respect to given due date $d_i \in \mathbb{Z}_{\geq 0}$ (see, e.g., Schwindt 2000c or Vanhoucke et al. 2001). Another example of a convex objective function is the negative *total weighted free float* of the project

$$f(S) = \sum_{i \in V} w_i^f \left(\max_{(j,i) \in E} [S_j + \delta_{ji}] - \min_{(i,j) \in E} [S_j - \delta_{ij}] \right)$$

For given schedule S, the total weighted free float of the project is the weighted sum of all early and late free floats of activities $i \in V$ if the earliest and latest start times ES_i and LS_i are set to be equal to S_i (cf. Subsection 1.1.3). A schedule with maximum total weighted free float can be regarded as robust in the sense that when executing the project, deviations of individual start times S_i from schedule will minimally affect the start times of other activities. In Section 6.5 we shall discuss how the total weighted earliness-tardiness and total weighted free float objective functions can be used for project scheduling under uncertainty.

Before concluding this subsection, we notice that all objective functions discussed above are continuous, which of course implies their lower semicontinuity.

2.3.2 Locally Regular and Locally Concave Objective Functions

In this subsection we move on to objective functions that are regular or concave on individual equal-preorder sets. Those objective functions play an important role for resource levelling, where one strives at smoothing loading profiles $r_k(S, \cdot)$ of renewable resources $k \in \mathcal{R}^\rho$ over time. Resource levelling problems typically arise when resource capacities may, at a certain cost, be adapted to the respective requirements. In that case, the resource capacities are regarded as being unlimited and the problem is to find a feasible minimum-cost schedule. However, besides the cost point of view, levelling loading profiles over time is of interest in its own right because in practice, evenly used resources tend less to be subject to disruption than resources whose usage is highly fluctuating over time. Accordingly, it has been proposed to use resource levelling as a technique for capacitated master production scheduling in production planning, where for a planning horizon of about one year, the monthly production quantities matching the gross requirements for the main products of a company are determined (see Franck et al. 1997, Neumann and Schwindt 1998, and Section 6.2).

Definition 2.31 (Locally regular and locally concave objective functions). *Let $f : \mathcal{S}_T \to \mathbb{R}$ be some objective function. We call f locally regular, if f is regular on all equal-preorder sets. f is termed locally concave if f is concave on all equal-preorder sets.*

The following proposition establishes the connection between locally regular and locally concave objective functions and the sets of quasiactive and quasistable schedules introduced in Subsection 2.2.2.

Proposition 2.32 (Neumann et al. 2000). *Let f be some lower semicontinuous objective function and assume that $\mathcal{S} \neq \emptyset$.*

(a) *If f is locally regular, the set of quasiactive schedules contains an optimal schedule.*

(b) *If f is locally concave, the set of quasistable schedules contains an optimal schedule.*

Proof. The lower semicontinuity of f and the compactness of $\mathcal{S}$ imply that f attains its minimum on $\mathcal{S}$. We first show statement (a). From the regularity of f on equal-preorder sets we can conclude that this minimum is taken at the minimal point of some equal-preorder set, which at the same time represents the minimal point of some schedule polytope (see Proposition 2.16, which applies to cumulative resources as well). We now show statement (b). From the concavity of f on equal-preorder sets it follows that f assumes its minimum at a vertex of some equal-preorder set. Proposition 2.16 says that this vertex is also a vertex of a schedule polytope. □

In contrast to regular or convexifiable objective functions, locally regular and locally concave objective functions cannot be minimized efficiently on relation polytopes in general. In particular this means that a resource allocation problem with a locally regular or a locally concave objective function generally does not become more tractable when the resource constraints are deleted. Below we shall give an example of a locally regular objective function for which time-constrained project scheduling is NP-hard. Note that minimizing such a function on an equal-preorder set constitutes an easy (though possibly unsolvable) problem because any equal-preorder set possesses at most one minimal point. Concerning locally concave functions, it is well-known that already the minimization of concave functions on hypercubes is NP-hard (cf. Horst and Tuy 1996, Sect. A.1.2). Proposition 2.28 indicates a simple way of generating all quasiactive or all quasistable schedules by constructing all spanning out-trees rooted at node 0 (resp. spanning trees) of relation networks belonging to feasible schedule-induced preorders. A corresponding schedule-generation scheme will be discussed in Section 4.1.

Next we consider locally regular and locally concave objective functions of resource levelling problems that have been discussed in literature. The objective functions express the variability in the utilization of renewable resources over time in terms of the range, the variance, and the total variation, respectively, of the loading profiles $r_k(S, \cdot)$ of renewable resources $k \in \mathcal{R}^\rho$.

An example of a locally regular objective function is the *total procurement cost* for renewable resources

$$f(S) = \sum_{k \in \mathcal{R}^\rho} c_k \max_{0 \leq t \leq \overline{d}} r_k(S, t)$$

where $c_k \in \mathbb{Z}_{\geq 0}$ denotes the unit procurement cost of renewable resource $k \in \mathcal{R}^\rho$. The total procurement cost equals the weighted sum of the maximum resource requirements (or, in other words, the weighted sum of the *ranges* of the loading profiles $r_k(S, \cdot)$).

Proposition 2.33. *The total procurement cost f is a lower semicontinuous and locally regular objective function.*

Proof. The lower semicontinuity can be seen as follows. Let S be some time-feasible schedule. The closedness of relation polytopes $\mathcal{S}_T(\rho)$ with $\rho \nsubseteq \theta(S)$ implies that there exists some $\varepsilon > 0$ such that $\theta(S') \subseteq \theta(S)$ for all S' contained in the relative ball $B_\varepsilon(S) \cap \mathcal{S}_T$ in $\mathcal{S}_T$ around S. Since for each resource $k \in \mathcal{R}^\rho$, $\max_{0 \leq t \leq \overline{d}} r_k(S, t)$ coincides with the weight of a maximum-weight antichain in $\theta(S)$, we obtain $f(S') \geq f(S)$ for all $S' \in B_\varepsilon(S) \cap \mathcal{S}_T$. The lower semicontinuity now follows from the fact that f is lower semicontinuous precisely if $f(S) \leq \liminf_{S' \to S} f(S')$ for all $S \in \mathcal{S}_T$ (see, e.g., Hiriart-Urruty and Lemaréchal

1993, Sect. A.1). Since $f(S)$ equals the weight of a maximum-weight antichain in $\theta(S)$, f is constant and thus regular on equal-order sets.   □

The total procurement cost is the objective function of the resource investment problem introduced by Möhring (1984). The resource investment problem arises in applications where installing resources incurs fixed transportation or setup costs per unit capacity. The recognition version (i.e., the question whether there is a feasible solution whose objective function value is smaller than or equal to a given threshold value, see, e.g., Papadimitriou and Steiglitz 1998, Sect. 15.2) of a resource investment problem with one resource coincides with the feasibility version (i.e., the question whether there is a feasible solution) of the corresponding resource-constrained project duration problem. The latter decision problem has been shown to be NP-complete by Theorem 1.12, which implies that the resource investment problem is NP-hard even if $R_k = \infty$ for all $k \in \mathcal{R}^\rho$. A classical objective function in the field of resource levelling that has been studied since the early work of Burgess and Killebrew (1962) is the *total squared utilization cost* for renewable resources

$$f(S) = \sum_{k \in \mathcal{R}^\rho} c_k \int_0^{\bar{d}} r_k^2(S, t) dt$$

where $c_k \in \mathbb{Z}_{\geq 0}$. Since workload $\int_0^{\bar{d}} r_k(S, t) dt = \sum_{i \in V^a} r_{ik} p_i$ does not depend on schedule S, $f(S)$ equals the weighted sum of the *variances* of the loading profiles $r_k(S, \cdot)$ plus a constant.

Proposition 2.34. *The total squared utilization cost f is a lower semicontinuous and locally concave objective function.*

Proof. The lower semicontinuity of f follows from its continuity. We show that f is concave on equal-order sets. For given schedule S, let $\mathcal{AC}(S)$ be the set of antichains in strict order $\theta(S)$, let $r_k(U) = \sum_{i \in U} r_{ik}$ be the weight of antichain $U \in \mathcal{AC}(S)$, and let $p(U, S) = \int_{t:\mathcal{A}(S,t)=U} dt$ be the time during which precisely the activities $i \in U$ overlap in time given schedule S. By $w_k(U, S) = r_k(U)p(U, S)$ we denote the corresponding workload on resource $k \in \mathcal{R}^\rho$. The total squared utilization cost can then be written as $f(S) = \sum_{k \in \mathcal{R}^\rho} c_k \sum_{U \in \mathcal{AC}(S)} r_k(U)w_k(U, S)$.

Now consider two schedules S and S' inducing the same strict order $\theta(S) = \theta(S')$. For any $\alpha \in [0, 1]$ we have $\mathcal{AC}(S) = \mathcal{AC}(S') = \mathcal{AC}(\alpha S + (1-\alpha)S')$. With respect to schedule S, the activities i from a nonempty antichain $U \in \mathcal{AC}(S)$ overlap during $\bar{p}(U, S) = \min_{i \in U} C_i - \max_{i \in U} S_i > 0$ units of time, where $\bar{p}(U, S) = p(U, S)$ if U is $\subseteq$-maximal in $\mathcal{AC}(S)$. Since function $\bar{p}(U, \cdot)$ is concave on $\mathcal{S}_T^=(\theta(S))$, we have $\bar{p}(U, \alpha S + (1-\alpha)S') \geq \alpha \bar{p}(U, S) + (1-\alpha)\bar{p}(U, S')$. Consequently, $w_k(U, \alpha S + (1-\alpha)S') \geq \alpha w_k(U, S) + (1-\alpha)w_k(U, S')$ for all $\subseteq$-maximal antichains $U \in \mathcal{AC}(S)$ and all $k \in \mathcal{R}^\rho$. As $\sum_{U \in \mathcal{AC}(S)} w_k(U, S) = \sum_{U \in \mathcal{AC}(S)} w_k(U, S') = \sum_{U \in \mathcal{AC}(S)} w_k(U, \alpha S + (1-\alpha)S') = \sum_{i \in U} r_{ik} p_i$ for all $k \in \mathcal{R}^\rho$, a positive difference $w_k(U, \alpha S + (1-\alpha)S') - [\alpha w_k(U,S) + (1-\alpha)w_k(U,S')]$ for the latter antichains U weighted by $r_k(U)$ corresponds to an equally large negative difference for the remaining (not $\subseteq$-maximal) antichains $U' \subset U$ weighted by $r_k(U') \leq r_k(U)$. By recursively applying the above reasoning to the function which arises from f by deleting the $\subseteq$-maximal elements from set $\mathcal{AC}(S)$ until $\mathcal{AC}(S) = \emptyset$, we finally obtain $f(\alpha S + (1-\alpha)S') \geq \alpha f(S) + (1-\alpha)f(S')$ for any $\alpha \in [0,1]$, which provides the concavity of f on equal-order sets. $\qquad\square$

By transformation from 3-PARTITION, Neumann et al. (2003b), Sect. 3.4, have shown that finding a time-feasible schedule with minimum total squared utilization cost is NP-hard.

Now let $t_1 < \cdots < t_\nu$ denote the start and completion times of real activities $i \in V^a$. Any jump discontinuity in loading profiles $r_k(S, \cdot)$ for $k \in \mathcal{R}^\rho$ occurs at some start or completion time t_μ where $1 \leq \mu \leq \nu$. A further resource-levelling objective function that has been studied in literature is the *total adjustment cost* for renewable resources

$$f(S) = \sum_{k \in \mathcal{R}^\rho} c_k \sum_{\mu=1}^{\nu} |r_k(S, t_\mu) - r_k(S, t_{\mu-1})|$$

where $t_0 := -1$ and $c_k \in \mathbb{Z}_{\geq 0}$ is the cost arising from increasing or decreasing the availability of resource $k \in \mathcal{R}^\rho$ by one unit (see, e.g., Younis and Saad 1996 or Neumann and Zimmermann 2000). Note that since $r_k(S, t_0) = r_k(S, t_\nu) = 0$ for all $k \in \mathcal{R}^\rho$, $f(S)$ equals $2\sum_{k \in \mathcal{R}^\rho} c_k \sum_{\mu=1}^{\nu}[r_k(S, t_\mu) - r_k(S, t_{\mu-1})]^+$. Thus, the case where decreasing the availability of (certain) resources does not incur additional cost is contained in the total adjustment cost problem. The total adjustment cost coincides with the weighted sum of the *total variations* of the loading profiles $r_k(S, \cdot)$.

Proposition 2.35. *The total adjustment cost f is a lower semicontinuous and locally concave objective function.*

Proof. Apparently, $f(S)$ can be expressed as a function of all pairs $(i,j) \in \theta(S)$ for which the precedence constraints $S_j \geq S_i + p_i$ are active. Consequently, f is constant on the relative interior of any face of an equal-order set. Moreover, it is easily seen that for any such face, the objective function values of relative boundary points are less than or equal to the objective function values of corresponding relative interior points. Hence, f is concave on equal-order sets and lower semicontinuous. $\qquad\square$

Finally, we notice that in contrast to the total procurement and total squared utilization costs, f is in general not continuous on equal-order sets. In Neumann et al. (2003b), Sect. 3.4, it is shown by the same polynomial transformation from 3-PARTITION as for the total squared utilization cost that minimizing the total adjustment cost on set $\mathcal{S}_T$ is NP-hard as well.

2.3.3 Preorder-Decreasing Objective Functions

In certain cases, the number of schedules to be enumerated for minimizing a locally regular or a locally concave objective function can be decreased by restricting the search to schedules inducing a maximum number of precedence relationships.

Definition 2.36 (Preorder-decreasing objective function). *An objective function f is called preorder-decreasing if $\theta' \supseteq \theta$ implies $\inf_{S \in \mathcal{S}_T^=(\theta')} f(S) \leq \inf_{S \in \mathcal{S}_T^=(\theta)} f(S)$ for all schedule-induced preorders θ and θ'.*

It follows from the definition of preorder-decreasing objective functions that, if $\mathcal{S} \neq \emptyset$, such functions possess a minimizer on some schedule polytope belonging to an $\subseteq$-maximal schedule-induced preorder. The total procurement cost is an example of a preorder-decreasing objective function, as has already been noticed by Möhring (1984). As an alternative to the construction of spanning trees (see preceding Subsection 2.3.2), a preorder-decreasing locally regular or locally concave objective function can be minimized on $\mathcal{S}$ by generating the set of $\subseteq$-maximal feasible schedule-induced preorders. Nübel (1999) has proposed a branch-and-bound algorithm for the resource investment problem that is implicitly based on this concept. The approach generally proves advantageous if the minimization of the objective function on equal-preorder sets already constitutes an NP-hard problem (which in particular may be the case for locally concave objective functions) because only the vertices of the generated $\subseteq$-minimal schedule polytopes have to be investigated.

In conclusion, Table 2.1 summarizes the relationships between the different classes of objective functions introduced and the sets of candidate schedules discussed in Section 2.2.

Table 2.1. Objective functions f and minimizers on $\mathcal{S}$

Objective function	Minimizer
Regular	Minimal point of $\mathcal{S}$
Convexifiable	Local minimizer on $\subseteq$-max. relation polytope $\mathcal{S}_T(\rho) \subseteq \mathcal{S}$
Locally regular	Minimal point of schedule polytope $\mathcal{S}_T(\theta(S)) \subseteq \mathcal{S}$
Locally concave	Vertex of schedule polytopes $\mathcal{S}_T(\theta(S)) \subseteq \mathcal{S}$
Preorder-decreasing locally regular	Minimal point of $\subseteq$-minimal schedule polytopes $\emptyset \neq \mathcal{S}_T(\theta(S)) \subseteq \mathcal{S}$
Preorder-decreasing locally concave	Vertex of $\subseteq$-minimal schedule polytopes $\emptyset \neq \mathcal{S}_T(\theta(S)) \subseteq \mathcal{S}$

3

Relaxation-Based Algorithms

Relaxation-based algorithms for resource-constrained project scheduling with regular or convexifiable objective functions rely on the first basic representation of the set $\mathcal{S}$ of all feasible schedules as a union of relation polytopes. By deleting the resource constraints we obtain the resource relaxation, which coincides with the time-constrained project scheduling problem. The latter problem can be solved efficiently by computing the minimal point ES of set $\mathcal{S}_T$ if f is regular or some local minimizer of the objective function f in set $\mathcal{S}_T$ if f is convexifiable. Clearly, the tractability of the problem is preserved when moving from set $\mathcal{S}_T$ to arbitrary nonempty relation polytopes $\mathcal{S}_T(\rho)$. Starting with the resource relaxation, i.e., with the empty relation, relaxation-based algorithms iteratively put the resource constraints into force by branching over time-feasible extensions ρ' of the respective parent relation ρ. Each relation ρ' defines a collection of precedence constraints that break up some forbidden active set $\mathcal{A}(S,t)$ belonging to a minimizer S of f on search space $\mathcal{P} = \mathcal{S}_T(\rho)$. The branching process is continued until either $\mathcal{S}_T(\rho) = \emptyset$ or the minimizer S of f on $\mathcal{S}_T(\rho)$ is feasible. The latter condition is necessarily satisfied as soon as relation ρ is feasible. Note, however, that schedule S may be feasible even before ρ has been extended to a feasible relation. When dealing with regular objective functions, the ordinary precedence constraints given by relations ρ may be replaced by disjunctive precedence constraints (cf. Subsections 1.2.3 and 1.3.3). Since a disjunctive precedence constraint corresponds to the disjunction of several ordinary precedence constraints, branching is then performed over sets of relations and consequently, the search spaces $\mathcal{P}$ on which f is to be minimized represent unions of relation polytopes.

From now on we assume that the project under consideration comprises renewable and cumulative resources, where the renewable resources are used by real activities $i \in V^a$ and the cumulative resources are depleted and replenished by events $i \in V^e$. Accordingly, for given schedule S the active sets

$$\mathcal{A}(S,t) := \{i \in V^a \mid S_i \le t < S_i + p_i\} \cup \{i \in V^e \mid S_i \le t\}$$

at times t contain both real activities and events, and resource-feasible schedules satisfy both the renewable-resource constraints (1.7) and the cumulative-resource constraints (1.20). The set of all feasible schedules is now $\mathcal{S} = \mathcal{S}_T \cap \mathcal{S}_R \cap \mathcal{S}_C$. As a straightforward extension of the definitions from Subsections 2.1.1 and 2.1.2, we say that a relation ρ *in set* V is time-feasible if $\mathcal{S}_T(\rho) \neq \emptyset$ and is feasible if $\emptyset \neq \mathcal{S}_T(\rho) \subseteq \mathcal{S}$. It is easily seen that first, relation ρ is again time-feasible precisely if relation network $N(\rho)$ does not contain any cycle of positive length and that second, a time-feasible relation ρ is feasible exactly if both induced sub-relations $\rho \cap (V^a \times V^a)$ and $\rho \cap (V^e \times V^e)$ are feasible in the sense of Definitions 2.3 and 2.17. As a consequence of the latter statement, the feasibility of a time-feasible relation ρ in set V can be verified by sequentially applying the network flow techniques discussed in Subsections 2.1.1 and 2.1.2 to the respective sub-relations.

The *resource-constrained project scheduling problem* to be dealt with reads as follows:

$$\left. \begin{array}{ll} \text{Minimize} & f(S) \\ \text{subject to} & S \in \mathcal{S}_T \cap \mathcal{S}_R \cap \mathcal{S}_C \end{array} \right\} \ (\mathrm{P})$$

where f is some regular or convexifiable objective function. In Section 3.1 we treat the case of regular objective functions. Section 3.2 is devoted to convexifiable objective functions.

3.1 Regular Objective Functions

We first develop an enumeration scheme based on the concept of disjunctive precedence constraints that either generates a set of candidate schedules containing an optimal schedule or proves that there is no feasible schedule for the project under consideration. We are then concerned with the relaxation to be solved at each enumeration node. The latter problem amounts to minimizing a regular objective function subject to temporal and disjunctive precedence constraints. Next, we discuss the extension of the enumeration scheme to a branch-and-bound algorithm and review alternative solution procedures for resource-constrained project scheduling with regular objective functions.

3.1.1 Enumeration Scheme

In this subsection we are concerned with an enumeration scheme for problem (P) with regular objective function f which forms the basis of branch-and-bound procedures by Schwindt (1998a) and Neumann and Schwindt (2002) for solving the project duration problem with renewable or cumulative resources, respectively. Consider an optimal solution S to the time-constrained project scheduling problem (1.2) with a regular objective function f, e.g., $S = ES = \min \mathcal{S}_T$. If S satisfies the renewable-resource constraints (1.7) and the cumulative-resource constraints (1.20), S is an optimal schedule. Otherwise, there is some point in time $t \in [0, \bar{d}]$ such that $F := \mathcal{A}(S, t) \cap V^a$ or $F := \mathcal{A}(S, t) \cap V^e$ represents a forbidden set. In the former case, the joint requirements by real activities $i \in F$ exceed the capacity of some renewable resource $k \in \mathcal{R}^\rho$, and in the latter case, the depletions and replenishments by events $i \in F$ create a surplus or a shortage in some cumulative resource $k \in \mathcal{R}^\gamma$. Forbidden set F can be broken up by introducing a disjunctive precedence constraint (see Subsections 1.2.3 and 1.3.3)

$$\min_{j \in B} S_j \geq \min_{i \in A}(S_i + p_i) \tag{3.1}$$

between some appropriate set A and a minimal delaying alternative B, where by definition $p_i = 0$ for $i \in V^e$. If resource k is renewable, we choose $A := F \backslash B$. Otherwise, we put $A := V_k^{e^-} \backslash F$ if F is a k-surplus set and $A := V_k^{e^+} \backslash F$ if F is a k-shortage set. Let

$$P(A, B) := \bigcup_{i \in A} \{\{i\} \times B\}$$

denote the set of irreflexive relations $\{i\} \times B$ with $i \in A$, which each give rise to the (ordinary) precedence constraints between activity i and all activities $j \in B$. Introducing disjunctive precedence constraint (3.1) refines the resource relaxation by restricting the initial search space $\mathcal{P} = \mathcal{S}_T$ to the set of all schedules S contained in the union of relation polytopes $\mathcal{S}_T(\rho)$ with $\rho \in P(A, B)$.

After the selection of a minimal delaying alternative B, we minimize f on the restricted search space. Checking the resource-feasibility of the resulting minimizer, refining the relaxation by disjunctive precedence constraints, and re-optimizing f on the restricted search space is performed until either the search space has become void or the resulting minimizer S of f is resource-feasible. The disjunctive precedence constraints are represented as a collection P of relations ρ whose relation polytopes $\mathcal{S}_T(\rho)$ cover the search space. In each iteration, when adding a disjunctive precedence constraint of type (3.1) we put $P := P \otimes P(A, B)$ where $P = \{\emptyset\}$ at the root node and

$$P \otimes P(A, B) := \bigcup_{\rho \in P, \rho' \in P(A, B)} \{\rho \cup \rho'\}$$

As we shall see in Subsection 3.1.2, each of the nonempty search spaces $\mathcal{P} = \cup_{\rho \in P} \mathcal{S}_T(\rho)$ generated in this way possesses a unique minimal point, which represents a minimizer S of f on set $\mathcal{P}$.

We now consider the enumeration scheme in more detail. The corresponding procedure is given by Algorithm 3.1. Let Q denote a list of relation sets P in set V and let $\mathcal{C}$ designate the set of candidate schedules generated. Starting with $Q = \{\{\emptyset\}\}$ and $\mathcal{C} = \emptyset$, at each iteration we remove some relation set P from Q and solve the relaxation by either computing the minimal point S of search space $\mathcal{P} = \cup_{\rho \in P} \mathcal{S}_T(\rho)$ or showing that $\mathcal{P} = \emptyset$. In the latter case, we write $S = S^\infty := (\infty, \ldots, \infty)$. For $S < S^\infty$, we proceed as follows. If schedule S is resource-feasible, we have found a candidate schedule and put $\mathcal{C} := \mathcal{C} \cup \{S\}$. Otherwise, there is a start time $t = S_i$ of some activity $i \in V$ such that active set $\mathcal{A}(S, t)$ includes a forbidden set of real activities or a forbidden set of events. In the former case, we compute the set $\mathcal{B}$ all minimal delaying alternatives B for $F := \mathcal{A}(S, t) \cap V^a$ by using Algorithm 1.4. Otherwise, $F := \mathcal{A}(S, t) \cap V^e$ is a k-surplus or a k-shortage set for some cumulative resource $k \in \mathcal{R}^\gamma$, and calling Algorithm 1.6 provides the set $\mathcal{B}$ of all minimal delaying alternatives for F and k. For each minimal delaying alternative $B \in \mathcal{B}$ we then introduce disjunctive precedence constraint (3.1) between the corresponding set A and set B by setting $P' := P \otimes P(A, B)$ and adding the expanded relation set P' on list Q. We return to the (refined) relaxation and reiterate these steps until all relation sets P in list Q have been investigated, i.e., until $Q = \emptyset$. Finally, we return the set $\mathcal{C}$ of all candidate schedules found.

Algorithm 3.1. Enumeration scheme for regular objective functions

---

Input: A project.
Output: Set $\mathcal{C}$ of candidate schedules.

    initialize list of relation sets $Q := \{\{\emptyset\}\}$ and set of candidate schedules $\mathcal{C} := \emptyset$;
    repeat
        delete some relation set P from list Q;
        determine schedule $S = \min(\cup_{\rho \in P} \mathcal{S}_T(\rho))$;
        if $S < S^\infty$ **then** (∗ search space is nonempty ∗)
            if S is resource-feasible **then** $\mathcal{C} := \mathcal{C} \cup \{S\}$; (∗ candidate schedule found ∗)
            else (∗ introduce disjunctive precedence constraints ∗)
                determine time t such that resource constraints (1.7) or (1.20) are violated
                for some $k \in \mathcal{R}^\rho \cup \mathcal{R}^\gamma$;
                if $k \in \mathcal{R}^\rho$ **then**
                    set $F := \mathcal{A}(S, t) \cap V^a$;
                    compute set $\mathcal{B}$ of all minimal delaying alternatives for F;
                    (∗ Algorithm 1.4 ∗)
                else
                    set $F := \mathcal{A}(S, t) \cap V^e$;
                    compute set $\mathcal{B}$ of all minimal delaying alternatives for F and k;
                    (∗ Algorithm 1.6 ∗)
                for all $B \in \mathcal{B}$ **do**
                    if $k \in \mathcal{R}^\rho$ **then** set $A := F \setminus B$; **elsif** $B \subseteq V_k^{e^+}$ **then** set $A := V_k^{e^-} \setminus F$;
                    else set $A := V_k^{e^+} \setminus F$;
                      set $P' := P \otimes P(A, B)$ and add P' on list Q;
    until $Q = \emptyset$;
    return $\mathcal{C}$;

The following proposition establishes the correctness of the enumeration scheme from Algorithm 3.1.

Proposition 3.1 (Neumann et al. 2003b, Sect. 2.5). *Let C be the set of candidate schedules generated by Algorithm 3.1 and let $\mathcal{OS}$ denote the set of all optimal schedules.*

(a) *Algorithm 3.1 is finite.*
(b) *Algorithm 3.1 is complete, i.e., $C \cap \mathcal{OS} = \emptyset$ if and only if $S = \emptyset$.*
(c) *All schedules generated by Algorithm 3.1 are quasiactive, i.e., $C \subseteq \mathcal{QAS}$.*

Proof.

(a) At each iteration a relation set P is removed from list Q and a finite number of expanded relation sets P' are added to Q. For each $\rho \in P$, sets P' contain a relation $\rho' \supset \rho$ each. Since the cardinality of any irreflexive relation in set V is bounded from above by $(n+1)(n+2)$, this implies that the number of iterations performed by Algorithm 3.1 is finite.

(b) Clearly, the search space $\mathcal{P} = \mathcal{S}_T(\emptyset) = \mathcal{S}_T$ associated with the initial relation set $P = \{\emptyset\}$ is a superset of the feasible region S and thus $S = \mathcal{S}_T(\emptyset) \cap S$. Now let S be the minimal point of some search space $\mathcal{P}$ enumerated in the course of Algorithm 3.1. If S is not resource-feasible, there is a time t such that active set $\mathcal{A}(S,t)$ includes a forbidden set F. Let $\mathcal{B}$ be the set of minimal delaying alternatives for F. Then Theorems 1.17 and 1.28 say that any resource-feasible schedule in set $\mathcal{P}$ satisfies one of the disjunctive precedence constraints (3.1) with $B \in \mathcal{B}$ and appropriate set A. Since in addition all enumerated schedules S minimize f on the respective search spaces, there is at least one optimal candidate schedule $S \in C$ provided that $S \neq \emptyset$. Conversely, all candidate schedules $S \in C$ are feasible and the lower semicontinuity of f implies that $\mathcal{OS} = \emptyset$ only if $S = \emptyset$. Consequently, from $C \neq \emptyset$ it follows that $\mathcal{OS} \neq \emptyset$.

(c) Each candidate schedule $S \in C$ is the minimal point of some relation polytope $\mathcal{S}_T(\rho)$ and feasible. Due to $\theta(S) \supseteq \rho$ and thus $\mathcal{S}_T(\theta(S)) \subseteq \mathcal{S}_T(\rho)$, it follows from $S \in \mathcal{S}_T(\theta(S))$ that S is the minimal point of its schedule polytope $\mathcal{S}_T(\theta(S))$ as well, i.e., $S \in \mathcal{QAS}$. $\square$

We notice that as a direct consequence of the proof of Proposition 3.1a, the maximum depth of the enumeration tree generated by Algorithm 3.1 is $\mathcal{O}(n^2)$. Moreover, the candidate schedules $S \in C$ are generally not active but only quasiactive. Recall that already deciding on whether or not a given feasible schedule is active constitutes an NP-hard problem.

3.1.2 Solving the Relaxations

In this subsection we are concerned with the problem of minimizing a regular objective function f on a search space $\mathcal{P}$ defined by temporal constraints and disjunctive precedence constraints. We assume that the disjunctive precedence constraints are given by a collection of ν relation sets $P(A_1, B_1), \ldots, P(A_\nu, B_\nu)$ with $P(A_\mu, B_\mu) = \cup_{i \in A_\mu}(\{i\} \times B_\mu)$ for $\mu = 1, \ldots, \nu$.

With $P = \otimes_{\mu=1}^{\nu} P(A_\mu, B_\mu)$ we then have

$$\mathcal{P} = \cup_{\rho \in P}\mathcal{S}_T(\rho) = \cap_{\mu=1}^{\nu} \cup_{i \in A_\mu} \mathcal{S}_T(\{i\} \times B_\mu)$$

Proposition 3.2 (Neumann and Schwindt 2002). *Let ψ be the operator on partially ordered set $(\mathbb{R}_{\geq 0}^{n+2}, \leq)$ with $\psi(S) = (\psi_j(S))_{j \in V}$ and*

$$\psi_j(S) = \max\left(0, \max_{(i,j) \in E}(S_i + \delta_{ij}), \max_{\substack{\mu=1,\dots,\nu: \\ j \in B_\mu}} \min_{i \in A_\mu}(S_i + p_i)\right) \quad (j \in V).$$

(a) *If $\mathcal{P} \neq \emptyset$, set $\mathcal{P}$ has a unique minimal point S^+.*

(b) *ψ possesses a fixed point if and only if $\mathcal{P} \neq \emptyset$. Minimal point S^+ coincides with the unique fixed point S of ψ with $S_0 = 0$.*

(c) *If $\mathcal{P} \neq \emptyset$, S^+ arises as the limit of the sequence $\{S^\lambda\}$ with $S^1 = ES$ and $S^{\lambda+1} = \psi(S^\lambda)$ for $\lambda \in \mathbb{N}$.*

(d) *If $\mathcal{P} \neq \emptyset$, there is a $\kappa \leq n\bar{d}$ with $\psi(S^\lambda) = S^\lambda = S^+$ for all $\lambda \geq \kappa$.*

Proof.

(a) Let S^+ be the schedule given by $S_j^+ := \min_{S \in \mathcal{P}} S_j$ for all $j \in V$ and assume that $\mathcal{P} \neq \emptyset$. We show that S^+ is the unique minimal point of $\mathcal{P}$. Since ψ is isotonic and $S^+ \leq S$ holds for all $S \in \mathcal{P}$, we have $\psi(S^+) \leq \min_{S \in \mathcal{P}} \psi(S)$. By definition of ψ, set $\mathcal{P}$ can be represented as $\mathcal{P} = \{S \in \mathbb{R}_{\geq 0}^{n+2} \mid S_0 = 0,\ S \geq \psi(S)\}$. Now assume that $S^+ \notin \mathcal{P}$. Then there is an activity $j \in V$ such that $S_j^+ < \psi_j(S^+) \leq \min_{S \in \mathcal{P}} \psi_j(S) \leq \min_{S \in \mathcal{P}} S_j = S_j^+$, which contradicts the assumption.

(b) Since S^+ is *componentwise* minimal in set $\mathcal{P} = \{S \in \mathbb{R}_{\geq 0}^{n+2} \mid S_0 = 0,\ S \geq \psi(S)\}$, we have $S^+ = \psi(S^+)$, i.e., S^+ is a fixed point of ψ. Due to the connectivity of network N, a point S is a fixed point of ψ exactly if there is an $\alpha \geq 0$ with $S = S^+ + \alpha(1, \dots, 1)$. Thus, $S = S^+$ is the unique fixed point of ψ with $S_0 = 0$. Now assume that $\mathcal{P} = \emptyset$. Then there is no point $S \in \mathbb{R}_{\geq 0}^{n+2}$ such that $S_0 = 0$ and $S \geq \psi(S)$. Since the set of fixed points of ψ equals $\{S \in \mathbb{R}_{\geq 0}^{n+2} \mid S = S^+ + \alpha(1, \dots, 1)$ for some $\alpha \geq 0\}$ and $S_0^+ = 0$, the latter statement implies that ψ does not possess any fixed point.

(c) We first show by induction on λ that $S^\lambda \leq S^+$ for all $\lambda \in \mathbb{N}$. From $\mathcal{P} \subseteq \mathcal{S}_T$ it follows that $S^1 = ES = (\min_{S \in \mathcal{S}_T} S_j)_{j \in V} \leq (\min_{S \in \mathcal{P}} S_j)_{j \in V} = S^+$. Now assume that $S^\lambda \leq S^+$. Since operator ψ is isotonic, we have $S^{\lambda+1} = \psi(S^\lambda) \leq \psi(S^+) \leq S^+$, where the last inequality results from $S^+ \in \mathcal{P}$. For $S^1 = ES$ it holds that $S_j^1 = [\max_{(i,j) \in E}(S_i^1 + \delta_{ij})]^+$ for all $j \in V$. This provides $S^2 = \psi(S^1) \geq S^1$, which proves the sequence $\{S^\lambda\}$ to be componentwise nondecreasing. Thus, the existence of an upper bound S^+ implies the convergence of $\{S^\lambda\}$. Then $\lim_{\lambda \to \infty} S^\lambda = \lim_{\lambda \to \infty} S^{\lambda+1} = \lim_{\lambda \to \infty} \psi(S^\lambda) = \psi(\lim_{\lambda \to \infty} S^\lambda)$, and the limit of $\{S^\lambda\}$ represents a fixed point of ψ. The last equation is due to the continuity of ψ. From $S_0^1 = ES_0 = 0 \leq \lim_{\lambda \to \infty} S_0^\lambda \leq S_0^+ = 0$ we obtain $\lim_{\lambda \to \infty} S_0^\lambda = 0$. Since $S = S^+$ is the unique fixed point S of ψ with $S_0 = 0$, S^+ coincides with the limit of sequence $\{S^\lambda\}$.

(d) The assertion is immediate with the monotonicity of $\{S^\lambda\}$ and the property that as long as $S^{\lambda+1} \neq S^\lambda$, there is an activity $h \in V$ with $S_h^{\lambda+1} \geq S_h^\lambda + 1$. □

According to Proposition 3.2, minimizing a regular objective function f on set $\mathcal{P}$ can be achieved by starting with $S = ES$ and putting $S := \psi(S)$ until either $S = \psi(S)$ or $S_{n+1} > \overline{d}$. In the latter case, $\mathcal{P}$ has been shown to be empty. The number of iterates needed for reaching minimal point S^+ can be decreased by the following modifications. First, we may start the procedure with any time-feasible schedule $S \leq S^+$. Second, each time the start time S_j of some activity j has been increased due to a disjunctive precedence constraint, we may immediately restore the time-feasibility of schedule S by putting $S_h := \max(S_h, S_j + d_{jh})$ for all $h \in V$. The resulting schedule is time-feasible precisely if $S_{n+1} \leq \overline{d}$, which is easily seen by adding arc $(0, j)$ with weight $\delta_{0j} = S_j$ to project network N and applying Algorithm 1.3 for updating distance matrix D (see Remark 1.8). For $\mu = 1, \ldots, \nu$ let $t_\mu := \min_{i \in A_\mu}(S_i + p_i)$ be the earliest completion time of some activity $i \in A_\mu$ with respect to current iterate $S \in \mathcal{S}_T$ and let $d_\mu^h := \max_{j \in B_\mu} d_{jh}$ denote the "distance" between set B_μ and activity $h \in V$. Then the start time of activity $h \in V$ has to be increased precisely if $S_h < t_\mu + d_\mu^h$. In this case, we set $S_h := t_\mu + d_\mu^h$ and update the earliest completion times t_λ for all sets A_λ containing activity h. Algorithm 3.2 shows an implementation of this method as a label-correcting procedure where queue Q contains all indices $\lambda = 1, \ldots, \nu$ for which time t_λ has to be updated.

Algorithm 3.2. Minimizing regular objective functions subject to temporal and disjunctive precedence constraints

---

Input: A schedule $S' \in \mathcal{S}_T$, distance matrix D, relation sets $P(A_\mu, B_\mu)$
    $(\mu = 1, \ldots, \nu)$.
Output: Minimal schedule $S \geq S'$ in set $\mathcal{P} = \cap_{\mu=1}^\nu \cup_{i \in A_\mu} \mathcal{S}_T(\{i\} \times B_\mu)$.

      set $S := S'$ and $Q := \{1, \ldots, \nu\}$;
      for all $\mu = 1, \ldots, \nu$ **do**
3:    $t_\mu := \min_{i \in A_\mu}(S_i + p_i)$;
4:    **for all** $h \in V$ **do** $d_\mu^h := \max_{j \in B_\mu} d_{jh}$;
      repeat
        dequeue index μ from Q;
7:    **for all** $h \in V$ with $S_h < t_\mu + d_\mu^h$ **do**
8:      set $S_h := t_\mu + d_\mu^h$;
        for all $\lambda = 1, \ldots, \nu$ with $h \in A_\lambda$ and $t_\lambda < \min_{g \in A_\lambda}(S_g + p_g)$ **do**
10:    set $t_\lambda := \min_{g \in A_\lambda}(S_g + p_g)$;
        if $\lambda \notin Q$ **then** enqueue λ to Q;
      until $Q = \emptyset$ or $S_{n+1} > \overline{d}$;
      if $Q = \emptyset$ **then return** S; **else return** S^∞;

Next we analyze the time complexity of Algorithm 3.2. To this end, we assume that sets V and A_μ with $\mu = 1, \ldots, \nu$ are stored as Fibonacci heaps (see, e.g., Knuth 1998, Sect. 6.2) sorted respectively according to nondecreasing start times S_i or nondecreasing completion times $S_i + p_i$. The initialization of earliest completion times t_μ and distances d_μ^h on lines 3 and 4 takes $\mathcal{O}(\nu n^2)$ time. Since the algorithm stops as soon as $S_{n+1} > \bar{d}$, line 8 is executed at most $\mathcal{O}(n\bar{d})$ times. On the other hand, on line 10 each point in time t_λ cannot be increased more than $\mathcal{O}(\nu \bar{d})$ times, which implies that the repeat-loop is iterated $\mathcal{O}(\min[n, \nu]\bar{d})$ times. At each iteration, identifying activities $h \in V$ with $S_h < t_\mu + d_\mu^h$ on line 7 requires $\mathcal{O}(\log n)$ time and rearranging the Fibonacci heaps V and A_μ after having increased start time S_h on line 8 takes $\mathcal{O}(\nu \log n)$ time. Thus, the time complexity of Algorithm 3.2 is $\mathcal{O}(\nu n^2 + \min[n, \nu]\bar{d}\nu \log n)$.

Alternative solution procedures with pseudo-polynomial time complexity have been devised by Zwick and Paterson (1996), Chauvet and Proth (1999), and Schwiegelshohn and Thiele (1999). Möhring et al. (2004) provide a review on papers dealing with applications of disjunctive precedence constraints that arise in fields outside project scheduling, such as analyzing functional dependencies among data in relational data bases (Ausiello et al. 1983), optimizing the partial disassembly of products when removing single components (Goldwasser and Motwani 1999), or computing optimal strategies for mean-payoff games on directed bipartite graphs (Zwick and Paterson 1996). In the latter paper it is shown that the problem to decide whether the outcome of such a game is positive is contained in $NP \cap coNP$. In addition, Möhring et al. (2004) have shown that this decision problem is polynomially equivalent to minimizing a regular objective function subject to disjunctive temporal constraints where p_i in inequality (1.11) is replaced with an arbitrary time lag δ_{ij}. Despite this observation, however, no algorithm is available thus far for solving the latter scheduling problem in polynomial time. For the case where all time lags δ_{ij} are nonnegative, Möhring et al. (2004) exhibit a label-setting algorithm that runs in $\mathcal{O}(n + [\sum_{\mu=1}^{\nu} |B_\mu|][m + \sum_{\mu=1}^{\nu} |A_\mu||B_\mu|])$ time.

3.1.3 Branch-and-Bound

The enumeration scheme given by Algorithm 3.1 defines the **branching strategy** of a branch-and-bound algorithm for problem (P) with regular objective function f. In this subsection we present the complete branch-and-bound procedure. Besides the branching strategy, a branch-and-bound algorithm for a minimization problem is characterized by the *search strategy* for selecting one of the generated enumeration nodes for further branching, *consistency tests*, which are applied to restrict the search spaces of enumeration nodes, and *lower bounds* on the minimum objective function value.

The **search strategy** of the branch-and-bound algorithm is as follows. We always branch from one of the child nodes v of the node u currently selected, i.e., we perform a *depth-first search*. The depth-first strategy can be implemented by simply choosing the list Q of unexplored nodes u to be a stack. The main advantages of depth-first search are that first, this strategy minimizes the memory requirements necessary for storing list Q and that second, the number of branchings for reaching the first leaf u of the enumeration tree (and thus often the time for computing a first feasible solution) is minimum. Child nodes v are pushed onto stack Q according to nonincreasing lower bounds. One drawback of the depth-first search strategy is that typically, two enumeration nodes visited consecutively belong to similar relation sets, which share a large number of common elements. As a consequence, it may take a long time before any schedule located in a given part of the feasible region is investigated, and thus the algorithm may spend much time in useless parts of the enumeration tree. This shortcoming can be avoided by partitioning the enumeration tree into a number of subtrees, which are simultaneously traversed according to a depth-first search strategy each (*scattered search*, cf. Klein and Scholl 2000).

Basically, each of the **consistency tests** discussed in Subsections 1.2.4 and 1.3.4 can be applied at any enumeration node. Since disjunctive precedence constraints cannot be represented by a distance matrix D, the tests using distances d_{ij} between arbitrary nodes $i, j \in V$ (the disjunctive activities, energy precedence, and balance tests) refer to a modified distance matrix $D' = (d'_{ij})_{i,j \in V}$ reflecting the temporal constraints $S_j - S_i \geq d'_{ij}$ that are implied by the original temporal constraints and the added disjunctive precedence constraints. For example, the modified distance matrix can be chosen to be equal to the elementwise minimal matrix D' with $d'_{gh} \geq \max(d_{gh}, \min_{i \in A_\mu} \max_{j \in B_\mu}(d'_{gi} + p_i + d'_{jh}))$ for all $g, h \in V$ and all $\mu = 1, \ldots, \nu$ which satisfies the triangle inequalities (1.6). For distances d'_{0h} we may choose $d'_{0h} = S_h$ ($h \in V$), where S is the minimal point of search space $\mathcal{P}$ computed by Algorithm 3.2.

The question which consistency test should actually be used at which node has to be investigated with care. The reason for this is that intuitively there is a tradeoff between the efficiency (i.e., the computation time required) and the effectiveness (i.e., the decrease in size of the search space) of a test. As a rule, the deeper the enumeration node, the less time should be spent with consistency tests. In any case, the search space reduction algorithm (cf. Algorithm 1.5) should be implemented in the form of a label-correcting procedure iterating the hypothetical temporal constraints whose validity may be affected by the last constraint added (either an imposed disjunctive precedence constraint or a temporal constraint arising from applying a consistency test). In branch-and-bound algorithms for the project duration problem with renewable resource constraints, De Reyck and Herroelen (1998*a*) and Schwindt (1998*c*) have applied the disjunctive activities test to two-element forbidden sets (De Reyck and Herroelen used the test as a preprocessing technique at the root node). Dorndorf et al. (2000*a*) report on favorable results using the workload-based disjunctive activities test and the unit-interval capacity test in a time-oriented branch-and-bound procedure for the same problem (the latter algorithm is briefly sketched in Subsection 3.1.4). Dorndorf et al. have also experimented with the activity interval and general interval consistency tests, but on their testbed (projects with 100 or 500 activities) the additional search space reduction has been, on the average, outweighed by the increase in computation time. Finally, Laborie (2003) has been able to improve upon the results obtained by Neumann and Schwindt (2002) for the project duration problem with cumulative resources by using the balance test.

Next, we turn to **lower bounds** on the minimum objective function value. Let S be the minimal point of search space $\mathcal{P}$ under study (possibly reduced by applying consistency tests). Obviously, $lb_0 = f(S)$ represents a lower bound on the objective function value $\min_{S' \in \mathcal{P} \cap \mathcal{S}} f(S')$ of a best feasible schedule in $\mathcal{P}$. Within a branch-and-bound algorithm for the project duration problem with renewable resources, Schwindt (1998a) has used two further lower bounds lb_1 and lb_2, respectively being based on disjunctive activities and energetic reasoning. We first deal with lower bound lb_1 (see also Klein and Scholl 1998). Let $\overline{d}' \in \mathbb{Z}_{\geq 0}$ with $S_{n+1} \leq \overline{d}' \leq \overline{d}$ denote some hypothetical upper bound on the project duration. Clearly, the latest start time $LS_i = -d_{i0}$ of activity i is, under the assumption of a project deadline $\overline{d}'$, less than or equal to $\overline{d}' - d_{i,n+1}$, and the earliest completion time $S_i + p_i$ of activity i is independent of $\overline{d}'$. Now let $\{i, j\}$ be a forbidden set such that $\overline{d}' - d_{j,n+1} < S_i + p_i$ and $\overline{d}' - d_{i,n+1} < S_j + p_j$. Then activities i and j must overlap in time, which is impossible due to their excessive joint resource requirements. Consequently, $\overline{d}' + 1$ is a lower bound on the shortest project duration of all schedules in the search space. Moreover, $\overline{d}'$ must be increased by $\min(S_i + p_i + d_{j,n+1}, S_j + p_j + d_{i,n+1})$ units of time to avoid the above contradiction. Thus, instead of performing a binary search in set $[S_{n+1}, \overline{d}] \cap \mathbb{Z}$, we may directly compute the smallest deadline $\overline{d}' = lb_1$ which cannot be disproved as

$$lb_1 = \max(S_{n+1}, \max_{\{i,j\} \in \mathcal{F}} \min(S_i + p_i + d_{j,n+1}, S_j + p_j + d_{i,n+1}))$$

For given two-element forbidden sets $\{i, j\}$, calculating smallest deadline $\overline{d}'$ requires $\mathcal{O}(n^2)$ time. By applying the profile test from Subsection 1.3.4 to the project termination event $n+1$, Neumann and Schwindt (2002) have obtained a similar lower bound on the minimum project duration of projects with cumulative resources. The algorithm iterates hypothetical upper bounds $\overline{d}'$, which may be refuted based on lower and upper approximations to the loading profiles.

Now recall the concept of lower bound $w_k(a, b)$ on the workload to be processed on renewable resource $k \in \mathcal{R}^\rho$ in interval $[a, b[$ (see equations (1.13) and (1.14)). By replacing the earliest completion time $EC_i = ES_i + p_i$ in (1.13) with $S_i + p_i$, we obtain a corresponding lower bound referring to the search space $\mathcal{P}$ rather than to set $\mathcal{S}_T$. In particular, $w_k(S_i, \overline{d})$ represents a lower bound on the workload for resource k that must be processed after the earliest start time S_i of activity i, which takes at least $\lceil w_k(S_i, \overline{d})/R_k \rceil$ units of time. By taking the maximum with respect to all real activities $i \in V^a$ and all renewable resources $k \in \mathcal{R}^\rho$, we obtain lower bound

$$lb_2 = \max_{i \in V^a}(S_i + \max_{k \in \mathcal{R}^\rho} \left\lceil \frac{w_k(S_i, \overline{d})}{R_k} \right\rceil)$$

on the minimum project duration. Computing value lb_2 can be done in $\mathcal{O}(|\mathcal{R}^\rho|n \log n)$ time.

We briefly touch upon further, more time-expensive lower bounds on the minimum duration of projects with renewable resources, which can be found in Heilmann and Schwindt (1997), Brucker and Knust (2003), and Möhring et al. (2003) and will be used for the performance analysis of exact and heuristic methods for the project duration problem in Subsection 3.1.4. The latter two lower bounds are also described in more detail in Neumann et al. (2003b), Subsect. 2.5.8.

Heilmann and Schwindt (1997) discuss several lower bounds based on disjunctive activities, energetic reasoning, and a relaxation of the resource-constrained project scheduling problem (1.8) leading to a preemptive one-machine problem with release dates d_{0i}^{min} and quarantine times $d_{i,n+1}^{min}$ ($i \in V^a$).

Similarly to lower bound lb_1, the lower bound on the minimum project duration devised by Brucker and Knust (2003) is based on falsifying hypothetical project deadlines $\overline{d}'$. For a given value of $\overline{d}'$, the procedure of testing the consistency of deadline $\overline{d}'$ constructs a linear program and tries to show that it is unsolvable. At first, several consistency tests are applied in order to tighten the time windows $[S_i, LS_i]$ of individual activities $i \in V^a$ (recall that minimal point S coincides with the earliest schedule in set $\mathcal{P}$). For each pair (t, t') of consecutive earliest start or latest completion times of activities $i \in V^a$, the set of all tentative active sets $\mathcal{A}$ for interval $[t, t'[$ is then computed, where $S_i < t'$ and $LC_i > t$ for all $i \in \mathcal{A}$ and $d_{ij} < p_i$ for all $i, j \in \mathcal{A}$. For each set $\mathcal{A}$, a continuous decision variable $y_{\mathcal{A}} \geq 0$ is introduced providing the time during which $\mathcal{A}$ is in progress in interval $[t, t'[$ (i.e., during which precisely the activities $i \in \mathcal{A}$ overlap in time). The project duration is then minimized subject to the constraints that first, each real activity i is carried out for p_i units of time in the different sets $\mathcal{A}$ and second, the total execution time of all sets $\mathcal{A}$ belonging to some pair (t, t') is less than or equal to interval length $t' - t$. The latter problem can be formulated as a linear program in decision variables $y_{\mathcal{A}}$ and corresponds to the relaxation of problem (1.8) where the temporal constraints are replaced with the weaker release dates $d_{0i}^{min} = S_i$ and deadlines $d_{0i}^{max} = LS_i$. Moreover, activities are allowed to be interrupted during their execution. Since the number of tentative active sets $\mathcal{A}$ grows exponentially in n, it is expedient to solve the linear program by *column-generation techniques* (see, e.g., Goldfarb and Todd 1989, Sect. 2.6). The basic idea is to consider only a restricted working set of decision variables that are generated when needed. Each time the linear program with the current working set of decision variables has been solved to optimality, new decision variables are added to the working set or it is shown that the current basic solution is optimal. For finding an improving decision variable $y_{\mathcal{A}}$

to be added to the working set, Brucker and Knust use a branch-and-bound algorithm enumerating binary incidence vectors for sets $\mathcal{A}$.

Möhring et al. (2003) use a formulation of problem (1.8) as a binary linear program with time-indexed binary variables x_{it}, which has been proposed by Pritsker et al. (1969) for the first time. Decision variable x_{it} equals one if activity i is started at time t and zero, otherwise. For (approximatively) solving the continuous relaxation of the latter binary program, Möhring et al. apply a standard subgradient method (cf. Held et al. 1974) to a Lagrangean relaxation of the latter linear program, which substitutes the resource constraints into a linear penalty function. For given multipliers, the Lagrangean relaxation can be solved efficiently by transforming the problem into a minimum-cut problem in a cyclic network with upper arc capacities, where each node stands for one decision variable x_{it} (the time complexity of this approach is studied in more detail in Möhring et al. 2001). The main advantage of this approach is that it can be used for each objective function f which can be written in the form $\sum_{i \in V} w_{it} x_{it}$, where $w_{it} \in \mathbb{Z}$ and variables x_{it} are used in the above meaning. In addition, the approach can straightforwardly be generalized to the case of cumulative resources (see Selle 1999).

3.1.4 Additional Notes and References

Algorithm 3.1 combines the enumeration schemes of the branch-and-bound algorithms by Schwindt (1998a) and Neumann and Schwindt (2002) for the project duration problems with renewable-resource and cumulative-resource constraints, respectively (see also Schwindt 1999). In this subsection we briefly present alternative solution procedures that have been proposed in literature and present the results of an experimental performance analysis of the algorithms. We only consider algorithms coping with general temporal constraints. For the special case where instead of minimum and maximum time lags between activities precedence constraints are prescribed, we refer to the survey papers by Herroelen et al. (1998), Brucker et al. (1999), Hartmann and Kolisch (2000), and Kolisch and Padman (2001) and the literature cited therein.

We first deal with exact procedures for the **project duration problem with renewable resources**. By using ordinary precedence constraints instead of disjunctive precedence constraints for breaking up forbidden active sets, we obtain the enumeration scheme of a branch-and-bound algorithm that has been devised by De Reyck and Herroelen (1998a). Accordingly, the enumeration nodes correspond to time-feasible relations ρ which arise from the union of *minimal delaying modes* $\{i\} \times B$. This enumeration scheme will be discussed in more detail in Subsection 3.2.1.

The earliest branch-and-bound algorithm for the project duration problem is due to Bartusch et al. (1988). Their approach differs from the algorithm by De Reyck and Herroelen in the forbidden sets considered in the course of the algorithm. The forbidden sets F broken up in the latter algorithm (and, likewise, in Algorithm 3.1) are always active sets $\mathcal{A}(S, t)$ belonging to the minimal point S of the search space $\mathcal{S}_T(\rho)$. If there is no forbidden active set $\mathcal{A}(S,t)$ for S at any time $t \geq 0$, schedule S is feasible, and no further pairs (i,j) are added to ρ. As we have already noticed in Subsection 3.1.1, the feasibility of S does not necessarily imply the feasibility of relation ρ. The algorithm of Bartusch et al. first computes all minimal forbidden sets $F \in \mathcal{F}$ for which the temporal constraints allow the simultaneous processing of all activities $i \in F$. Similarly to the enumeration scheme of the algorithm by De Reyck and Herroelen, enumeration nodes correspond to relations ρ in set V^a. The child nodes ρ', however, now arise from branching, for given minimal forbidden set F, over all pairs (i,j) of activities $i,j \in F$ such that relation $\rho' := \rho \cup \{(i,j)\}$ breaks up F. Leaves of the enumeration tree are either feasible relations ρ or relations ρ for which no further minimal forbidden set can be broken up by any time-feasible relation $\rho' \supset \rho$.

By substituting the disjunctive precedence constraints (3.1) into release dates

$$d_{0j}^{min} = \min_{i \in A}(S_i + p_i) \quad (j \in B) \tag{3.2}$$

where the right-hand side is the smallest completion time of some activity $i \in A$ with respect to the schedule S under consideration, one obtains the enumeration scheme of the branch-and-bound algorithm by Fest et al. (1999). The main advantage of this approach is that given distance matrix D, minimizers S of the project duration on the search space can be calculated in $\mathcal{O}(|B|n)$ time. Furthermore, there exists a very simple and effective dominance criterion, which enables fathoming nodes by comparing corresponding release date vectors. The drawback of the release-date based enumeration scheme is that constraints (3.2) only temporarily establish a precedence relationship between sets A and B. Since in contrast to the case of disjunctive precedence constraints, the right-hand side of (3.2) is a constant, the resource conflict caused by forbidden set $F = A \cup B$ is not definitely settled and thus one and the same resource conflict may be resolved repeatedly along a path from the root to some leaf of the enumeration tree. Computational experience, however, indicates that this situation can often be avoided by discarding enumeration nodes which due to unnecessary idle times cannot lead to quasiactive schedules (total-idle-time dominance rule, cf. Fest et al. 1999).

All algorithms mentioned thus far are based on breaking up forbidden sets. The constraint propagation algorithm by Dorndorf et al. (2000c) branches over the binary decision whether to schedule a given activity $i \in V^a$ at its (current) earliest possible start time ES_i or delaying i by introducing a release date $d_{0i}^{min} \geq ES_i + 1$. The large size of the corresponding complete enumeration tree is significantly reduced by applying the disjunctive activities and unit-interval capacity consistency tests and exploiting specific properties of active schedules.

We proceed with heuristic procedures for the project duration problem with renewable resources. Franck (1999), Ch. 4, has proposed the following *priority-rule method*. Preliminary variants of this algorithm have been devised by Neumann and Zhan (1995) and Brinkmann and Neumann (1996). A streamlined version of Franck's algorithm is described in Franck et al. (2001b). At first, a preprocessing step is performed by applying the disjunctive activities consistency test to two-element forbidden sets. To construct a feasible schedule, a *serial schedule-generation scheme* is used (cf. Kolisch 1996), which in each iteration schedules one eligible activity $j \in V^a$ by fixing its start time S_j. An activity j is called eligible if all of its predecessors $i \in Pred^\prec(j)$ with respect to strict order $\prec$ in set V^a have been scheduled, where $i \prec j$ if (1) $d_{ij} > 0$ or (2) $d_{ij} = 0$ and $d_{ji} < 0$. From the set of eligible activities, the activity to be scheduled next is chosen according to a priority rule. Let C denote the set of all activities already scheduled. The activity j selected is started at the earliest point in time $t \in [ES_j, LS_j]$, where $ES_j = \max[d_{0j}, \max_{i \in C}(S_i + d_{ij})]$ and $LS_j = \min[-d_{0j}, \min_{i \in C}(S_i - d_{ji})]$, such that in interval $[t, t+p_j[$ the joint resource requirements by j and the activities $i \in C$ do not exceed the resource capacities. Due to the presence of maximum time lags, it may happen that for a selected activity j there is no such point in time t. Let $t' := \min_{i \in C}(S_i - d_{ji})$ then denote the latest start time of j due to the (induced) maximum time lags between scheduled activities $i \in C$ and activity j. To resolve the deadlock, an *unscheduling step* is performed, which cancels the start times of all scheduled activities $i \in C$ with $S_i \geq t'$ and increases the earliest start time ES_i of all scheduled activities $i \in C$ with $S_i = t'$ by one unit of time. The procedure is terminated if a prescribed maximum number of unscheduling steps have been performed or if all activities $j \in V^a$ have been scheduled. The number of required unscheduling steps can be markedly decreased on the average if activities of strong components in project network N are scheduled directly one after another, where N does not contain backward arc $(n+1, 0)$ (recall that when minimizing the project duration, we may delete the deadline $\overline{d}$ on the project termination).

Based on this priority-rule method, Franck (1999), Ch. 6, has also developed a schedule-improvement procedure of type *parallel genetic algorithm* (see also Franck et al. 2001b), which is an adaptation of a genetic algorithm by Hartmann (1998) for the project duration problem without maximum time lags. The genetic algorithm works on several subpopulations of equal size, where each island evolves separately until after a given number of iterations, some individuals migrate from one subpopulation to another one. The individuals are represented by feasible activity lists (i.e., complete strict orders $<$ in set V^a extending strict order $\prec$), which are transformed into schedules by applying the serial schedule-generation scheme with strict order $\prec$ substituted into $<$. The initial subpopulations are created by randomly biasing priority rules and transforming the resulting priority values $\pi(i)$ of activities i in an activity list $<$ by putting $i < j$ if (1) $i \prec j$ or (2) $j \not\prec i$ and $\pi(i) < \pi(j)$. At each iteration, two individuals are selected for crossover in each subpopulation according to a double roulette-wheel selection. By applying a one-point and a two-point crossover operation to those two individuals two new activity lists are generated. With a certain probability, the new activity lists are then subjected to mutation by interchanging the positions of two adjacent activities in the list. Subsequently, the two activity lists are decoded into schedules using the serial schedule-generation scheme. If in the course of the schedule generation a maximum number of unscheduling steps has been performed, the violation of maximum time lags is allowed, which means that the resulting schedule is not time-feasible. Based on the resulting schedules, the fitness of the activity lists is calculated as the sum of the project duration and a penalty term for time-infeasibility of the schedule. Eventually, the worst two individuals in the subpopulation are replaced with the two new activity lists, provided that the new activity lists have a better fitness. These steps are iterated until one of five stop criteria is met: all individuals have the same fitness, a lower bound on the shortest project duration has been attained, a prescribed number of schedules have been evaluated, a feasible schedule has not been found within a given number of iterations, or the best feasible schedule found has not been improved within a given number of iterations.

A variant of the enumeration scheme of De Reyck and Herroelen (1998a) has been used by Cesta et al. (2002) for a *multi-pass heuristic*, where relation $\{i\} \times B$ is replaced with a pair (i, j) such that the addition of (i, j) to relation ρ breaks up some selected minimal forbidden set F. Set F is chosen from a given number of sampled minimal forbidden sets $F' \in \mathcal{F}$ with $F' \subseteq \mathcal{A}(S, t)$ for some $t \geq 0$. F is one of the sampled minimal forbidden sets with minimum "temporal flexibility" in terms of total slack times TF_h with $h \in F$, and pair (i, j) is chosen such that the resulting temporal flexibility for set F is maximum. The addition of pairs (i, j) to ρ is repeated until $\mathcal{S}_T(\rho) = \emptyset$ or minimal point $S = \min \mathcal{S}_T(\rho)$ is a feasible schedule. Within the multi-pass procedure, the temporal flexibility used for selecting pairs (i, j) is randomly biased, and thus in general several different feasible schedules are generated.

We now turn to the results of an experimental performance analysis. All of the above algorithms for the project duration problem with renewable resources except the branch-and-bound algorithm of Bartusch et al. (1988) have been tested on a test set consisting of 1080 problem instances with 100 real activities and 5 renewable resources each. The instances have been generated randomly by using the project generator ProGen/max (see Schwindt 1998b and Kolisch et al. 1999). The construction of projects can be influenced by means of control parameters for the problem size, shape of the project network, activity durations, time lags, and resource constraints. From the 1080 instances, 1059 possess a feasible solution. For 785 instances, an optimal solution is known.

Table 3.1 shows, in historical order, the results obtained by the different procedures, where the computation times refer to a Pentium personal computer with 200 MHz clock pulse (to account for different hardware, we have linearly scaled the computation times for De Reyck and Herroelen's and Franck's algorithms according to the corresponding clock pulse ratio). The results for the branch-and-bound procedure of De Reyck and Herroelen (1998a) are given as quoted by Dorndorf et al. (2000c). "Schwindt (1998a)

Table 3.1. Performance of algorithms for the project duration problem with renewable resources

Algorithm	t_{cpu}	p_{opt}	p_{ins}	p_{nopt}	p_{unk}	Δ_{lb}
De Reyck and Herroelen (1998a)	3 s	54.8 %	1.4 %	42.5 %	1.1 %	n. a.
	30 s	56.4 %	1.4 %	41.1 %	1.1 %	n. a.
Schwindt (1998a) BB	3 s	58.0 %	1.9 %	40.1 %	0.0 %	7.5 %
	30 s	62.5 %	1.9 %	35.6 %	0.0 %	7.0 %
	100 s	63.4 %	1.9 %	34.7 %	0.0 %	6.9 %
Schwindt (1998a) FBS	28.1 s	59.4 %	1.9 %	38.7 %	0.0 %	6.4 %
Fest et al. (1999)	3 s	58.1 %	1.9 %	34.1 %	5.9 %	10.9 %
	30 s	69.4 %	1.9 %	28.7 %	0.0 %	7.7 %
	100 s	71.1 %	1.9 %	27.0 %	0.0 %	7.0 %
Franck (1999) PR	0.16 s	57.2 %	1.9 %	40.9 %	0.0 %	7.3 %
Franck (1999) GA	12.1 s	60.1 %	1.9 %	38.0 %	0.0 %	5.3 %
Dorndorf et al. (2000c)	3 s	66.2 %	1.9 %	31.6 %	0.3 %	5.2 %
	30 s	70.4 %	1.9 %	27.7 %	0.0 %	4.8 %
	100 s	71.7 %	1.9 %	26.4 %	0.0 %	4.6 %
Cesta et al. (2002)	100 s	63.2 %	1.9 %	34.9 %	0.0 %	7.3 %

BB" and "Schwindt (1998a) FBS" designate the branch-and-bound algorithm of Schwindt (1998a) and its truncation to a filtered beam search heuristic (see Franck et al. 2001b). "Franck (1999) PR" and "Franck (1999) GA" stand for the priority-rule method and genetic algorithm by Franck (1999). The priority-rule method is performed with 14 different priority rules and the best schedule is returned. For the branch-and-bound procedures, t_{cpu} denotes an imposed time limit after which the enumeration is stopped. For the heuristics, t_{cpu} is the mean computation time. p_{opt}, p_{ins}, p_{nopt}, and p_{unk} denote the percentages of instances for which respectively an optimal schedule is found and optimality is proven, insolvability is shown, a feasible schedule is found whose optimality cannot be shown, or the solvability status remains unknown. In addition, we provide the mean percentage deviation Δ_{lb} of the project duration found from a lower bound lb on the minimum project duration, which has been calculated using techniques described in Heilmann and Schwindt (1997), the lower bound of Möhring et al. (2003) based on Lagrangean relaxation, and the lower bound of Brucker and Knust (2003) using column generation (see Subsection 3.1.3). For the algorithm of De Reyck and Herroelen (1998a), the published mean deviations from lower bound are based on values different from lb and are thus not listed. The mean refers to the instances which have been solved to feasibility by the respective algorithm. For the heuristic methods, we say that optimality is proven if the project duration obtained equals lower bound lb

and insolvability is shown if the consistency tests included reduce the search space to void.

As far as the exact algorithms are concerned, the results suggest that the most recent of the branch-and-bound procedures (Dorndorf et al. 2000c) is also the algorithm which performs best with respect to all five evaluation criteria. The good performance of the constraint propagation algorithm is primarily due to a clever search strategy and the effectiveness of the consistency tests, which are applied at every enumeration node. In particular, the mean deviation Δ_{lb} from lower bound is significantly smaller than for all remaining algorithms and for almost three quarters of the instances, the enumeration is completed within a time limit of 100 seconds. It is worth mentioning that all algorithms compared, except De Reyck and Herroelen's branch-and-bound procedure, are able to identify all insolvable instances and to find a feasible schedule for each solvable instance. The comparison of the results obtained when varying the time limit of the branch-and-bound procedures, however, indicates that solving all of the remaining open instances would probably require a prohibitively large computation time.

The priority-rule method provides feasible schedules with an acceptable deviation from lower bound within a very short amount of time. If more computation time is available, the genetic algorithm may be used to improve the initial schedule calculated by the priority-rule method. The comparison with Dorndorf et al.'s algorithm stopped after three seconds, however, shows that the latter algorithm also outperforms the heuristics. In addition, the data for the filtered beam search version of the branch-and-bound procedure of Schwindt (1998a) suggest that even better results may be obtained by a truncated version of Dorndorf et al.'s algorithm.

We proceed with the **project duration problem with cumulative resources**. To the best of our knowledge, there are only two algorithms for solving this problem: the branch-and-bound procedure devised by Neumann and Schwindt (2002), which is based on the enumeration scheme given by Algorithm 3.1, and a branch-and-bound algorithm that has been proposed by Laborie (2003).

The enumeration scheme of the latter procedure picks two distinct events i, j with $d_{ij} < 0$ and $d_{ji} < 0$ in each iteration and branches over the binary decision whether or not i occurs before j (i.e., $S_i \leq S_j - 1$ or $S_i \geq S_j$). The selection of events i, j is based on the upper and lower bounds $\overline{r}_k^{\leq}(h)$, $\overline{r}_k^{\leq}(h)$, $\underline{r}_k^{\geq}(h)$, $\underline{r}_k^{\leq}(h)$ on the inventory levels in resources $k \in \mathcal{R}^\gamma$ just before and at the occurrence, respectively, of events $h \in V^e$ (see Subsection 1.3.4). At each node of the enumeration tree, the balance test is used to reduce the time windows $[ES_h, LS_h]$ of events $h \in V^e$.

Table 3.2 shows the results of an experimental performance analysis of Neumann and Schwindt's and Laborie's algorithms. The test set has again been generated by ProGen/max and contains 360 instances with 10, 20, 50, or 100 events and 5 cumulative resources each. The computations have been performed on a Pentium personal computer with 200 MHz clock pulse. For each instance we have imposed a time limit of 100 seconds. The mean deviation from lower bound Δ_{lb} is based on the lower bound lb_1 that is obtained by applying the profile test to the project termination event $n + 1$ (see Subsection 3.1.3).

Table 3.2. Performance of algorithms for the project duration problem with cumulative resources

Algorithm	n	p_{opt}	p_{ins}	p_{nopt}	p_{unk}	Δ_{lb}
Neumann and Schwindt (2002)	10	66.7%	33.3%	0.0%	0.0%	0.3%
	20	48.9%	51.1%	0.0%	0.0%	2.2%
	50	51.1%	45.6%	1.1%	2.2%	1.3%
	100	55.6%	34.4%	7.8%	2.2%	1.2%
Laborie (2003)	50	53.3%	46.7%	0.0%	0.0%	1.5%
	100	63.4%	36.6%	0.0%	0.0%	0.9%

We first discuss the results obtained with the algorithm by Neumann and Schwindt (2002). For all 180 instances with 10 and 20 events, the enumeration is completed within the time limit. Even for the projects with 100 events, 90% of the instances can be either solved to optimality or proved to be insolvable. Put into perspective with the data displayed in Table 3.1, those results may indicate that problems with cumulative-resource constraints are more tractable than problems with renewable resources. As far as the computation of feasible schedules is concerned, the picture is different. There exist projects with 50 events for which after 100 seconds neither a feasible schedule can be found nor insolvability can be shown. With the branch-and-bound algorithm by Laborie (2003), however, the twelve open instances with 50 or 100 activities can be solved within less than 100 seconds (56 seconds on a HP 9000/785 workstation), which again confirms the benefit of efficient and effective consistency tests. The results for the projects with 10 or 20 activities are the same as for the algorithm by Neumann and Schwindt (2002).

3.2 Convexifiable Objective Functions

For convexifiable objective functions, time-constrained project scheduling with disjunctive precedence constraints can no longer be performed efficiently, and thus resource conflicts are settled by introducing ordinary precedence constraints. After the treatment of an enumeration scheme for generating candidate schedules, we discuss two alternative approaches to solving the relaxations: the primal approach, which will be used to solve the time-constrained project scheduling problem at the root node of the enumeration tree, and the dual approach for adding precedence constraints between activities of the project. Whereas the primal steepest descent algorithm iterates over time-feasible schedules, the dual flattest ascent algorithm consecutively enforces the precedence constraints. Both algorithms are used within a branch-and-bound algorithm for minimizing convexifiable objective functions. In addition, we provide an overview of alternative solution procedures that have been devised in literature for specific convexifiable objective functions and discuss the results of an experimental performance analysis of the methods treated.

3.2.1 Enumeration Scheme

Precursors of the enumeration scheme to be discussed in this subsection have been proposed, independently, by Icmeli and Erengüç (1996) for the net present value problem with renewable resources and by De Reyck and Herroelen (1998a) for the project duration problem with renewable resources. Icmeli and Erengüç (1996) have considered the case of precedence constraints among activities instead of general temporal constraints. The enumeration scheme has arisen from the combination of the relaxation-based approach by Bell and Park (1990) and the concept of minimal delaying alternatives introduced by Demeulemeester and Herroelen (1992). Later on, Schwindt (2000c) has used the enumeration scheme within a branch-and-bound algorithm for the total earliness-tardiness cost problem with renewable resources. For solving the capital-rationed net present value problem, Schwindt (2000a) has expanded the enumeration scheme to cope with cumulative resources.

The algorithm mainly differs from the enumeration scheme considered in Subsection 3.1.1 in that forbidden active sets are broken up by ordinary instead of disjunctive precedence constraints. Hence, each enumeration node is associated with a relation ρ rather than with a set P of relations, and the search spaces $\mathcal{P}$ represent relation polytopes $\mathcal{S}_T(\rho)$. The relations ρ arise from the union of minimal delaying modes $\{i\} \times B$, where B is a minimal delaying alternative for some forbidden set F and $i \in A$ with $A \subseteq V \setminus B$ being an appropriate set of activities to be chosen depending on the type of the underlying resource conflict. Accordingly, we obtain one enumeration node for each combination of activity $i \in A$ and minimal delaying alternative B. The relaxation to be solved at an enumeration node belonging to relation ρ consists in finding a (local) minimizer of objective function f on search space $\mathcal{S}_T(\rho)$. In contrast to the case of regular objective functions, it can easily be verified whether or not the search space becomes void when passing from ρ to a child node's relation $\rho' = \rho \cup (\{i\} \times B)$ by checking the condition $d_{ji}^\rho + p_i \leq 0$ for each $j \in B$ (see Proposition 1.9). Updating the distance matrix $D(\rho)$ after the addition of pairs (i,j) with $j \in B$ can be achieved in $\mathcal{O}(n^2)$ time by using Algorithm 1.3 and observing that $\max_{j \in B}(d_{gi} + \delta_{ij} + d_{jh}) = d_{gi} + p_i + \max_{j \in B} d_{jh}$ for all $g, h \in V$.

The enumeration scheme is now as follows (cf. Algorithm 3.3). Q is a list of relations in set V and $\mathcal{C}$ again denotes the set of candidate schedules to be generated. At first, we put the empty relation $\rho = \emptyset$ on list Q and set $\mathcal{C} := \emptyset$.

We then check whether there is a cycle of positive length in project network N, in which case we return the empty set of candidate schedules. At each iteration we take some relation ρ from list Q and determine a minimizer S of f on relation polytope $\mathcal{S}_T(\rho)$. If schedule S is resource-feasible, we have found a candidate schedule, which is added to set $\mathcal{C}$. Otherwise, we scan S for a start time $t = S_i$ of some activity $i \in V$ such that active set $\mathcal{A}(S, t)$ includes a forbidden set F and compute the corresponding set $\mathcal{B}$ of all minimal delaying alternatives. For each minimal delaying alternative $B \in \mathcal{B}$ and each activity i from the respective set A we obtain one minimal delaying mode $\{i\} \times B$, which is joined with relation ρ and gives rise to the extension ρ' of ρ. If relation polytope $\mathcal{S}_T(\rho')$ is nonempty, ρ' is added to the list Q of unexplored enumeration nodes. We then take the next relation ρ from list Q and proceed in the same way until no more relations ρ remain in list Q and the set $\mathcal{C}$ of all candidate schedules is returned.

Algorithm 3.3. Enumeration scheme for convexifiable objective functions

---

Input: A project, convexifiable objective function f.
Output: Set $\mathcal{C}$ of candidate schedules.

> initialize list of relations $Q := \{\emptyset\}$ and set of candidate schedules $\mathcal{C} := \emptyset$;
> **if** $\mathcal{S}_T = \emptyset$ **then return** $\mathcal{C}$; ($*$ cycle of positive length in N $*$)
> **repeat**
> > delete some relation ρ from list Q;
> > determine minimizer S of f on $\mathcal{S}_T(\rho)$;
> > **if** S is resource-feasible **then** $\mathcal{C} := \mathcal{C} \cup \{S\}$; ($*$ candidate schedule found $*$)
> > **else** ($*$ introduce ordinary precedence constraints $*$)
> > > determine time t such that resource constraints (1.7) or (1.20) are violated for some $k \in \mathcal{R}^\rho \cup \mathcal{R}^\gamma$;
> > > **if** $k \in \mathcal{R}^\rho$ **then**
> > > > set $F := \mathcal{A}(S, t) \cap V^a$;
> > > > compute set $\mathcal{B}$ of all minimal delaying alternatives for F;
> > > **else**
> > > > set $F := \mathcal{A}(S, t) \cap V^e$;
> > > > compute set $\mathcal{B}$ of all minimal delaying alternatives for F and k;
> > > **for all** $B \in \mathcal{B}$ **do**
> > > > **if** $k \in \mathcal{R}^\rho$ **then** set $A := F \setminus B$; **elsif** $B \subseteq V_k^{e^+}$ **then** set $A := V_k^{e^-} \setminus F$;
> > > > **else** set $A := V_k^{e^+} \setminus F$;
> > > > **for all** $i \in A$ **do**
> > > > > set $\rho' := \rho \cup (\{i\} \times B)$;
> > > > > **if** $\mathcal{S}_T(\rho') \neq \emptyset$ **then** add ρ on list Q; ($*$ search space is nonempty $*$)
> **until** $Q = \emptyset$;
> **return** $\mathcal{C}$;

3.2.2 Solving the Relaxations: The Primal Approach

The relaxation to be solved at each node of the enumeration tree generated by Algorithm 3.3 corresponds to a time-oriented scheduling problem of type (1.2) where $\mathcal{S}_T$ is substituted into some relation polytope $\mathcal{S}_T(\rho)$ and f is a convexifiable objective function. To simplify writing, we consider the relaxation at the root node, where $\rho = \emptyset$, i.e., the resource relaxation of problem (P).

Recall that if objective function $f : \mathcal{S}_T \to \mathbb{R}$ is convexifiable, there exists a C^1-diffeomorphism $\varphi : \mathcal{S}_T \to X$ such that composite function $\psi : X \to \mathbb{R}$ with $\psi(x) = (f \circ \varphi^{-1})(x)$ for all $x \in X$ is convex and the image $X = \varphi(\mathcal{S}_T)$ of $\mathcal{S}_T$ under φ is a convex set. The continuity of φ and the compactness of $\mathcal{S}_T$ imply that the domain X of ψ is compact as well. If for given convexifiable objective function f, a diffeomorphism φ satisfying the conditions of Definition 2.29 is known, the relaxation can be solved by computing a minimizer x of ψ on X and returning schedule $S = \varphi^{-1}(x)$. The existence of such a minimizer x is easily seen as follows. By definition of ψ, the lower-level set L_α^ψ of ψ for given $\alpha \in \mathbb{R}$ equals the image of lower-level set L_α^f of f under φ, which is closed because of the lower semicontinuity of f. Consequently, the continuity of φ provides the closedness of any lower-level set L_α^ψ of ψ, which means that ψ is lower semicontinuous as well. Since X is compact, ψ always assumes its minimum on X. A minimizer x of ψ on X can be determined by the ellipsoid method, whose time complexity is polynomial in the input length of function ψ and set X. We stress, however, that the latter time complexity is not necessarily polynomial in the input length of the original relaxation (1.2).

For two special cases, which cover most convexifiable objective functions occurring in practice, the relaxation can be solved more efficiently on the average. We first consider the case where f is piecewise affine, convex, and sum-separable in the nodes $i \in V$ and the arcs $(i, j) \in E$ of project network N, i.e., f can be written in the form

$$f(S) = \sum_{i \in V} f_i(S_i) + \sum_{(i,j) \in E} f_{ij}(S_j - S_i)$$

where functions $f_i : [ES_i, LS_i] \to \mathbb{R}$ $(i \in V)$ and $f_{ij} : [d_{ij}, -d_{ji}] \to \mathbb{R}$ $((i, j) \in E)$ are piecewise affine and convex. The problem of minimizing a sum-separable function on set $\mathcal{S}_T$ is known as the *optimal-potential problem* in literature (cf. e.g., Rockafellar 1998, Sect. 1J). It is well-known that the optimal-potential problem with piecewise affine and convex functions f_i and f_{ij} is dual to the *convex-cost flow problem*

$$\text{Minimize} \quad \sum_{(i,j) \in E} f_{ij}^*(u_{ij}) + \sum_{i \in V} f_i^*\left(\sum_{(j,i) \in E} u_{ji} - \sum_{(i,j) \in E} u_{ij} \right)$$

$$\text{subject to} \quad \underline{c}_i \le \sum_{(j,i) \in E} u_{ji} - \sum_{(i,j) \in E} u_{ij} \le \overline{c}_i \quad (i \in V : i \neq 0)$$

where the functions f_i and f_i^* and the functions f_{ij} and f_{ij}^* are conjugate to each other (see Rockafellar 1998, Sect. 8G). Recall that a function ϕ^* with effective domain X^* (i.e., $\phi^*(y) < \infty$ for all $y \in X^*$) is conjugate to a function $\phi : X \to \mathbb{R}$ if $\phi^*(y) = \sup_{x \in X}(y^\top x - \phi(x))$ for all $y \in X^*$. For given functions f_i and f_{ij}, the corresponding conjugate functions f_i^* and f_{ij}^* are piecewise affine as well. The functions f_i^* and f_{ij}^* (up to an additive constant) and the lower and upper bounds $\underline{c}_i$ and $\overline{c}_i$ on supplies at nodes $i \in V$ can be determined by reversing the roles of breakpoints and slopes in passing from functions f_i and f_{ij} to their respective conjugates f_i^* and f_{ij}^*. The additive constants arise from evaluating a convenient point on the characteristic curves of f_i and f_{ij} (see Rockafellar 1998, Example 3 in Sect. 8F). The characteristic curve Γ of a convex function of one variable is the set of all points $(x, y) \in \mathbb{R}^2$ such that y is between the left-hand and the right-hand derivative of the function at x. The convex-cost flow problem can be solved in $\mathcal{O}(mn^2 \log[\sum_{i \in V}(|\overline{c}_i| + |\underline{c}_i|)])$ time by a generalization of the capacity-scaling algorithm for the min-cost flow problem (see Ahuja et al. 1993, Sect. 14.5).

The subcase where $f_i(S_i) = w_i S_i$ for all $i \in V$ and $f_{ij}(S_j - S_i) = 0$ for all $(i, j) \in E$ leads to the following min-cost flow problem (cf. e.g., Russell 1970):

$$\text{Minimize} \quad \sum_{(i,j) \in E} -\delta_{ij} u_{ij}$$

$$\text{subject to} \quad \sum_{(i,j) \in E} u_{ij} - \sum_{(j,i) \in E} u_{ji} = \begin{cases} \sum_{j=1}^{n+1} w_j, & \text{if } i = 0 \\ -w_i, & \text{otherwise} \end{cases} \quad (i \in V)$$

$$u_{ij} \geq 0 \quad ((i, j) \in E)$$

We now turn to the second special case, where convexifiable objective function f is assumed to be continuously differentiable or sum-separable in the nodes $i \in V$ of N. In that case, the relaxation is amenable to an efficient *primal steepest descent approach*, which has been used by Schwindt (2000c) for solving the time-constrained total earliness-tardiness cost problem and by Schwindt and Zimmermann (2001) for solving the time-constrained net present value problem. We first review some basic concepts required for what follows. For notational convenience, we assume that function f possesses a continuation $\bar{f}$ from an open set $C \subseteq \mathbb{R}^{n+2}$ to $\mathbb{R}$ which is differentiable at the boundary points of $\mathcal{S}_T$. The *directional derivative* of $\bar{f}$ at point $S \in \mathcal{S}_T$ in direction $z \in \mathbb{R}^{n+2}$ is defined to be

$$d\bar{f}|_S(z) := \lim_{\lambda \downarrow 0} \frac{\bar{f}(S + \lambda z) - \bar{f}(S)}{\lambda} \tag{3.3}$$

if the limit exists. Now recall that function $\psi = f \circ \varphi^{-1}$ is convex and thus is directionally differentiable in any direction at any interior point of its domain (cf. Shor 1998, Sect. 1.2). Since $f = \psi \circ \varphi$ is a composition of a C^1-function and a finite convex function, f is directionally differentiable in any direction at any interior point of its domain as well. The latter property implies that the limit in (3.3) always exists. The derivative $d\bar{f}|_S(z)$ in direction of the i-th unit vector $z = e_i$ coincides with the right-hand S_i-derivative $\partial^+ \bar{f}/\partial S_i(S)$ of

$\bar{f}$ at S, and the left-hand S_i-derivative $\partial^-\bar{f}/\partial S_i(S)$ of $\bar{f}$ at S equals $-d\bar{f}|_S(z)$ where $z = -e_i$. The vectors of right-hand and left-hand S_i-derivatives of $\bar{f}$ at S are denoted by $\nabla^+\bar{f}(S)$ and $\nabla^-\bar{f}(S)$, respectively. For fixed schedule S, derivative $d\bar{f}|_S(z)$ is a positively homogeneous function g of z (i.e., $g(\alpha z) = \alpha g(z)$ for all $\alpha > 0$ and all $z \in \mathbb{R}^{n+2}$). Under our assumption that objective function f is continuously differentiable or sum-separable in $i \in V$, derivative $g(z) = d\bar{f}|_S(z)$ at point S in direction z takes the form

$$g(z) = \sum_{i \in V:z_i>0} \frac{\partial^+\bar{f}}{\partial S_i}(S)z_i + \sum_{i \in V:z_i<0} \frac{\partial^-\bar{f}}{\partial S_i}(S)z_i$$

In particular, if f is continuously differentiable, then $g(z) = \nabla\bar{f}(S)^\top z$, where $\nabla\bar{f}(S)$ is the derivative of $\bar{f}$ at S. As we will see later on (see Lemma 3.4), $\partial^+\bar{f}/\partial S_i(S) \geq \partial^-\bar{f}/\partial S_i(S)$ for all $i \in V$, which implies that $g(z) = \sum_{i \in V} \max(\partial^+\bar{f}/\partial S_i(S)z_i, \partial^-\bar{f}/\partial S_i(S)z_i)$. Consequently, g is a convex and thus sublinear function.

A direction $z \in \mathbb{R}^{n+2}$ is called a *descent direction* at $S \in \mathcal{S}_T$ if $d\bar{f}|_S(z) < 0$. z is termed a *feasible direction* at S if for some $\varepsilon > 0$, $S + \delta z \in \mathcal{S}_T$ for all $0 < \delta < \varepsilon$. Due to the convexity of $\mathcal{S}_T$, the latter condition is equivalent to the existence of some $\varepsilon > 0$ with $S + \varepsilon z \in \mathcal{S}_T$. Now let for given schedule $S \in \mathcal{S}_T$, $E(S) := \{(i,j) \in E \mid S_j - S_i = \delta_{ij}\}$ denote the set of arcs $(i,j) \in E$ for which temporal constraint $S_j - S_i \geq \delta_{ij}$ is active at S. Then direction z is feasible at S precisely if $z_0 = 0$ and $z_j - z_i \geq 0$ for all $(i,j) \in E(S)$. A (normalized first-order) *steepest feasible descent direction* at S is a feasible descent direction z at S with $\|z\| \leq 1$ minimizing derivative $g(z) = d\bar{f}|_S(z)$, where $\|\cdot\|$ is some vector norm in $\mathbb{R}^{n+2}$.

Now recall that any local minimizer of f on $\mathcal{S}_T$ is a global minimizer as well (cf. Proposition 2.30d). Obviously, a schedule S can only be a local minimizer of f on $\mathcal{S}_T$ if there is no feasible descent direction at S. Thus, any local minimizer S of f on $\mathcal{S}_T$ must satisfy the following necessary optimality condition (defining an *inf-stationary point*, see Kiwiel 1986):

$$\inf\{g(z) \mid z_0 = 0 \text{ and } z_j - z_i \geq 0 \text{ for all } (i,j) \in E(S)\} \geq 0 \qquad (3.4)$$

Condition (3.4) is sufficient for S to be a local minimizer of f on $\mathcal{S}_T$ if f is convex or if f is differentiable and $\nabla\bar{f}(S) \neq 0$. The objective function of the net present value problem is an example of a convexifiable and differentiable objective function f for which $\nabla\bar{f}(S) \neq 0$ for all $S \in \mathcal{S}_T$.

A classical approach to computing local minimizers are so-called *steepest descent algorithms*, which construct a sequence $S^1, S^2, \ldots, S^\nu$ of iterates such that $f(S^{\mu+1}) < f(S^\mu)$ for all $\mu = 1, \ldots, \nu - 1$. Steepest descent algorithms belong to the class of *feasible direction methods* introduced by Zoutendijk (1960). Feasible direction methods offer an efficient way of solving nonlinear programming problems with linear inequality constraints (cf. e.g., Jacoby et al. 1972, Sect. 7.5, or Simmons 1975, Sect. 8.1), in particular if the directional derivatives are easily obtained. Iterations of steepest descent algorithms consist of two main phases: the *direction-finding phase* and the *line-search phase* (see Hiriart-Urruty and Lemaréchal 1993, Sect. II.2). The direction-finding phase determines a steepest feasible descent direction z at the current iterate S or establishes that there is no feasible descent direction at S. Line search provides a feasible destination $S' = S + \sigma z$ with $f(S + \sigma z) < f(S)$. σ is termed the *stepsize*. Algorithm 3.4 specifies a generic (primal) steepest descent algorithm.

Algorithm 3.4. Primal steepest descent algorithm

Input: MPM project network $N = (V, E, \delta)$, objective function f.
Output: Local minimizer S of f on set $\mathcal{S}_T$.

    determine some time-feasible schedule S, e.g., $S = ES$;
    repeat
        determine normalized feasible direction z at S with minimum $g(z)$; ($*$ direction-finding phase $*$)
        if $g(z) < 0$ **then** ($* z$ is a descent direction $*$)
            determine stepsize σ in N at S; ($*$ line-search phase $*$)
            set $S := S + \sigma z$;
    until $g(z) \geq 0$;
    return S;

We now deal with the **direction-finding phase** in more detail. The problem of finding a normalized steepest feasible descent direction at schedule S reads as follows:

$$\left.\begin{array}{ll} \text{Minimize} & g(z) \\ \text{subject to} & z_j - z_i \geq 0 \quad ((i,j) \in E(S)) \\ & z_0 = 0 \\ & \|z\| \leq 1 \end{array}\right\} \tag{3.5}$$

The feasible region of problem (3.5) is compact and nonempty since $z = 0$ is always a feasible solution. The choice of vector norm $\| \cdot \|$ is of crucial importance for the efficiency of the steepest descent algorithm. For what follows, we assume that $\| \cdot \|$ is chosen to be supremum norm, i.e., $\|z\| = \|z\|_\infty := \max_{i \in V} |z_i|$, which means that normalization constraint $\|z\| \leq 1$ can be stated as $-1 \leq z_i \leq 1$ for all $i \in V$. In this case, all constraints of problem (3.5) are linear, and (3.5) can easily be transformed into a linear program by introducing an additional variable y_i for each $i \in V$ together with the constraints $y_i \geq \partial^+ \bar{f} / \partial S_i(S) z_i$ and $y_i \geq \partial^- \bar{f} / \partial S_i(S) z_i$ and replacing $g(z)$ with $\sum_{i \in V} y_i$.

    In the following we consider a relaxation of problem (3.5) which can be solved in linear time. To this end, we again assume that $\|z\| = \|z\|_\infty$, but we only consider a subset of the temporal constraints that are active at S. The active temporal constraints to be taken into account are chosen such that the corresponding rows of the coefficient matrix are linearly independent. As it is well-known from the theory of network flows, the directed graph $G = (V, E_G)$ whose arc set E_G contains the arcs belonging to the selected active temporal constraints represents a spanning forest of project network N (see, e.g., Ahuja et al. 1993, Sect. 11.2). Proposition 2.28b tells us that G can be chosen to be a spanning tree of N precisely if S is a vertex of $\mathcal{S}_T$. The *steepest descent problem* (SDP) at schedule S can now be formulated as follows:

$$
\left.
\begin{aligned}
\text{Minimize} \quad & g(z) \\
\text{subject to} \quad & z_j - z_i \geq 0 \quad ((i,j) \in E_G) \\
& z_0 = 0 \\
& -1 \leq z_i \leq 1 \quad (i \in V)
\end{aligned}
\right\} \quad \text{(SDP)}
$$

A direction z solving steepest descent problem (SDP) is called an *optimal direction* at S. Of course, we have to pay a price for the efficiency with which (SDP) can be solved. At degenerate points S of $\mathcal{S}_T$, where $E_G \subset E(S)$, optimal directions may no longer be feasible directions at S. In the latter case, line search will provide the stepsize $\sigma = 0$, and the set of selected active constraints is modified without leaving the current iterate S. Since (SDP) is a relaxation of problem (3.5), schedule S satisfies the necessary optimality condition (3.4) if $z = 0$ is an optimal direction at S.

We show how for a given schedule $S \in \mathcal{S}_T$ the steepest descent problem can be solved in linear time. The procedure is based on two fundamental properties of problem (SDP). First, it always possesses an integral solution and second, it can be decomposed into two independent subproblems with linear objective functions.

Proposition 3.3. *Let f be a differentiable or sum-separable convexifiable objective function. Then there is an integer-valued solution z to (SDP).*

Proof. If f is differentiable or sum-separable, then objective function $g(z) = \sum_{i \in V : z_i > 0} \partial^+ \bar{f} / \partial S_i(S) z_i + \sum_{i \in V : z_i < 0} \partial^- \bar{f} / \partial S_i(S) z_i$. It follows that g is linear on each octant and continuous. Since $z = 0$ is a feasible solution to (SDP), the continuity of g implies that (SDP) is solvable. In addition, the coefficient matrix of (SDP) is totally unimodular, which means that a feasible solution z minimizing g on a given octant can always be chosen to be integral. $\square$

We proceed with the decomposition of the steepest descent problem (SDP) into two independent subproblems where we only consider nonnegative directions $z \geq 0$ or nonpositive directions $z \leq 0$ and which are respectively denoted by (SDP$^+$) and (SDP$^-$). For (SDP$^+$) objective function $g(z)$ equals $\nabla^+ \bar{f}(S)^\top z$, and for (SDP$^-$) we have $g(z) = \nabla^- \bar{f}(S)^\top z$.

$$
\left.
\begin{aligned}
\text{Minimize} \quad & g(z) = \nabla^+ \bar{f}(S)^\top z \parallel \nabla^- \bar{f}(S)^\top z \\
\text{subject to} \quad & z_j - z_i \geq 0 \quad ((i,j) \in E_G) \\
& z_0 = 0 \\
& 0 \leq z_i \leq 1 \parallel -1 \leq z_i \leq 0 \quad (i \in V)
\end{aligned}
\right\} \quad \text{(SDP}^+\text{)} \parallel \text{(SDP}^-\text{)}
$$

We first need two preliminary lemmas.

Lemma 3.4. *Let f be some convexifiable objective function and let S be a time-feasible schedule. Then*

$$\nabla^+ \bar{f}(S) \geq \nabla^- \bar{f}(S)$$

Proof. We only consider the case where S is an interior point of $\mathcal{S}_T$ since by assumption, $\bar{f}$ is differentiable at boundary points of $\mathcal{S}_T$. Let $\varphi : \mathcal{S}_T \to X$ be a C^1-diffeomorphism satisfying the conditions of Definition 2.29 and let $\psi = f \circ \varphi^{-1}$. Since φ is continuous, $x = \varphi(S)$ is an interior point of X. Let $\nabla \varphi(S)$ be the Jacobian matrix of φ at point S. For given direction $z \in \mathbb{R}^{n+2}$, applying the chain rule (see Shapiro 1990, Proposition 3.6 (ii) or Scholtes 1990, Theorem 3.1) then provides $d\bar{f}|_S(z) = d\psi|_x(y)$ where $y = \nabla \varphi(S) z$ (recall that φ is continuously differentiable and that ψ is finite-valued convex and thus continuously Bouligand-differentiable at interior point of its domain). We then have $-d\bar{f}|_S(-z) = -d\psi|_x(-y)$. The convexity of ψ implies that $-d\psi|_x(-y) \leq d\psi|_x(y)$ and thus $-d\bar{f}|_S(-z) \leq d\bar{f}|_S(z)$ (see Hiriart-Urruty and Lemaréchal 1993, Sect. VI.1). The assertion follows from $\frac{\partial^+ \bar{f}}{\partial S_i}(S) = d\bar{f}|_S(e_i)$ and $\frac{\partial^- \bar{f}}{\partial S_i}(S) = -d\bar{f}|_S(-e_i)$. $\qquad \square$

Lemma 3.5. *z is a feasible solution to* (SDP) *if and only if* $\max(0, z)$ *and* $\min(0, z)$ *are feasible solutions to* (SDP).

Proof. Let $z^+ := \max(0, z)$ and $z^- := \min(0, z)$. Trivially, for any direction $z \in \mathbb{R}^{n+2}$ we have $z = z^+ + z^-$.

Sufficiency: Let H denote the coefficient matrix of constraints $z_j - z_i \geq 0$ $((i, j) \in E_G)$, which coincides with the negative arc-node incidence matrix of spanning forest G. If z^+ and z^- are feasible solutions to (SDP), then $Hz^+ \geq 0$ and $Hz^- \geq 0$, which implies that $Hz^+ + Hz^- = H(z^+ + z^-) = Hz \geq 0$. In addition, $z_0 = z_0^+ + z_0^- = 0$ and $z_i = z_i^+ + z_i^- \geq 0 - 1 = -1$ and $z_i = z_i^+ + z_i^- \leq 1 - 0 = 1$ for all $i \in V$.

Necessity: Let z and z' be two feasible solutions to (SDP). Then it follows from elementary calculus that $\max(z, z')$ and $\min(z, z')$ are feasible solutions to (SDP) as well. By choosing $z' = 0$ we obtain the feasibility of directions z^+ and z^-. $\qquad \square$

Theorem 3.6. *Let z^+ be a solution to* (SDP$^+$) *and let z^- be a solution to* (SDP$^-$). *Then* $z = z^+ + z^-$ *solves problem* (SDP).

Proof. We first show that $g(z) = g(z^+) + g(z^-)$. As a consequence of Lemma 3.4 we have $g(z) = \sum_{i \in V} \max(\partial^+ \bar{f}/\partial S_i(S)z_i, \partial^- \bar{f}/\partial S_i(S)z_i)$, from which it follows that g is convex. The positive homogeneity of g then implies the sublinearity and thus the subadditivity of g. Hence, $g(z) = g(z^+ + z^-) \leq g(z^+) + g(z^-)$. Since $\max(0, z)$ is a feasible solution to (SDP$^+$) (see Lemma 3.5), we have $g(z^+) \leq g(\max(0, z))$. Symmetrically it holds that

$g(z^-) \leq g(\min(0, z))$. By definition $g(\max(0, z)) = \sum_{i \in V: z_i > 0} \partial^+ \bar{f}/\partial S_i(S) z_i = g(z) - \sum_{i \in V: z_i < 0} \partial^- \bar{f}/\partial S_i(S) z_i$ and $g(\min(0, z)) = \sum_{i \in V: z_i < 0} \partial^- \bar{f}/\partial S_i(S) z_i$. Thus, $g(z^+) \leq g(z) - g(\min(0, z)) \leq g(z) - g(z^-)$, i.e., $g(z) \geq g(z^+) + g(z^-)$.

Due to Lemma 3.5, problem (SDP) can now equivalently be stated as

$$\text{Minimize} \quad g(z') + g(z'')$$
$$\text{subject to} \quad z'_j - z'_i \geq 0, \; z''_j - z''_i \geq 0 \quad ((i, j) \in E_G)$$
$$z'_0 = z''_0 = 0$$
$$0 \leq z'_i \leq 1, \; -1 \leq z''_i \leq 0 \quad (i \in V)$$

Since in the latter problem the vectors z' and z'' are unrelated, the problem decomposes into the two independent problems (SDP$^+$) and (SDP$^-$) with corresponding solutions z^+ and z^-. □

For solving problem (SDP$^+$) we make use of the following property of forests. A forest G with at least one node possesses a source i with at most one successor or a sink i with exactly one predecessor. We call such a node i an extremal node of G. Now let $c_i := \partial^+ \bar{f}/\partial S_i(S)$ be the right-hand S_i-derivative of $\bar{f}$ at point S. If there is a source $i \neq 0$ of spanning forest G with $c_i \leq 0$, then there is a solution z^+ to (SDP$^+$) satisfying $z_i^+ = 0$. Conversely, if there is a sink $i \neq 0$ of G with $c_i > 0$, then $z_i^+ = 1$ for any solution to (SDP$^+$). In both cases node i (and all incident arcs) can be deleted from G. If there is no source i with $c_i \leq 0$ and no sink i with $c_i > 0$, then V necessarily contains a source i with at most one successor j (and $c_i > 0$) or a sink i with exactly one predecessor j (and $c_i \leq 0$). In both cases, i is delayed exactly if j is delayed, i.e., $z_i^+ = z_j^+$. Thus, nodes i and j can be coalesced into an aggregate activity with partial derivative $c_i + c_j$ (which corresponds to the directional derivative of $\bar{f}$ at S in direction z with $z_h^+ = 1$ for $h \in \{i, j\}$ and $z_h^+ = 0$, otherwise). We perform these steps until all nodes aside from 0 have been deleted from G.

Algorithm 3.5 provides an $\mathcal{O}(n)$-time implementation of the above procedure, where $Pred(i) := \{j \in V \mid (j, i) \in E_G\}$ and $Succ(i) := \{j \in V \mid (i, j) \in E_G\}$ denote the sets of immediate predecessors and successors of node i in G. To achieve the linear time complexity, we use an indices-representation of forests, which is similar to the data structure discussed in Ahuja et al. (1993), Sect. 11.3. We associate two indices $pred_i$ and $orient_i$ with each node $i \in V$. For each component C of G, we identify a specially designated node, called the root of C. If i is not a root node, $pred_i$ provides the predecessor of i in G on the unique (undirected) path from the root to i, and the orientation index $orient_i$ equals 1 if G contains arc $(pred_i, i)$ and -1, otherwise. For a root node i, we set $pred_i := -1$ and $orient_i := 0$. In addition, the nodes i of G are stored in some depth-first traversal order of G, starting in each component C at the root node. Then the last unvisited node $i \in U$ with respect to that order is always an extremal node of the subgraph G_U of G induced by set U. If $orient_i \leq 0$, i is a source of G_U, and if $orient_i = 1$, i is a sink of G_U. For $orient_i \neq 0$, the predecessor $j \in Pred(i)$ or successor $j \in Succ(i)$, respectively, is given by $pred_i$. The sets $C(j)$ of coalesced nodes can efficiently be identified via a labelling technique.

Algorithm 3.5. Direction-finding phase

Input: Objective function f, schedule S, spanning forest G of project network N.
Output: Solution z^+ to (SDP$^+$).

    set $U := V$, $z^+ := 0$, $c := \nabla^+ \bar{f}(S)$, and $C(i) := \{i\}$ for all $i \in V$;
    while $U \neq \{0\}$ **do**
        if U contains a node $i \neq 0$ with $Pred(i) \cap U = \emptyset$ and $|Succ(i) \cap U| \leq 1$ **then**
            set $U := U \setminus \{i\}$;
            if $c_i > 0$ and $Succ(i) \cap U = \{j\}$ **then** set $c_j := c_j + c_i$ and $C(j) := C(j) \cup C(i)$;
        else
            determine a node $i \in U$, $i \neq 0$ with $Succ(i) \cap U = \emptyset$ and $Pred(i) \cap U = \{j\}$;
            set $U := U \setminus \{i\}$;
9:           **if** $c_i > 0$ **then** set $z_h^+ := 1$ for all $h \in C(i)$;
           else set $c_j := c_j + c_i$ and $C(j) := C(j) \cup C(i)$;
    return z^+;

The mirror problem (SDP$^-$) can be solved by a similar procedure where z^+ is replaced with z^-, vector c is initialized with the left-hand derivative $\nabla^- \bar{f}(S)$ at schedule S, the roles of predecessors and successors in G are reversed, and z_h^- is put to -1 on line 9. Theorem 3.6 says that $z = z^+ + z^-$ is an optimal direction at S.

In general, the **line-search phase** at schedule S is performed by computing an optimal stepsize $\sigma \geq 0$ such that destination schedule $S' = S + \sigma z \in \mathcal{S}_T$ minimizes f on the line segment ℓ in $\mathcal{S}_T$ passing through S in direction z. In certain cases, however, it is more efficient to proceed with a suboptimal descent step (see Jacoby et al. 1972, Sect. 5.1) because first, finding an optimal stepsize is expensive or second, moving to a minimizer S' on line segment ℓ may cause a zigzagging phenomenon. Schwindt (2000c) and Schwindt and Zimmermann (2001) have used the following stepsize σ in their steepest descent algorithms for the total earliness-tardiness cost and the net present value problems. Each activity $i \in V$ with $z_i \neq 0$ can at most be shifted until some temporal constraint $S_j - S_i \geq \delta_{ij}$ with $(i, j) \notin E_G$ becomes active, i.e.,

$$\sigma \leq \sigma_1(i) := \min_{(i,j)\in E:z_i>z_j} \frac{S_j - S_i - \delta_{ij}}{z_i - z_j}$$

$\sigma_1(i)$ may be equal to 0 if S is a degenerate point of $\mathcal{S}_T$. If f is not binary-monotone (see Subsection 2.3.1), we stop shifting i when crossing a kink of $\bar{f}$, i.e.

$$\sigma \leq \sigma_2(i) := \min\{\sigma' > 0 \mid \frac{\partial^- \bar{f}}{\partial S_i}(S + \sigma' z) < \frac{\partial^+ \bar{f}}{\partial S_i}(S + \sigma' z)\}$$

where for convenience we define $\min \emptyset := \infty$. Note that we have $\min_{i \in V} \sigma_2(i) = \min\{\sigma' > 0 \mid -d\bar{f}|_{S+\sigma' z}(-z) < d\bar{f}|_{S+\sigma' z}(z)\}$.

Accordingly, stepsize σ is chosen to be

$$\sigma = \min(\min_{i \in V} \sigma_1(i), \min_{i \in V} \sigma_2(i)) \tag{3.6}$$

where $\sigma_2(i) := \infty$ for all $i \in V$ if f is binary-monotone. For the general case of an objective function that is neither piecewise affine nor binary-monotone, we in addition have

$$\sigma \leq \min\{\sigma' > 0 \mid d\bar{f}|_{S+\sigma'z}(z) = 0\}$$

When moving from S to destination $S' = S + \sigma z$, spanning forest G is updated as follows. At first, we delete all arcs (g, h) from G for which $z_h > z_g$. If $\sigma = \sigma_1(i)$ for some $i \in V$, a new temporal constraint $S_j - S_i \geq \delta_{ij}$ becomes active and the corresponding arc (i, j) is added to G.

For the time-constrained net present value problem, Schwindt and Zimmermann (2001) have shown the following plausible statement, which readily carries over to the more general case of piecewise affine or binary-monotone objective functions f.

Proposition 3.7 (Schwindt and Zimmermann 2001). *If in Algorithm 3.3 the initial schedule is chosen to be the earliest schedule ES and the stepsizes σ are calculated according to (3.6), then at each iterate S there is a solution z to steepest descent problem (SDP) with $z \geq 0$.*

Under the assumptions of Proposition 3.7, it is thus sufficient to solve subproblem (SDP$^+$) for computing optimal directions z.

For piecewise affine or binary-monotone objective functions, the number of iterates needed to reach a schedule S satisfying necessary optimality condition (3.4) can markedly be decreased by using an acceleration technique. Consider the spanning forest G arising from deleting all arcs (i, j) with $z_j > z_i$ and let i be an activity with $\sigma = \min(\sigma_1(i), \sigma_2(i))$. All components C of G consist of nodes j with identical z_j. If there is a component of G which does not contain node i and for whose nodes j we have $z_j \neq 0$, those nodes can be shifted further without recomputing a new steepest descent direction. By shifting the components in order of nondecreasing minimum slacks between component nodes i and nodes j with $z_i > z_j$, we obtain the acceleration step displayed in Algorithm 3.6. If the one-sided S_i-derivatives of $\bar{f}$ are obtained in constant $\mathcal{O}(1)$ time, the algorithm can be implemented to run in $\mathcal{O}(m \log m)$ time by maintaining a Fibonacci heap of arcs $(i, j) \in E$ with $z_i > z_j$ and a Fibonacci heap of nodes $i \in V$ with $z_i \neq 0$ that are sorted according to nondecreasing slack times $\frac{S_j - S_i - \delta_{ij}}{z_i - z_j}$ and $\sigma_2(i)$, respectively.

We finally notice that if f is binary-monotone and $z \geq 0$, the resulting destination schedule S is always a vertex. Furthermore, it can be shown that in case of regular and in case of so-called *antiregular* objective functions f, which are componentwise nonincreasing in start times S_i, the steepest descent algorithm with the acceleration step included reaches the respective minimizers ES and LS after one iteration, independently of the initial schedule chosen (see Schwindt and Zimmermann 2001).

Algorithm 3.6. Acceleration step

Input: MPM project network $N = (V, E, \delta)$, schedule S, direction z, spanning forest G of project network N.
Output: Destination schedule S, updated spanning forest G.

> **for all** $(i, j) \in E_G$ with $z_j > z_i$ **do** set $E_G := E_G \setminus \{(i, j)\}$;
> **while** $z \neq 0$ **do**
>> determine a node $i \in V$ with $z_i \neq 0$ and minimum slack $\sigma = \min(\sigma_1(i), \sigma_2(i))$;
>> **if** $\sigma = \sigma_1(i)$ **then** ($*$ update spanning forest $G *$)
>>> set $E_G := E_G \cup \{(i, j)\}$ for some arc $(i, j) \in E$ with $z_i > z_j$ and $\frac{S_j - S_i - \delta_{ij}}{z_i - z_j}$
>>> $= \sigma(i)$;
>> determine node set $C(h)$ of component with $i \in C(h)$;
>> **for all** $g \in C(h)$ **do** set $S_g := S_g + \sigma$ and $z_g := 0$;
> **return** schedule S;

3.2.3 Solving the Relaxations: The Dual Approach

Let ρ be a relation in activity set V to be extended by a minimal delaying mode $\{i\} \times B$ in the course of Algorithm 3.3. For computing a minimizer on the reduced search space $\mathcal{S}_T(\rho')$ of the resulting relation $\rho' = \rho \cup \{\{i\} \times B\}$, it is often more expedient to use a dual approach rather than re-performing the primal steepest descent algorithm from scratch. The basic principle of the *dual flattest ascent approach* is to start with the minimizer S of f on $\mathcal{S}_T(\rho)$ and to perform an outer approximation towards set $\mathcal{S}_T(\rho')$, where the distance to $\mathcal{S}_T(\rho')$ is stepwise decreased at locally minimal cost. More precisely, at each iteration we consider moving in feasible directions z such that first, $z_j - z_i \geq 1$ for all $j \in B$ and second, the directional derivative $g(z)$ at iterate S is minimum. We refer to such a direction as a *flattest feasible ascent direction* at S. Let $\Delta(S, \mathcal{S}_T(\rho')) := \inf_{S' \in \mathcal{S}_T(\rho')} \|S' - S\|_\infty = \max_{j \in B}(S_i + p_i - S_j)^+ = (S_i + p_i - \min_{j \in B} S_j)^+$ denote the distance between S and set $\mathcal{S}_T(\rho')$. The first condition ensures that $\Delta(S + \sigma z, \mathcal{S}_T(\rho')) < \Delta(S, \mathcal{S}_T(\rho'))$ provided that stepsize $\sigma > 0$, whereas the second requirement means that the first-order approximation of the increase in the objective function value when moving from S to $S + \sigma z$ is minimum. We notice that if f is not a convex and piecewise affine function, this increase may also be negative, and thus in the general case we have to consider *normalized* flattest ascent directions z at S.

Algorithm 3.7 shows a generic flattest ascent algorithm, where for simplicity we assume that $\rho = \emptyset$ and $\mathcal{S}_T(\rho') \neq \emptyset$. At each iteration of the algorithm we first remove those activities j from minimal delaying alternative B for which precedence constraint $S_j \geq S_i + p_i$ has already been enforced. The arcs (i, j) corresponding to the latter precedence constraints are added to project network N in order to ensure that they are observed at all subsequent iterations. Next, we compute a normalized flattest ascent direction z at S. If $B = \emptyset$ and $g(z) = 0$, we have reached set $\mathcal{S}_T(\rho')$ and there is no feasible descent direction z at S. Otherwise, we determine an appropriate stepsize σ, move to destination schedule $S + \sigma z$, and put $S := S + \sigma z$.

Algorithm 3.7. Dual flattest ascent algorithm

Input: MPM project network $N = (V, E, \delta)$, objective function f, time-optimal schedule S, minimal delaying mode $\{i\} \times B$.
Output: Local minimizer S of f on set $\mathcal{S}_T(\{i\} \times B)$.

    repeat
        for all $j \in B$ with $S_j \geq S_i + p_i$ **do**
            remove j from set B and add arc (i, j) with weight $\delta_{ij} = p_i$ to N;
            determine normalized flattest feasible ascent direction z at S; (*direction-finding phase*)
        if $B \neq \emptyset$ or $g(z) < 0$ **then**
            determine stepsize σ in N at S; (*line-search phase*)
        set $S := S + \sigma z$;
    until $B = \emptyset$ and $g(z) = 0$;
    return S;

In what follows, we study the direction-finding and line-search phases in more detail. During the **direction-finding phase** of the algorithm we have to determine a flattest feasible ascent direction z at the given iterate S. In analogy to (3.5), the latter problem can be formulated as follows, where $\{i\} \times B$ is the minimal delaying mode under consideration:

$$\left.\begin{array}{ll} \text{Minimize} & g(z) \\ \text{subject to} & z_h - z_g \geq 0 \quad ((g, h) \in E(S)) \\ & z_0 = 0 \\ & z_j - z_i \geq 1 \quad (j \in B) \\ & \|z\| \leq 1 \end{array}\right\} \tag{3.7}$$

The normalization constraint $\|z\| \leq 1$ may be deleted if f is convex and piecewise affine (the objective functions of the total inventory holding cost and total earliness-tardiness cost problems are examples of such an objective function). We notice that in contrast to the steepest descent problem (3.5), problem (3.7) does not necessarily possess a feasible solution. It is easily seen, however, that under the assumption that relation ρ' is time-feasible, i.e., $\mathcal{S}_T(\rho') \neq \emptyset$, there is always a flattest ascent direction at S.

In analogy to the primal steepest descent algorithm treated in Subsection 3.2.2, we choose the vector norm $\| \cdot \|$ in (3.7) to be the supremum norm and relax the problem by replacing the arc set $E(S)$ belonging to all active constraints at S with the arc set $E_G \subseteq E(S)$ of some spanning forest G of project network N. The resulting problem will be referred to as the *flattest ascent direction problem* (FAP) at S.

$$\left. \begin{array}{ll} \text{Minimize} & g(z) \\ \text{subject to} & z_h - z_g \geq 0 \quad ((g,h) \in E_G) \\ & z_0 = 0 \\ & z_j - z_i \geq 1 \quad (j \in B) \\ & -1 \leq z_h \leq 1 \quad (h \in V) \end{array} \right\} \quad \text{(FAP)}$$

A solution z to (FAP) is again called an *optimal direction* at S. Our approach to solving the flattest ascent direction problem is based on a decomposition of the problem into two subproblems, where we respectively enforce all activities $j \in B$ to be right-shifted (i.e., $z_j = 1$) or activity i to be left-shifted (i.e., $z_i = -1$). The problems where in (FAP) we replace $z_j - z_i \geq 1$ ($j \in B$) by the corresponding constraints $z_i = 0$ and $z_j = 1$ ($j \in B$) or $z_i = -1$ and $z_j \geq 0$ ($j \in B$) are denoted by (FAP$^+$) or (FAP$^-$), respectively.

Proposition 3.8. *Flattest ascent problem* (FAP) *is unsolvable if and only if both problems* (FAP$^+$) *and* (FAP$^-$) *are unsolvable. If* (FAP) *is solvable, it is solved by any solution* z^+ *to* (FAP$^+$) *or by any solution* z^- *to* (FAP$^-$).

Proof. Analogously to the proof of Proposition 3.3 it can again be shown that, if (FAP) is solvable, there exists an integral solution z to (FAP). In the latter case, z_i may assume the two values 0 and -1. If $z_i = 0$, we have $z_j = 1$ for all $j \in B$. For $z_i = -1$, the constraints $z_j - z_i \geq 1$ ($j \in B$) turn into $z_j \geq 0$ ($j \in B$).   □

As a consequence of Proposition 3.8, an optimal direction z at S can be computed by solving both subproblems (FAP$^+$) and (FAP$^-$) and choosing $z = z^+$ if $g(z^+) \leq g(z^-)$ and $z = z^-$, otherwise (where we write $g(z^+) = \infty$ or $g(z^-) = \infty$ if the respective subproblem is unsolvable). Like the steepest descent problem (SDP), problem (FAP$^+$) can be solved by using Algorithm 3.5 for (SDP$^+$) and its analogue for the mirror problem (SDP$^-$). To this end, we put $c_i := \infty$ and $c_j := -\infty$ for all $j \in B$ when we apply Algorithm 3.5, and we put $c_i := -\infty$ and $c_j := \infty$ for all $j \in B$ when using the algorithm for the mirror problem. Problem (FAP$^-$) can be dealt with analogously. In sum, computing an optimal direction z at S necessitates four calls to the direction-finding algorithms from Subsection 3.2.2 and thus can again be achieved in linear time.

The following proposition shows that if at current iterate S moving in any feasible descent direction z at S would increase the distance between S and $S_T(\rho')$, then (FAP) can be solved by only one application of Algorithm 3.5 and its adaptation for the mirror problem. It can easily be seen (cf. Schwindt 2000c) that the conditions of the proposition are satisfied at each iterate if f is convex and piecewise affine.

Proposition 3.9. *Let* S *be a time-feasible schedule and assume that for given minimal delaying mode* $\{i\} \times B$, $z = 0$ *solves the steepest descent problem*

(SDP) *at point S with additional constraints $z_j - z_i \geq 0$ for all $j \in B$. If* (FAP$^+$) *is solvable, it is solved by some direction $z^+ \geq 0$, and if* (FAP$^-$) *is solvable, it is solved by some direction $z^- \leq 0$.*

Proof. Let z' be an optimal solution to (FAP$^+$). Since $z^+ := \max(0, z')$ satisfies all constraints of problem (SDP) (compare the proof of Lemma 3.5) and $z_j^+ - z_i^+ = 1$ for all $j \in B$, z^+ is a feasible solution to (FAP)$^+$ as well, and thus from the optimality of z' it follows that $g(z^+) \geq g(z')$. Moreover, direction $z'' := \min(0, z')$ is a feasible solution to problem (SDP) with $z_j - z_i \geq 0$ for all $j \in B$. For z' we have $g(z') = \sum_{i \in V : z_i' > 0} \partial^+ \bar{f} / \partial S_i(S) z_i' + \sum_{i \in V : z_i' < 0} \partial^- \bar{f} / \partial S_i(S) z_i' = g(z^+) + g(z'')$. Since the optimal objective function value of problem (SDP) with $z_j - z_i \geq 0$ for all $j \in B$ equals 0, it holds that $g(z'') \geq 0$. We conclude that $g(z^+) = g(z') - g(z'') \leq g(z')$, which due to $g(z^+) \geq g(z')$ provides $g(z^+) = g(z')$. From the feasibility of direction z^+ then follows the assertion. The proof for problem (FAP$^-$) is analogous, where $z^- := \min(0, z')$ and $z'' := \max(0, z')$. $\square$

For given optimal direction z, the **line-search phase** yields an appropriate stepsize $\sigma \geq 0$ such that

$$\sigma \leq \sigma_3(j) := S_i + p_i - S_j$$

for all $j \in B$. $\sigma_3(j)$ is the amount by which the time lag between the starts of activities i and j has to be increased for satisfying precedence constraint $S_j \geq S_i + p_i$. In addition, σ is chosen such that destination schedule $S' = S + \sigma z$ is time-feasible and we do not move beyond a kink of g, i.e.,

$$\sigma = \min(\min_{h \in V} \sigma_1(h), \min_{h \in V} \sigma_2(h), \min_{j \in B} \sigma_3(j))$$

3.2.4 Branch-and-Bound

By providing the enumeration scheme given by Algorithm 3.3 with a search strategy, consistency tests, and lower bounds, we obtain a branch-and-bound procedure for problem (P) with convexifiable objective function f. For the same reasons as in Subsection 3.1.3 it is generally expedient to store list Q of unexplored enumeration nodes in a stack, i.e., to perform a depth-first search. Since the consistency tests discussed in Subsections 1.2.4 and 1.3.4 do not refer to the objective function, we may again apply all those tests in principle. The effectiveness of a given test, however, among other things strongly depends on the particular objective function under consideration. As for the case of regular objective functions, the objective function value $f(S)$ of a minimizer S of f on some search space $\mathcal{S}_T(\rho)$ may again serve as a lower bound lb_0 on the objective function value of the best feasible schedule in $\mathcal{S}_T(\rho)$. Selle (1999) and Kimms (2001b) have used the technique devised by Möhring et al. (2003) based on Lagrangean relaxation of the resource constraints (see Subsection 3.1.3) to compute lower bounds for the net present value and total earliness-tardiness cost problems, respectively, with renewable resources.

Sometimes relations ρ can be excluded from further consideration because they are dominated by other relations ρ' in the sense that either the absence of feasible schedules in $\mathcal{S}_T(\rho')$ excludes the existence of feasible schedules in $\mathcal{S}_T(\rho)$ or the minimum objective function value of the best feasible schedule in $\mathcal{S}_T(\rho')$ can be proved to be not greater than for the best feasible schedule in $\mathcal{S}_T(\rho)$. The simplest type of dominance between relations is given by the set inclusion of relation polytopes: relation ρ' dominates ρ if $\mathcal{S}_T(\rho) \subseteq \mathcal{S}_T(\rho')$. Since such *dominance rules* define a reflexive relation in the set of relations, one has to ensure by appropriate tie-breakers that "cross-pruning" (i.e., relation ρ' dominates relation ρ and vice versa) does not occur. The branch-and-bound algorithm may apply several dominance rules to newly generated relations ρ with corresponding minimal delaying mode $\{i\} \times B$.

The first dominance rule is as follows (cf. De Reyck and Herroelen 1998a). We add all activities $h \in \mathcal{A}(S,t) \setminus B$ with $d_{jh} \geq 0$ for some $j \in B$ to set B because they are delayed as well when shifting activities $j \in B$ behind the completion of activity i. If there is a minimal delaying alternative $B' \in \mathcal{B}$ with $B' \subset B$, relation ρ is dominated by relation ρ' belonging to minimal delaying mode $\{i\} \times B'$. The second dominance rule refers to a (possibly induced) minimum time lag between activity i and some activity i' of a delaying mode $\{i'\} \times B$ with the same minimal delaying alternative. If either (1) $d_{i'i} + p_i > p_{i'}$ or (2) $d_{i'i} + p_i = p_{i'}$ and (as tie-breaker) $i' < i$, then relation ρ can be fathomed because the completion time of activity i is greater than or equal to the completion time of activity i'.

Whereas the first two rules establish dominance between child nodes ρ of one and the same parent node, the following *subset-dominance rules* compare the recent child nodes ρ with (arbitrary) relations ρ' from which we have branched formerly or which remain on stack Q. The first subset-dominance rule has again been proposed by De Reyck and Herroelen (1998a). If the whole search space $\mathcal{S}_T(\rho')$ of a relation ρ' has been explored and if ρ' is a subset of ρ, relation ρ can be fathomed. This rule can be implemented to run quite efficiently by exploiting two properties of the enumeration tree (see Schwindt 1998c). First, $\rho' \subset \rho''$ for all descendants ρ'' of relations ρ' and second, in case of a depth-first search the parents ρ'' of relations ρ' with $\subseteq$-maximal completely explored search spaces $\mathcal{S}_T(\rho')$ are ancestors of ρ.

Neumann and Zimmermann (2002) have used a generalization of the latter rule in their branch-and-bound algorithm for the net present value problem with renewable resources. Comparing relations ρ and ρ' does not take into account the time lags that are induced by the distance matrix D. In other words, we may have $\mathcal{S}_T(\rho) \subseteq \mathcal{S}_T(\rho')$ though $\rho \not\supseteq \rho'$. Rather, condition $\mathcal{S}_T(\rho) \subseteq \mathcal{S}_T(\rho')$ can be checked by (elementwise) comparing the corresponding relation matrices $D(\rho)$ and $D(\rho')$, i.e., $\mathcal{S}_T(\rho) \subseteq \mathcal{S}_T(\rho')$ precisely if $d_{ij}^\rho \geq d_{ij}^{\rho'}$ for all $i, j \in V$.

The following subset-dominance rule by Schwindt (1998c) compares the recent child nodes ρ with relations ρ' on stack Q. If Q contains a relation $\rho' \subseteq \rho$ that is not an ancestor of ρ, then relation ρ can be deleted because $\mathcal{S}_T(\rho) \subseteq \mathcal{S}_T(\rho')$. This rule offers the advantage that no additional memory is required for storing enumeration nodes already visited. Of course, the rule can also be applied in a way to compare relation matrices rather than relations.

3.2.5 Additional Notes and References

In this subsection we briefly survey procedures for project scheduling with specific convexifiable objective functions and general temporal constraints. We first deal with primal algorithms for the time-constrained case, which may be used for solving the resource relaxation of problem (P). Kamburowski (1990) was probably the first who studied the **time-constrained net present value problem** with general minimum and maximum time lags between the start times of activities. He has proposed an adaptation of the approach by Grinold (1972) for ordinary precedence constraints to the case of general temporal constraints. Grinold's procedure is based on the transformation of the problem into a linear program by specifying a C^1-diffeomorphism φ which satisfies the conditions of Definition 2.29. Using specific properties of the linear program, the problem is solved by a vertex-following algorithm, the methods by Grinold (1972) and by Kamburowski (1990) differing in the pivot rule used. De Reyck and Herroelen (1998b) have generalized the recursive-search procedure by Herroelen et al. (1996) for the precedence-constrained net present value problem to the case of general temporal constraints. Starting at the earliest schedule, the activities of subtrees representing active temporal constraints and possessing a negative net present value are stepwise delayed in order to increase the net present value of the project. In contrast to all other procedures, the temporal constraints are represented by the distance matrix, i.e., their transitive closure, rather than by the project network. Neumann and Zimmermann (2000) have combined Kamburowski's procedure, equipped with a new pivot rule, and a preprocessing method proposed by Herroelen et al. (1996). The latter method delays all terminal activities with negative cash flows up to their latest start time (an activity is called terminal if it does not have successors in project network N aside from the project termination event $n + 1$).

Table 3.3 compiles the results of an experimental performance analysis comparing the algorithms for the time-constrained net present value problem. The rows "Grinold (1972)" and "CPLEX" refer to the adaptation of Grinold's procedure to general temporal constraints with the original pivot rule and the primal simplex algorithm implemented in LP solver CPLEX 6.0 (among the different LP solvers available in the CPLEX package, the primal simplex method has shown the best performance). The performance of the algorithms has been evaluated on the basis of two test sets generated with ProGen/max. The test sets contain 1440 and 90 projects with 100 and 1000 activities, respectively (see Schwindt and Zimmermann 2001 for details). The results for the algorithm by De Reyck and Herroelen (1998*b*) are quoted from De Reyck (1998). We provide the mean number #*it* of iterations needed to reach an optimal solution (where "n. a." indicates that this number is not available) and the corresponding mean computation time t_{cpu} on an Intel 486 personal computer with 50 MHz clock pulse ($n = 100$) and a Pentium personal computer with 200 MHz clock pulse ($n = 1000$).

Table 3.3. Performance of primal algorithms for the time-constrained net present value problem

Algorithm	n	#it	t_{cpu}
Grinold (1972)	100	22	26 ms
	1000	473	1.7 s
CPLEX	100	n. a.	570 ms
	1000	n. a.	118.6 s
Kamburowski (1990)	100	24	30 ms
	1000	577	2.5 s
De Reyck and Herroelen (1998*b*)	100	n. a.	831 ms
Neumann and Zimmermann (2000)	100	12	17 ms
	1000	219	1.0 s
Schwindt and Zimmermann (2001)	100	4	10 ms
	1000	17	0.6 s

The results depicted in Table 3.3 permit several conclusions. First, the methods based on Grinold's vertex-following algorithm show a much better performance than the primal simplex method applied to the linearized problem. Second, the preprocessing method allows to save roughly one half of the computation time. Third, the efficiency of the recursive-search method is poor, which is presumably less due to the recursion itself than rather to the use of the distance matrix, whose computation is expensive and which causes almost any vertex of set $\mathcal{S}_T$ to be degenerate. As a consequence, the algorithm performs many pivot steps that do not lead to a new vertex. Fourth, the steepest descent method appears as the most efficient solution procedure for the time-constrained net present value problem. If we reduce t_{cpu} by the time needed for computing the earliest schedule, the speed-up factor between the procedure of Neumann and Zimmermann (2000) and the steepest descent algorithm is more than six (cf. Schwindt and Zimmermann 2001). The small value for #it can be mainly attributed to the acceleration step, which for $n = 1000$ reduces the number of iterations by more than 90 %. This reduction does not lead to an equally large saving in computation time because the acceleration step is more time consuming than simple line search (recall that the time complexity of the acceleration step is $\mathcal{O}(m \log m)$, whereas line search can be done in $\mathcal{O}(m)$ time).

Next, we consider the **time-constrained total earliness-tardiness cost problem**. The only algorithm for this problem we are aware of is the steepest descent procedure proposed by Schwindt (2000c). For the special case where only minimum time lags are present, Vanhoucke et al. (2001) have devised a recursive-search procedure, which is an adaptation of Herroelen et al.'s algorithm for the net present value problem. The time-constrained total earliness-tardiness cost problem can readily be transformed into a linear program by introducing two continuous variables $e_i \geq 0$ and $t_i \geq 0$ for each activity $i \in V$ along with the constraints $e_i \geq d_i - S_i - p_i$ and $t_i \geq S_i + p_i - d_i$. The objective function of the linear program then is $\sum_{i \in V}(w_i^e e_i + w_i^t t_i)$. Obviously, for $\mathcal{S}_T \neq \emptyset$ there is always an optimal solution satisfying $e_i = (d_i - S_i - p_i)^+$ and $t_i = (S_i + p_i - d_i)^+$ for all $i \in V$, i.e., e_i equals the earliness and t_i equals the tardiness of i. Notice that the existence of an equivalent linear program does not imply that the total earliness-tardiness cost is a linearizable objective function in the sense of Definition 2.29, which is obviously not true.

Table 3.4 compares the primal simplex algorithm with the steepest descent procedure. The analysis is based on two test sets with 100 and 1000 activities, respectively, containing 90 instances each (details are given in Neumann et al. 2003b, Sect. 3.5). The computations have been performed on a 200 MHz Pentium personal computer.

Table 3.4. Performance of primal algorithms for the time-constrained earliness-tardiness problem

Algorithm	n	#it	t_{cpu}
CPLEX	100	367	539 ms
	1000	5035	58.3 s
Schwindt (2000c)	100	15	7 ms
	1000	139	3.8 s

The results are in line with those obtained for the net present value problem. Again, the steepest descent algorithm clearly outperforms the LP solver. However, the gap between both approaches is less important, which is due to two reasons. First, though the linear program contains more variables and constraints than for the net present value problem, the computation time decreases since the coefficient matrix of the constraints is now binary instead of real-valued. Second, since the objective function is no longer binary-monotone, the stepsizes for the steepest descent algorithm are typically much smaller, which is also indicated by the large increase in the number of iterations.

We proceed to the net present value and total earliness-tardiness cost problems with renewable or cumulative resources. We restrict ourselves to procedures that are dedicated to the case of general temporal constraints between activities. For a review of various types of precedence-constrained net present value problems and solution procedures we refer to the survey paper by Herroelen et al. (1997). Algorithms for total earliness-tardiness cost problems with precedence constraints and renewable resources have been devised by Serafini and Speranza (1994*a*,*b*) and Vanhoucke et al. (2001). For solving the resource relaxation, Serafini and Speranza exploit the duality relationship between the latter problem and the convex-cost flow problem (see Subsection 3.2.2).

We first consider the **net present value problem with renewable resources**. The branch-and-bound algorithms by De Reyck and Herroelen (1998*b*) and Neumann and Zimmermann (2002) are both based on the enumeration scheme discussed in Subsection 3.2.1. The algorithms mainly differ in the procedures for solving the relaxations at the enumeration nodes. Whereas De Reyck and Herroelen (1998*b*) use their (primal) recursive-search method, Neumann and Zimmermann (2002) solve the initial resource relaxation at the root node by the primal steepest descent algorithm by Schwindt and Zimmermann (2001) and the relaxations at descendant nodes with a dual method resembling the flattest ascent algorithm dealt with in Subsection 3.2.3. In addition, De Reyck and Herroelen (1998*b*) and Neumann and Zimmermann (2002) have used disjunctive activities tests and dominance rules for reducing the size of the enumeration tree. Selle and Zimmermann (2003) have proposed a bidirectional priority-rule method for approximatively solving large-scale net present value problems. Similarly to the heuristic by Franck (1999) for the project duration problem (see Subsection 3.1.4), one activity is scheduled per iteration, where the essential difference is that certain activities, namely those with negative cash flows, are started at their *latest* feasible start time. An analysis of this schedule-generation scheme in Section 4.1 will show that the schedules obtained in this way are stable, provided that no unscheduling step is performed. Since the set of all optimal schedules may not contain a stable schedule, the heuristic may systematically miss the optimal solution. A similar result is known for the minimization of regular objective functions, where the parallel schedule-generation scheme yields nondelay schedules (see Kolisch 1996), among which there is not necessarily an optimal schedule.

Table 3.5 shows the results of an experimental performance analysis where we have compared the three algorithms on a test set containing 1440 projects with 50 activities and 5 renewable resources each. A detailed description of the remaining ProGen/max control parameters chosen can be found in De Reyck and Herroelen (1998*b*). We have imposed a limit t_{cpu} of 3 and 30 seconds on the maximum running time of the branch-and-bound algorithms, which refers to a Pentium personal computer operating at 200 MHz (for comparison purposes, the computation times have been scaled according to the clock pulse ratio by a factor of 0.3 for De Reyck and Herroelen's branch-and-bound algorithm and by a factor of 2.5 for the priority-rule method). Since De Reyck and Herroelen (1998*b*) only report on the number of instances for which the branch-and-bound algorithm has completed the enumeration within the respective time limit, the values p_{opt} and p_{ins} and the values p_{nopt} and p_{unk} have been aggregated.

Table 3.5. Performance of algorithms for the net present value problem with renewable resources

Algorithm	t_{cpu}	p_{opt}	p_{ins}	p_{nopt}	p_{unk}
De Reyck and Herroelen (1998b)	3 s	58.1 %		41.9 %	
	30 s	75.5 %		24.5 %	
Neumann and Zimmermann (2002)	3 s	79.1 %	4.4 %	16.5 %	0.0 %
	30 s	85.1 %	4.4 %	10.5 %	0.0 %
Selle and Zimmermann (2003)	3 ms	1.0 %	4.4 %	94.6 %	0.0 %

Not surprisingly, the branch-and-bound algorithm by Neumann and Zimmermann (2002) seems to be more efficient than the earlier algorithm by De Reyck and Herroelen (1998b). The improvement upon the latter algorithm is probably to be attributed to the tremendous difference in the time needed for solving the relaxations. The dual method typically runs in a small fraction of the time that is required for re-optimizing from scratch the minimizer with the primal steepest descent method after the addition of a minimal delaying mode to the current relation. Moreover, the primal method is by far less time-consuming than the recursive-search procedure (see Table 3.3). The priority-rule method provides feasible schedules within a very short amount of time. The small proportion p_{opt} of instances, however, for which the optimal objective function value computed by the branch-and-bound algorithm of Neumann and Zimmermann (2002) can be found, indicates that the low computational effort is paid for by some loss of quality. Nevertheless, experience with the project duration problem documented in Franck et al. (2001b) suggests that priority-rule methods may constitute a valuable alternative to exact procedures when coping with projects comprising hundreds of activities. Finally, we notice that we do not give a deviation Δ_{lb} from some lower bound lb on the minimum objective function value because the latter quantity may be positive, zero, or negative. The development of a suitable index measuring the mean remaining error of suboptimal solutions for this type of problem seems to be an open issue in literature.

Starting from the representation of minimizers of a convex objective function on relation polytopes as spanning forests G of the project network N, Schwindt (2000b) has developed a neighborhood function for local search procedures (see also Neumann et al. 2003a). Similarly to the steepest descent algorithm from Subsection 3.2.2, the arcs of forest G correspond to active temporal or precedence constraints. G is decoded into the corresponding time-feasible schedule by computing a local minimizer S on the relation polytope $\mathcal{S}_T(\rho)$

where ρ is the relation in set V^a arising from the arcs of G that belong to precedence constraints (precedence arcs, for short). Two types of neighborhood operations are considered, which transform forest G into a neighboring forest G'. If S is feasible, G' results from G by deleting some precedence arc. Otherwise, a precedence arc may be deleted or a new precedence arc may be added for which both the initial and terminal nodes are contained in a forbidden active set for S. The reason why precedence arcs may also be cancelled even if S is not resource-feasible is that due to maximum time lags, it may be necessary to perform backtracking before attaining a feasible solution. When some precedence arc is deleted from G, the new minimizer of f is determined by applying the primal method starting at S. In case a precedence arc is added to G, the dual method is used.

We have tested a simple randomized best-fit search implementation (cf. Kolisch and Hartmann 1999) of this approach for the **total earliness-tardiness cost problem with renewable resources**. At each iteration the algorithm moves to the best neighboring forest. The quality of a forest G is evaluated according to the objective function value $f(S)$ of the corresponding schedule S and its degree of infeasibility measured in terms of the excessive workload $\sum_{k \in \mathcal{R}^{\rho}} \int_0^d (r_k(S,t) - R_k)^+ dt$. In order to avoid cycling, the quality is randomly biased. Each time the local search gets stuck in a deadlock where S is not yet resource-feasible and no additional precedence arc can be added to G without generating a cycle of positive length in the corresponding relation network $N(\rho)$, we return to the best schedule found thus far. 10 % of the computation time is allotted to the branch-and-bound algorithm by Schwindt (2000c) for the computation of an initial feasible schedule serving as starting-point for the local search. If the branch-and-bound procedure fails in finding a feasible solution within the imposed time limit, the search starts at the minimizer of f on set $\mathcal{S}_T$.

The results for the branch-and-bound method and the best-fit search procedure are given in Table 3.6. They have been obtained for the test set with 90 instances comprising 100 activities and 5 renewable resources already used for the analysis of the algorithms for the time-constrained problem (see Table 3.4). Again, the tests have been performed on a 200 MHz Pentium personal computer.

Table 3.6. Performance of algorithms for the earliness-tardiness problem with renewable resources

Algorithm	t_{cpu}	p_{opt}	p_{ins}	p_{nopt}	p_{unk}	Δ_{lb}
Schwindt (2000c)	3 s	3.3 %	13.3 %	67.8 %	15.6 %	6.6 %
	30 s	5.6 %	13.3 %	70.0 %	11.1 %	6.5 %
	100 s	5.6 %	13.3 %	71.1 %	10.0 %	6.4 %
Schwindt (2000b)	83.4 s	3.3 %	13.3 %	75.6 %	7.8 %	6.0 %

Comparing the results from Tables 3.1 and 3.6 suggests that the earliness-tardiness problem is much more difficult to solve to optimality than the project duration problem. The mean deviation Δ_{lb} from the lower bound lb_0 arising from the resource relaxation, however, indicates that the quality of the schedules found is comparable to those computed for the project duration problem. This deviation can be further decreased by stopping the enumeration after a short amount of time and subsequently executing the best-fit search procedure based on the neighborhood function of Schwindt (2000b).

We conclude the subsection by considering the **capital-rationed net present value problem**, where the project is executed with a limited budget. In that case, the funds available for disbursement depend on the initial budget (possibly plus a credit line) and the difference of all past progress payments and paying outs. This situation frequently occurs in the building industry, where the receipts from completed subprojects serve to finance succeeding subprojects. It is readily seen that the cash balance can be interpreted as a cumulative resource with infinite storage capacity $\overline{R}$ and a safety stock of $\underline{R} = 0$. The initial inventory r_0 equals the project budget, and the resource requirements r_i of events $i \in V^e$, $i \neq 0$ coincide with the cash flows c_i^f. This project scheduling problem has been treated in an early paper by Doersch and Patterson (1977), who have devised an integer programming formulation based on time-indexed binary variables x_{it} being equal to one if $t = S_i$ and zero, otherwise. The objective function then reads $\sum_{i \in V} \sum_{t=ES_i}^{LS_i} c_i^f e^{-\alpha t} x_{it}$, and the resource constraints can be written as

$$\sum_{i \in V} \sum_{t'=ES_i}^{\min(t, LS_i)} c_i^f x_{it'} \geq \underline{R} \quad (t = 0, 1, \ldots, \overline{d})$$

A priority-rule method for solving the problem has been proposed by Smith-Daniels et al. (1996). The priority values are based on delay penalties, which arise from solving the dual of the time-constrained problem where the objective function is replaced by its first-order Taylor expansion (as it has been shown by Russell 1970, the dual then represents a transshipment problem).

Schwindt (2000a) has addressed the capital-rationed problem as a net present value problem with cumulative-resource constraints. His branch-and-bound algorithm is based on the enumeration scheme from Subsection 3.2.1, and the relaxations at the enumeration nodes are solved by the dual flattest ascent method discussed in Subsection 3.2.3. Kimms (2001a), Sect. 8.2, has proposed a mixed-integer linear program for a generalization of the problem setting where residual cash is lent from one period to the next and several projects from a given portfolio are considered simultaneously. The objective is to select the projects to be performed from the portfolio and to schedule the selected projects in a way that the cash balance at planning horizon $\overline{d}$ is maximized. Kolisch (1997) has investigated a variant of this problem where in addition, cash can be borrowed at an interest rate of $\alpha' \geq \alpha$ but only one project is considered. For a critique of the underlying assumptions of this model we refer to Kimms (2001a), Sect. 8.1.

Table 3.7 shows the results of an experimental performance analysis comparing the branch-and-bound algorithm with the CPLEX 6.0 MIP solver processing Doersch and Patterson's integer programming formulation. The four test sets used consist of 90 instances each with 10, 20, 50, or 100 activities. For the projects with 10 or 20 activities, the emphasis parameter of the MIP solver has been put to optimality, whereas for the projects with 50 and 100 activities, this parameter has been chosen to be feasibility. The MIP solver and the branch-and-bound algorithm have been stopped after a maximum computation time of 100 seconds on a Pentium personal computer with 200 MHz clock pulse.

Table 3.7. Performance of algorithms for the net present value problem with one cumulative resource

Algorithm	n	p_{opt}	p_{ins}	p_{nopt}	p_{unk}
Doersch and Patterson (1977)	10	73.3%	13.3%	0.0%	13.3%
	20	50.0%	0.0%	7.8%	42.2%
	50	0.0%	0.0%	5.6%	94.4%
	100	0.0%	0.0%	0.0%	100.0%
Schwindt (2000a)	10	74.4%	25.6%	0.0%	0.0%
	20	74.4%	25.6%	0.0%	0.0%
	50	75.6%	16.7%	1.1%	6.7%
	100	65.6%	8.9%	5.6%	20.0%

The analysis clearly demonstrates the suitability of the cumulative-resource concept for solving this type of problems. Whereas the MIP solver is only capable of solving small problem instances of academic interest, the branch-and-bound algorithm terminates the enumeration within 100 seconds for almost 75% of the projects with 100 activities. The instances with 10 and 20 activities are all either solved to optimality or shown to be unsolvable. It is worth noting that in contrast to the case of renewable resources (see Table 3.5), the difficulty resides rather in finding a feasible schedule than in proving optimality. Thus, developing advanced search strategies to overcome this difficulty may constitute a valuable field of future research.

4

Constructive Algorithms

If the objective function to be minimized is locally regular or locally concave, the relaxation of the resource constraints does not yield a tractable problem in general. Thus, the relaxation-based approach from Chapter 3 no longer proves useful. For solving resource allocation problems with locally regular or locally concave objective function f, we have to explicitly construct the schedules from an appropriate set that contains an optimal schedule if the problem is solvable. We refer to algorithms that proceed in such a way as *constructive algorithms*. The serial schedule-generation scheme for minimizing regular objective functions is an example of a constructive algorithm. In this chapter we develop constructive algorithms that are based on the second basic representation of the set S of all feasible schedules as a union of disjoint equal-preorder sets (recall that the term equal-preorder set may also designate an equal-order set). As we have seen in Subsections 2.1.1 and 2.1.2, the set of all minimal points or vertices of equal-preorder sets coincides with the set of all minimal points or vertices, respectively, of schedule polytopes. In Subsection 2.2.2 we have introduced the notion of quasiactive and quasistable schedules designating those feasible schedules which represent minimal points or vertices, respectively, of their schedule polytopes. The analysis in Subsection 2.3.2 has shown that for $S \neq \emptyset$, the set of all quasiactive schedules always contains some optimal schedule if the objective function f under study is locally regular. Likewise, the set of all quasistable schedules always contains an optimal schedule if f is locally concave provided that $S \neq \emptyset$.

Since we again consider the general case where both renewable and cumulative resources are present, we consider relations ρ in set V of all (real and fictitious) activities. Under our assumption that the real activities use the renewable resources and that the events deplete and replenish the cumulative resources, precedence relationships need only be defined among real activities and among events of the project. More formally, instead of considering schedule-induced preorders $\theta(S) = \{(i,j) \in V \times V \mid S_j \geq S_i + p_i\}$ in set V, we may restrict ourselves to schedule-induced relations arising from the union of the respective schedule-induced strict order in set V^a and the corresponding reflexive preorder in set V^e. Since the ground sets V^a and V^e of those two preorders are disjoint, the union of both preorders is again transitive and thus represents a preorder in ground set $V = V^a \cup V^e$. Accordingly, for given schedule S we define the schedule-induced preorder to be

$$\theta(S) := \{(i,j) \in (V^a \times V^a) \cup (V^e \times V^e) \mid S_j \geq S_i + p_i\}$$

We notice that preorder $\theta(S)$ is neither irreflexive nor reflexive.

Now recall that any quasiactive schedule can be represented as a spanning outtree $G = (V, E_G)$ of its schedule network $N(\theta(S))$ rooted at node 0, where each arc (i,j) of G belongs to one temporal constraint $S_j - S_i \geq \delta_{ij}$ or one precedence constraint $S_j \geq S_i + p_i$ that is active at S (cf. Proposition 2.28). Similarly, any quasistable schedule can be assigned to a spanning tree G of its schedule network. In addition, we assign the weights $\delta_{ij}^G := d_{ij}^{\theta(S)}$ to the arcs $(i,j) \in E_G$. The active temporal and precedence constraints can then be written in the form

$$S_j - S_i \geq \delta_{ij}^G \quad ((i,j) \in E_G)$$

The constructive algorithms are based on generating such spanning outtrees and spanning trees G. The corresponding schedule S is obtained from G by computing the unique solution to the system of linear equations $S_0 = 0$ and $S_j = S_i + \delta_{ij}^G ((i,j) \in E_G)$, which can be achieved in linear time. By constructing a spanning outtree or spanning tree G we perform two consecutive tasks simultaneously: first, finding a feasible schedule-induced preorder in set V and second, computing some appropriate vertex (the minimal point if G is an outtree) of the corresponding relation polytope.

Resource allocation problems with locally regular or locally concave objective functions, regardless of containing explicit resource constraints or not, are much harder to solve to optimality on the average than resource-constrained project scheduling problems where some regular or convexifiable objective function is to be minimized. That is why in the present chapter we are concerned with heuristic procedures. In Section 4.1 we first discuss a generic schedule-generation scheme producing one quasiactive or one quasistable schedule. This schedule-generation scheme has been proposed by Neumann et al. (2000) and goes back to priority-rule heuristics for resource levelling problems that have been devised by Neumann and Zimmermann (1999b, 2000). The schedule-generation scheme provides an initial quasiactive or quasistable schedule, from which we may subsequently move stepwise towards different quasiactive or quasistable schedules by using an iterative improvement procedure. In Section 4.2 we then deal with tree-based neighborhood functions presented in Neumann et al. (2003a). Neighborhood functions constitute the essential building block of local search algorithms such as hill climbing, tabu search, simulated annealing, or threshold accepting (for an overview of different local search techniques, see Aarts and Lenstra 2003b). In particular, we show that the proposed neighborhoods allow local search algorithms to reach optimal schedules independently of the initial schedule chosen. Section 4.3 is devoted to additional notes on alternative solution procedures and an experimental performance analysis of the methods discussed.

4.1 Schedule-Generation Scheme

The schedule-generation scheme for constructing quasistable schedules expands the node set C of a subtree G of some schedule network by one node j in each iteration until $C = V$. The algorithm starts with $C = \{0\}$ and iteratively links the activities $j \in V \setminus C$ not yet scheduled with activities $i \in C$. In this way, the start times S_i of all activities $i \in C$ are fixed. They are uniquely determined by the recursion $S_0 = 0$ and $S_i = S_h + \delta_{hi}^G$ if $(h, i) \in E_G$ or $S_i = S_h - \delta_{ih}^G$ if $(i, h) \in E_G$ ($i \in C$, $i \neq 0$), where h is the predecessor of node i on the (undirected) path from node 0 to node i in G. For a given pair (i, j) with $i \in C$, $j \in V \setminus C$, there are four alternatives of connecting nodes i and j. First, we may either introduce a *forward arc* (i, j) or a *backward arc* (j, i). Now assume that we have chosen forward arc (i, j). Then (i, j) may be weighted by $\delta_{ij}^G = \delta_{ij}$ if (i, j) is contained in project network N or weighted by $\delta_{ij}^G = p_i$ if $d_{ij} < p_i$. In the first case, we speak of a *temporal arc*, and in the second case, the arc is referred to as a *precedence arc*. Likewise, backward arc (j, i) may be weighted by $\delta_{ji}^G = \delta_{ji}$ or by $\delta_{ji}^G = p_j$. If i and j are events, then $S_i + p_i = S_i - p_j = S_i$ and thus the backward precedence arc may be omitted. The arcs have to be chosen in accordance with the temporal constraints. Let

$$ES_j^G := \max[ES_j, \max_{i \in C}(S_i + d_{ij})] \text{ and } LS_j^G := \min[LS_j, \min_{i \in C}(S_i - d_{ji})]$$

denote the earliest and latest start times of activity j given that activities $i \in C$ start at times S_i. The schedule S generated is time-feasible precisely if at any iteration it holds that $ES_j^G \leq S_i + \delta_{ij}^G \leq LS_j^G$ if a forward arc (i, j) is selected and $ES_j^G \leq S_i - \delta_{ji}^G \leq LS_j^G$ if a backward arc (j, i) is chosen.

From the viewpoint of implementation, it is expedient to allow the scheduling of activities j at their earliest or latest start times ES_j^G or LS_j^G even if the corresponding temporal arc connects activity j with an activity i that is not scheduled either. We then need not check whether or not activity j can already be linked to some activity $i \in C$, while the set of schedules which can be generated is not affected by this modification. The reason for this is that the same tree G could have been constructed by the original method just by processing the activities j in a different order. Figuratively speaking, the modification means that the directed graph G whose node set C is iteratively expanded may now be unconnected unless $C = V$. Nevertheless, the property that the start times of all scheduled activities $i \in C$ are known as soon as they are added to G is preserved.

Algorithm 4.1 shows an implementation of the procedure for the case where the availability of the resources is not limited, i.e., $R_k = \infty$ for all $k \in \mathcal{R}^\rho$ and

$\underline{R}_k = -\infty$, $\overline{R}_k = \infty$ for all $k \in \mathcal{R}^\gamma$. As we have mentioned in Subsection 2.3.2, this assumption is generally met in practice when dealing with resource level-ling problems, where only renewable resources are taken into account and the resource capacities may be chosen according to the respective requirements. How to modify the schedule-generation scheme in the presence of resource constraints will be explained below. For simplicity, we assume that $\mathcal{S}_T \neq \emptyset$. After the computation of the earliest and latest schedules ES and LS, at each iteration some activity $j \in V \setminus C$ not yet scheduled is selected. Then, the *de-cision set* $\mathcal{D}_j$ of tentative start times t for j is determined. The conditions on start times t ensure that the resulting schedule S is (time-)feasible and that precedence relationships are only established between activities of the same type (i.e., among real activities and among events; recall our discussion about the proper definition of schedule-induced preorder $\theta(S)$). Finally, some $t \in \mathcal{D}_j$ is selected to be the start time of j and the time windows $[ES_h, LS_h]$ for the activities $h \in V \setminus C$ are updated. These steps are reiterated until all activities have been scheduled. The resulting tree G is a spanning tree of all relation networks $N(\rho)$ for which ρ contains the precedence arcs added and thus in particular a spanning tree of schedule network $N(\theta(S))$. The time complexity of Algorithm 4.1 equals $\mathcal{O}(mn)$, which is the time required for calculating the initial earliest and latest schedules.

Algorithm 4.1. Schedule-generation scheme for locally concave objective functions

Input: A project without resource constraints.
Output: A quasistable schedule S.

    initialize set of scheduled activities $C := \{0\}$ and set $S_0 := 0$;
    compute earliest and latest schedules ES and LS;
    while $C \neq V$ **do** ($*$ not all activities $j \in V$ scheduled $*$)
      select an activity $j \in V \setminus C$;
      if $j \in V^a$ **then** put $V' := V^a$; **else** put $V' := V^e$;
      add j to C and set $\mathcal{D}_j := \{ES_j, LS_j\}$;
      for all $i \in V' \cap C$ with $ES_j < S_i + p_i < LS_j$ **do** add $S_i + p_i$ to $\mathcal{D}_j$;
8:     **if** $V' = V^a$ **then**
9:       **for all** $i \in V' \cap C$ with $ES_j < S_i - p_j < LS_j$ **do** add $S_i - p_j$ to $\mathcal{D}_j$;
10:    select some time $t \in \mathcal{D}_j$ and set $S_j := t$; ($*$ schedule j at time t $*$)
      for all $h \in V \setminus C$ **do** ($*$ update earliest and latest start times $*$)
        set $ES_h := \max(ES_h, S_j + d_{jh})$ and $LS_h := \min(LS_h, S_j - d_{hj})$;
    return S;

The following proposition (cf. Neumann et al. 2000) establishes the com-pleteness of the schedule-generation scheme. This means that, at least in the-ory, a resource allocation problem with locally concave objective function can be solved by a brute-force algorithm branching over the activity $j \in V \setminus C$ to be scheduled next and the tentative start time $t \in \mathcal{D}_j$ chosen.

Proposition 4.1 (Neumann et al. 2000).

(a) *Any schedule S generated by using Algorithm 4.1 is quasistable.*
(b) *Any quasistable schedule $S \in QSS$ can be generated by using Algorithm 4.1.*

Proof.

(a) Since the earliest and latest start times are updated in the course of the algorithm, schedule S is (time-)feasible if at each iteration $\mathcal{D}_j \subseteq [ES_j, LS_j]$. It follows from the definition of decision set $\mathcal{D}_j$ that we only need to show that $ES_j \leq LS_j$. Now assume that we have scheduled some activity j' and before the update of the earliest and latest start times it holds that $ES_h \leq LS_h$ for all $h \in V \setminus C$. Then $S_{j'} \leq LS_{j'} \leq LS_h - d_{j'h}$ and $S_{j'} \geq ES_{j'} \geq ES_h + d_{hj'}$ for all $h \in V \setminus C$ and in particular $S_{j'} + d_{j'j} \leq LS_j$ and $S_{j'} - d_{jj'} \geq ES_j$. Consequently, $ES_j > LS_j$ after the update would imply $S_{j'} + d_{j'j} > S_{j'} - d_{jj'}$, i.e., $d_{j'j} + d_{jj'} > 0$, which contradicts $S_T \neq \emptyset$. Thus, S is feasible. The quasistableness of S now follows from Proposition 2.28b.

(b) We consider some quasistable schedule S and show how to generate S by using Algorithm 4.1. Let G be a spanning tree of schedule network $N(\theta(S))$. The existence of such a spanning tree is guaranteed by Proposition 2.28b. Since G is a tree and the procedure starts with $C = \{0\}$, at each iteration there is some activity $j \in V \setminus C$ whose predecessor i on the path from node 0 to node j in G has already been scheduled. We may then connect j with i by selecting $t = S_i + \delta_{ij}^G \in \mathcal{D}_j$ if $S_j = S_i + \delta_{ij}^G$ and $t = S_i - \delta_{ji}^G \in \mathcal{D}_j$, otherwise. Thus, when $C = V$, the schedule generated coincides with schedule S. $\square$

Now recall that any quasiactive schedule S can be associated with a spanning outtree G of its schedule network $N(\theta(S))$ with root node 0. Such a spanning outtree is obtained if each activity j to be scheduled is linked with some activity $i \in C$ by a forward arc (i, j). Accordingly, a schedule-generation scheme for quasiactive schedules is readily obtained from Algorithm 4.1 by initializing decision set $\mathcal{D}_j$ with $\{ES_j\}$ instead of $\{ES_j, LS_j\}$ and deleting lines 8 and 9. The statements of Proposition 4.1 with "quasistable" and QSS replaced by "quasiactive" and QAS immediately carry over to this modification of Algorithm 4.1.

For what follows, we drop our assumption of infinite renewable-resource capacities. To take account of renewable-resource constraints, in line 10 of Algorithm 4.1 we only select *feasible start times* t from decision set $\mathcal{D}_j$ such that the residual resource capacities suffice to execute activity j in time interval $[t, t + p_j[$, i.e.,

$$\sum_{\substack{i \in C \cap V^a: \\ S_i \leq t' < S_i + p_i}} r_{ik} + r_{jk} \leq R_k \quad (k \in \mathcal{R}^\rho, \, t \leq t' < t + p_j) \tag{4.1}$$

Of course, inequality (4.1) only needs to be evaluated for real activities $j \in V^a$. By using a support-point representation of the resource demand over time that results from the real activities $i \in C \cap V^a$ scheduled, testing (4.1) for given $t \in \mathcal{D}_j$ takes $\mathcal{O}(|\mathcal{R}^\rho|n)$ time. If times t in decision set $\mathcal{D}_j$ are iterated in increasing order, the amortized time complexity for eliminating all infeasible start times from $\mathcal{D}_j$ is $\mathcal{O}(n \log n + |\mathcal{R}^\rho|n)$. By keeping a sorted list of all start and completion times of scheduled activities $i \in C \cap V^a$, the amortized time complexity for checking (4.1) is decreased to $\mathcal{O}(|\mathcal{R}^\rho|n)$ per iteration. Thus, the time complexity of Algorithm 4.1 including the test of inequality (4.1) is $\mathcal{O}(mn + |\mathcal{R}^\rho|n^2)$.

It may happen that no tentative start time $t \in \mathcal{D}_j$ is resource-feasible, which means that the current *partial schedule* $(S_i)_{i \in C}$ cannot be extended to a feasible schedule $S \in \mathcal{S}$. In that case, either the schedule generation is stopped or an unscheduling step is performed. Different unscheduling techniques are known from literature. The method by Franck (1999), Ch. 4, tailored to the case of regular objective functions, has been sketched in Subsection 3.1.4. Further unscheduling procedures have been devised by Neumann and Zimmermann (1999b, 2000) (see also Zimmermann 2001a, Sect. 3.2, and Neumann et al. 2003b, Sect. 3.7), where those activities $i \in C$ are unscheduled whose start at a different time frees capacity for processing activity j. Alternatively, one may also generate a time-feasible schedule S using Algorithm 4.1 first and then resolve resource conflicts by left- or right-shifting certain activities. This approach corresponds to *schedule-repair methods* described by Neumann and Zimmermann (2000). We finally notice that the proof of Proposition 4.1 remains valid for the case of renewable-resource constraints, which means that even without unscheduling, any quasistable schedule may still be generated using Algorithm 4.1 with reduced decision sets $\mathcal{D}_j$.

For certain choices of tentative start times $t \in \mathcal{D}_j$ one obtains specific types of schedules. If at each iteration we select $t = \min \mathcal{D}_j$ and no unscheduling step is performed, the resulting schedule is active because each activity is scheduled at its earliest feasible start time. Likewise, by always choosing $t = \min \mathcal{D}_j$ or $t = \max \mathcal{D}_j$ we obtain a stable schedule. The following example, however, shows that due to the presence of maximum time lags, not all active or stable schedules can be generated in this way.

Example 4.2. We consider a project with one renewable resource of capacity $R = 1$ and four real activities $i = 1, 2, 3, 4$ with durations $p_i = 1$ and resource requirements $r_i = 1$ $(i = 1, \ldots, 4)$. The project network N is depicted in Figure 4.1a. Clearly, there is precisely one feasible schedule $S = (0, 1, 2, 3, 4, 5)$, which, as a consequence, is active and stable. Schedule S is illustrated by the Gantt chart shown in Figure 4.1b, where each real activity $i \in V^a$ is represented as a box of length p_i and height r_i over the time axis from S_i to C_i.

The start times of activities 0, 1, 4, and 5 are fixed by the prescribed time lags because the corresponding nodes form a cycle of length zero in N. If in

(a)

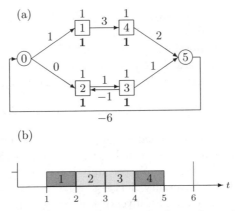

(b)

Fig. 4.1. Incompleteness of schedule-generation scheme for active or stable schedules: (a) project network N; (b) Gantt chart for unique feasible schedule S

the course of the algorithm, activity 2 is scheduled before activity 3, we obtain $\min \mathcal{D}_2 = 0$ and $\max \mathcal{D}_2 \geq 3$. Symmetrically, if activity 3 is scheduled before activity 2, we have $\min \mathcal{D}_3 \leq 2$ and $\max \mathcal{D}_3 = 5$. Hence, the unique feasible schedule S cannot be generated if solely scheduling at earliest or latest feasible start times is considered.

We obtain the schedule-generation scheme of the priority-rule methods for resource levelling proposed by Neumann and Zimmermann (1999b, 2000) if start time $t \in \mathcal{D}_j$ is always chosen to be the greatest minimizer of an *additional-cost function* f_j^a on $\mathcal{D}_j$, i.e., $t = \max \arg \min_{t' \in \mathcal{D}_j} f_j^a(t')$. For given $t' \in \mathcal{D}_j$, $f_j^a(t')$ is the increase in the objective function value if activity j is scheduled at time t' given partial schedule $(S_i)_{i \in C}$, where we put $r_{hk} := 0$ for all activities $h \in V \setminus C$ not yet scheduled and all $k \in \mathcal{R}^\rho$. Similarly to Example 4.2 it can be shown that the restriction to locally optimal tentative start times $t \in \arg \min_{t' \in \mathcal{D}_j} f_j^a(t')$ generally implies that the schedule-generation scheme is no longer complete, which means that one may miss the optimum even if all sequences in which activities j are scheduled are enumerated.

In the case where the availability of cumulative resources is limited as well, the feasibility of the generated schedule can no longer be ensured by iterating partial schedules which observe the resource constraints. The reason for this is that a partial schedule leading to a shortage or a surplus in some cumulative resource may be extended to a feasible schedule. Nevertheless, we may still exclude certain tentative start times from further consideration by computing, for given partial schedule, lower and upper bounds on the inventory in cumulative resources.

Let $(S_i)_{i \in C}$ be the partial schedule under consideration and assume that we want to test whether event $j \in V^e \setminus C$ can be scheduled at time $S_j = t \in \mathcal{D}_j$. By D' we denote the distance matrix for the expanded project network N' where for each $h \in C \cup \{j\}$ we add the two arcs $(0, h)$ and $(h, 0)$ weighted by

$\delta_{0h} = S_h$ and $\delta_{h0} = -S_h$ to project network N. The set $\mathcal{S}'_T \subseteq \mathcal{S}_T$ of all time-feasible schedules belonging to project network N' coincides with the set of all schedules that can be obtained by extending $(S_h)_{h \in C \cup \{j\}}$ to a time-feasible schedule. If for all schedules $S \in \mathcal{S}'_T$, the inventory level at time S_j either falls below the safety stock or exceeds the storage capacity, i.e.,

$$r_k(S, S_j) < \underline{R}_k \text{ or } r_k(S, S_j) > \overline{R}_k \text{ for some } k \in \mathcal{R}^\gamma \tag{4.2}$$

then event j cannot be scheduled at time $t = S_j$ because $\mathcal{S}'_T \cap S = \emptyset$. In this case, tentative start time t can be deleted from decision set $\mathcal{D}_j$. (4.2) holds true for any schedule $S \in \mathcal{S}'_T$ precisely if for some cumulative resource $k \in \mathcal{R}^\rho$, the maximum inventory $\max_{S \in \mathcal{S}'_T} r_k(S, S_j)$ at time S_j is less than safety stock $\underline{R}_k$ or the minimum inventory $\min_{S \in \mathcal{S}'_T} r_k(S, S_j)$ at time S_j exceeds storage capacity $\overline{R}_k$. The problems of computing the maximum and minimum inventories have been addressed in Subsection 2.1.2, where we have been concerned with checking the feasibility of a given relation ρ in set V^e. In the latter context, we have shown that maximizing or minimizing $r_k(\cdot, S_j)$ on a relation polytope $\mathcal{S}_T(\rho)$ can be stated as a binary program with totally unimodular coefficient matrix, the dual of whose continuous relaxation is a minimum-flow problem (see (2.2) and (2.4)). We obtain analogous formulations of our present problems if we choose reflexive preorder θ in (2.2) to be the preorder $\theta = \Theta(D')$ induced by distance matrix D'. Since solving a minimum-flow problem takes $\mathcal{O}(n^3)$ time, the computational effort for testing the feasibility of a tentative start time $t \in \mathcal{D}_j$ is $\mathcal{O}(|\mathcal{R}^\gamma|n^3)$. Hence, the time complexity of the variant of Algorithm 4.1 coping with renewable-resource and cumulative-resource constraints is $\mathcal{O}(|\mathcal{R}^\rho|n^2 + |\mathcal{R}^\gamma|n^5)$.

Alternatively, resource constraints can be taken into account by combining the relaxation-based and constructive approaches into a *two-phase method*. In phase 1, we determine a feasible relation ϱ in set V. In phase 2, we generate a vertex of relation polytope $\mathcal{S}_T(\varrho) \subseteq \mathcal{S}$ (i.e., a quasistable schedule) by using a variant of Algorithm 4.1 where the original project network N is replaced with relation network $N(\varrho)$. A feasible relation ϱ in set V can be generated using a modification of the enumeration scheme given by Algorithm 3.3. In the modified version, forbidden sets F are given by antichains U and unions of predecessor sets U in preorders $\theta = \Theta(D(\rho))$ rather than by active sets $\mathcal{A}(S, t)$ for minimizers S on relation polytopes $\mathcal{S}_T(\rho)$. For given relation ρ, those sets U can be determined by solving the minimum-flow problems discussed in Subsections 2.1.1 and 2.1.2 for the restrictions of ρ to sets V^a and V^e, respectively. The solutions to the dual problems, i.e., the maximum (s, t)-cuts in the respective flow networks, then provide the activity sets U sought (for details we refer to Section 5.2, where we shall use a similar technique for computing forbidden active sets when sequence-dependent changeover times arise between the execution of activities that are executed at different locations). If no set U is forbidden any longer, we have obtained a feasible relation $\varrho = \rho$.

4.2 Local Search

The schedule constructed by using the schedule-generation scheme may be improved by performing a local search in the set $\mathcal{QAS}$ of all quasiactive schedules if objective function f is locally regular or in the set $\mathcal{QSS}$ of all quasistable schedules if f is locally concave. Starting with some initial solution, local search algorithms try to find better solutions by exploring neighborhoods (cf. Aarts and Lenstra 2003a). The neighborhoods are given by a *neighborhood function* $\mathcal{N} : \Sigma \to \mathbb{P}(\Sigma)$ mapping the *set of solutions* Σ into the power set of Σ. For each solution $s \in \Sigma$, $\mathcal{N}$ defines a set $\mathcal{N}(s)$ of *neighboring solutions* s'. $\mathcal{N}(s)$ is called the *neighborhood* of s, and neighboring solutions $s' \in \mathcal{N}(s)$ are referred to as *neighbors* of s.

A neighborhood function $\mathcal{N}$ can be represented by its (directed) *neighborhood graph* $\mathcal{G}$ with node set Σ. Two nodes s and s' are linked by an arc (s, s') in $\mathcal{G}$ precisely if s' is a neighbor of s, where it may happen that s' is a neighbor of s but not vice versa. Local search can be regarded as a directed walk in neighborhood graph $\mathcal{G}$. Graph $\mathcal{G}$ is called *weakly optimally connected* if from any node s of $\mathcal{G}$, there is a directed path from s to some optimal solution s^*. If $\mathcal{G}$ is weakly optimally connected, an optimal solution s^* can be reached from any initial solution just by iteratively moving from solutions s to appropriate neighboring solutions s'. Obviously, $\mathcal{G}$ is weakly optimally connected if it is strongly connected.

In this section we review neighborhoods for resource allocation problems with locally regular or locally concave objective functions f that have been proposed by Neumann et al. (2003a). We first deal with the case of locally concave objective functions and then explain how to adapt the neighborhood to locally regular objective functions. Recall that each quasistable schedule S can be represented by a spanning tree $G = (V, E_G, \delta^G)$ of its schedule network $N(\theta(S))$ such that S is the unique solution to the system of linear equations $S_0 = 0$ and $S_j - S_i = \delta_{ij}^G$ $((i, j) \in E_G)$. That is why we identify the set of solutions Σ with the set Σ^{st} of all spanning trees of schedule networks $N(\theta)$ where $\theta \in \mathcal{SIP}$ is some schedule-induced preorder in set V.

The starting point for constructing a neighborhood function $\mathcal{N}^{st}$ on set Σ^{st} is the observation that first, two spanning trees in set Σ^{st} differing in only one arc always belong to either coinciding or adjacent vertices of some schedule polytope and that second, for any two adjacent vertices of a schedule polytope, there exist two corresponding spanning trees in set Σ^{st} which differ in exactly one arc. Roughly speaking, we determine neighbors G' of a spanning tree G by removing a *leaving arc* (i, j) from G and adding a different *entering arc* (i', j') to G such that the resulting directed graph G' is again a tree. By deleting arc (i, j), G decomposes into two subtrees with node sets $C \supseteq \{0\}$ and $C' = V \setminus C$. Let S and S' be the quasistable schedules that are represented by spanning trees G and G', respectively. Obviously, $S'_h = S_h$ for all $h \in C$ and $S'_h = S_h + \sigma$ for all $h \in C'$ or $S'_h = S_h - \sigma$ for all $h \in C'$ and some stepsize $\sigma \geq 0$. In other words, when moving from S to S' we uniformly shift all activities h of C' by some $\sigma \geq 0$ until a new inequality $S_{j'} - S_{i'} \geq \delta^{G'}_{i'j'}$ with $i' \in C'$, $j' \in C$ or $i' \in C$, $j' \in C'$ becomes active. Arc (i', j') may be a temporal arc or a precedence arc. Similarly to the steepest descent and flattest ascent methods discussed in Section 3.2, stepsize σ may be equal to 0 and thus $S' = S$ if S is a degenerate vertex of its schedule polytope $\mathcal{S}_T(\theta(S))$.

Now recall that we refer to (g, h) as a forward arc of G if g is the predecessor of h on the (undirected) path from 0 to h in G, and as a backward arc of G, otherwise. If leaving arc (i, j) is a forward arc of G, then $i \in C$ and $j \in C'$, and if (i, j) is a backward arc of G, then $i \in C'$ and $j \in C$. For what follows we associate a direction z with leaving arc (i, j) with $z_h = 0$ for all $h \in C$ and $z_h = 1$ for all $h \in C'$ if (i, j) is a forward arc and $z_h = -1$ for all $h \in C'$ if (i, j) is a backward arc. Let (g, h) be an arc in some schedule network. We say that set C' is *shifted along* arc (g, h) if $z_h - z_g = 1$. If $z_h - z_g = -1$, we speak of a *shift against* arc (g, h). Clearly, a shift of C' against leaving arc (i, j) is only meaningful if (i, j) is a precedence arc. In that case, the precedence relationship between activities i and j is deleted when passing from S to neighboring schedule S'. Symmetrically, a shift along an entering temporal arc is not possible. If we shift C' along leaving arc (i, j), then $S' = S + \sigma z$, and for a shift against leaving arc (i, j) we have $S' = S - \sigma z$. Before we describe neighborhood function $\mathcal{N}^{st}$ in more detail, we consider the four cases that may occur when shifting set C'. For illustration, we consider the spanning tree G and the corresponding Gantt chart displayed on the top of Figure 4.2, where for simplicity we have omitted the arc weights. We assume that the underlying project has one renewable resource and that the real activities $i = 1, 2, 3$ are unrelated and can be started at the project beginning. Thus, all arcs $(g, h) \in E_G$ are precedence arcs.

(a) We shift C' along leaving arc (i, j) and against entering arc (i', j'). This means that the schedule-induced preorder remains unchanged when passing from S to S', i.e., $\theta(S') = \theta(S)$, or, in other words, $S' \in \mathcal{S}_{\overline{T}}(\theta(S))$. This case is shown in Figure 4.2a, where $(i, j) = (0, 1)$ and $(i', j') = (4, 0)$. In the resulting spanning tree G', the activities $h \in C'$ shifted are drawn in bold.

(b) We shift C' along leaving arc (i, j) and along entering precedence arc (i', j'). This means that the schedule-induced preorder is augmented when passing from S to $S' \neq S$, i.e., $\theta(S') \supset \theta(S)$. This case is shown in Figure 4.2b, where $(i, j) = (1, 3)$ and $(i', j') = (2, 3)$.

(c) We shift C' against leaving precedence arc (i, j) and against entering arc (i', j'). This means that the schedule-induced preorder is reduced when passing from S to $S' \neq S$, i.e., $\theta(S') \subset \theta(S)$. Such a shift is always opposite to a shift augmenting the schedule-induced preorder (case (b)). This case is shown in Figure 4.2c, where $(i, j) = (1, 3)$ and $(i', j') = (0, 3)$.

(d) We shift C' against leaving precedence arc (i, j) and along entering precedence arc (i', j'). This means that $\theta(S') \not\supseteq \theta(S)$ and $\theta(S') \not\subseteq \theta(S)$ if $S' \neq S$. This case is shown in Figure 4.2d, where $(i, j) = (1, 2)$ and $(i', j') = (2, 3)$.

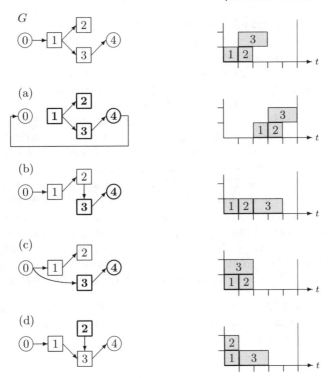

Fig. 4.2. Cases occurring when shifting set C': (a) shift along leaving and against entering arc; (b) shift along leaving and along entering arc; (c) shift against leaving and against entering arc; (d) shift against leaving and along entering arc

In all four cases, the resulting schedule S' either coincides with S (which may happen when S is a degenerate vertex of its schedule polytope) or S' is a vertex adjacent to S in the closure of equal-order set $\mathcal{S}_T^=(\theta(S''))$ of some schedule S''. In cases (a) and (b), S and S' are adjacent vertices of the closure of $\mathcal{S}_T^=(\theta(S))$. In cases (a) and (c), S and S' are adjacent vertices of the closure of $\mathcal{S}_T^=(\theta(S'))$. In case (d), S and S' are adjacent vertices of the closure of $\mathcal{S}_T^=(\theta(S''))$ with $S'' := \frac{1}{2}(S + S')$.

A neighbor $G' \in \mathcal{N}^{st}(G)$ can be determined in two steps. First, we delete an arc (i, j) from G. Then, we shift set C' until a temporal or precedence constraint corresponding to some arc (i', j') becomes active. If (i, j) is a temporal arc, C' can only be shifted along (i, j). C' can be shifted along or against (i, j) if (i, j) is a precedence arc. Finally, we add arc (i', j') to G and obtain spanning tree G'. Since G contains $n+1$ arcs (i, j), which all may leave G, and because we may shift either along or against (i, j), the size of neighborhood $\mathcal{N}^{st}(G)$ is of order $\mathcal{O}(n)$.

Next, we define a neighborhood function $\mathcal{N}^{ot}$ on the set $\Sigma^{ot} \subseteq \Sigma^{st}$ of spanning outtrees G of schedule networks $N(\theta)$ where $\theta \in \mathcal{SIP}$. Those spanning outtrees represent minimal points of schedule polytopes $\mathcal{S}_T(\theta)$. A tree G is an outtree with root node 0 precisely if all arcs $(g, h) \in E_G$ are forward arcs. Hence, to obtain a spanning outtree $G' \in \Sigma^{ot}$ from a spanning outtree $G \in \Sigma^{ot}$ such that G and G' differ in exactly one arc, the leaving arc (i, j) must be replaced by an entering arc $(i', j') \neq (i, j)$ such that G' is a tree and (i', j') is a forward arc in G'. Clearly, both conditions are satisfied precisely if $j' = j$. Since (i, j) is a forward arc in G, in addition we have $z_j \in \{0, 1\}$. This implies that if we shift along leaving arc (i, j), we necessarily shift along entering precedence arc (i', j), and if we shift against leaving precedence arc (i, j), we necessarily shift against entering arc (i', j) (see Figures 4.2b and 4.2c). We obtain a neighbor $G' \in \Sigma^{ot}$ of G as follows. An arc (i, j) can be chosen to be the leaving arc if the first constraint that becomes active when shifting set C' corresponds to an arc (i', j) with terminal node j. After the selection of an appropriate leaving arc (i, j) we proceed analogously as for neighborhood function $\mathcal{N}^{st}$. We first delete (i, j) from G, then shift set C' until the constraint corresponding to entering arc (i', j) becomes active, and finally add arc (i', j) to G. The size of neighborhood $\mathcal{N}^{ot}(G)$ is again of order $\mathcal{O}(n)$.

Proposition 4.3 (Neumann et al. 2003a). *The neighborhood graphs $\mathcal{G}^{st}$ and $\mathcal{G}^{ot}$ of (a) neighborhood function $\mathcal{N}^{st}$ and (b) neighborhood function $\mathcal{N}^{ot}$ are strongly connected.*

Proof.

(a) Clearly, each spanning outtree G representing the earliest schedule ES can be reached from any other spanning tree $G \in \Sigma^{st}$ by performing a sequence of (left-)shifts along a backward leaving arc or against a forward leaving arc. This proves $\mathcal{G}^{st}$ to be weakly connected. Moreover, each shift of type (a), (b), (c), or (d) transforming some spanning tree G into a different neighboring spanning tree G' is reversible because the opposite shift is of type (a), (c), (b), or (d), respectively. Consequently, any two adjacent nodes in $\mathcal{G}^{st}$ are linked by a pair of oppositely directed arcs, i.e., $\mathcal{G}^{st}$ is symmetric (see, e.g., Bang-Jensen and Gutin 2002, Sect. 1.6). From the weak connectivity and the symmetry of $\mathcal{G}^{st}$ it follows that $\mathcal{G}^{st}$ is strongly connected.

(b) $\mathcal{G}^{ot}$ is the subgraph of $\mathcal{G}^{st}$ that is induced by set Σ^{ot} and thus $\mathcal{G}^{ot}$ is symmetric as well. The weak connectivity of $\mathcal{G}^{ot}$ follows from the fact that the spanning outtrees representing schedule ES can be obtained from any outtree $G \in \Sigma^{ot}$ by successively shifting against leaving precedence arcs (i, j). □

4.3 Additional Notes and References

Locally regular and locally concave objective functions have essentially been studied in the context of resource levelling problems, where one strives at smoothing the utilization of renewable resources over time. Resource level-ling problems have been investigated since the very beginning of algorithmic project planning in the early 1960s. An overview of different problem set-tings and solution procedures can be found in Zimmermann (2001a), Ch. 5, and Kimms (2001a), Sect. 11.3. Resource levelling procedures for the case of general temporal constraints have first been proposed by Brinkmann and Neumann (1996), who have devised simple priority-rule methods where the activities are scheduled one after the other according to a *quasi-topological ordering* $\prec$ of the nodes in project network N. Strict order $\prec$ arises from arc set E by deleting all arcs with nonpositive weight (i.e., the maximum time lags) and taking the transitive hull of the resulting relation. An activity h becomes eligible for scheduling as soon as all its predecessors i with respect to strict order $\prec$ have been processed, i.e., $Pred^{\prec}(h) \subseteq C$. Among the eligible activities h, an activity j is selected by using a priority rule and j is scheduled at a minimizer t of additional-cost function f^a on set $[ES_j, LS_j] \cap \mathbb{Z}$. Since f^a is evaluated on set $[ES_j, LS_j] \cap \mathbb{Z}$ by complete enumeration, the heuristic shows a pseudo-polynomial time complexity.

Neumann and Zimmermann (1999b, 2000) have streamlined this ap-proach in different respects. First, instead of scanning all integral times $t \in [ES_j, LS_j]$, only the relevant tentative start times t from decision set $\mathcal{D}_j$ are investigated (see Section 4.1). Second, the concept of *core loading pro-files* r_k^c (see Subsection 1.2.4) is used to anticipate (a part of) the unavoidable resource usage by activities $h \in V^a \setminus C$ not yet scheduled. In doing so, dead-locks where $\mathcal{D}_j = \emptyset$ can more likely be avoided when resource constraints have to be taken into account. The definition of additional-cost function f_j^a is based on the core loading profiles, which means that the cost $f_j^a(t)$ of starting activity j at time $t \in \mathcal{D}_j$ arises from comparing the costs associated with the core loading profiles before and after putting $S_j := t$. A third improvement on Brinkmann and Neumann's procedure is the use of different unscheduling techniques invoked when no feasible start time can be assigned to activity j (for details see Section 4.1).

Neumann and Zimmermann (2000) have also proposed a *tabu search proce-dure* for resource levelling, which in principle is as follows (for an introduction to tabu search we refer to Glover and Laguna 1997 or Hertz et al. 2003). Given some time-feasible schedule S, a neighboring schedule S' is constructed by se-lecting a real activity $j \in V^a$ such that $r_k(S, S_j) \geq \lambda \max_{0 \leq t \leq \bar{d}} r_k(S, t)$, where λ with $0 < \lambda \leq 1$ is a control parameter. Then activity j is shifted behind or in front of some activity $i \in V^a$, i.e., $S_j' = S_i + p_i$ or $S_j' = S_i - p_j$. Subsequently, the time-feasibility of resulting schedule S' is restored. The move from S to S' is only accepted if $r_k(S', t) < r_k(S, t)$ for some resource $k \in \mathcal{R}^\rho$ and some "peak time" $t \in \arg\max_{0 < t' \leq \bar{d}} r_k(S, t')$. In general, the schedules S iterated are not resource-feasible. That is why they are evaluated on the basis of a cost function including a penalty term for violations of the resource constraints. The penalty term is similar to that used by Schwindt (2000b) in the local search algorithm for the earliness-tardiness problem with renewable resources (see Subsection 3.2.5).

For solving the resource investment problem, Nübel (1999) has proposed a branch-and-bound algorithm that (implicitly) makes use of the property that the total procurement cost represents a preorder-decreasing objective function (see Subsection 2.3.3). The principle of this branch-and-bound algorithm is to introduce fictitious resource capacities that are stepwise decreased at certain enumeration nodes. Starting with the earliest schedule $S = ES$ at the root node, the capacity R_k of some resource $k \in \mathcal{R}^\rho$ is put to $\max_{0 \le t \le \bar{d}} r_k(S,t) - 1$ and a new schedule S is sought with $r_k(S,t) \le R_k$ for all $0 \le t \le \bar{d}$ by using the enumeration scheme for regular objective functions given by Algorithm 3.1. Reduction of fictitious resource capacities and computation of quasiactive schedules with lower maximum resource requirements are reiterated until no feasible schedule with $S_{n+1} \le \bar{d}$ can be found any more. Each time a new feasible schedule has been found, one branches over the resource k whose capacity is decreased next.

Based on an enumeration scheme by Patterson et al. (1989) for project scheduling subject to precedence and renewable-resource constraints, Neumann and Zimmermann (2000) have developed a time-based branch-and-bound procedure. The algorithm is capable of solving arbitrary resource allocation problems for which an optimal schedule can be chosen to be integer-valued. The latter condition is obviously always satisfied if the objective function is locally regular or locally concave because any quasistable schedule is integral. The nodes of the enumeration tree are associated with partial schedules $(S_i)_{i \in C}$ satisfying the temporal and resource constraints. Starting with $C = \{0\}$ and $S_0 = 0$, at each level an activity j from set $V \setminus C$ with minimum total float $TF_j = LS_j - ES_j$ is added to C. For each integral start time t in the current time window $[ES_j, LS_j]$ of j, a corresponding child node with $S_j = t$ is generated and the time windows of the activities $h \in V \setminus C$ not yet scheduled are updated. Leaves of the enumeration node correspond to feasible, not necessarily quasistable schedules.

Next, we discuss the results of an experimental performance analysis for the time-constrained resource investment and total squared utilization cost problems. We compare a tabu search implementation of Neumann et al.'s local search principle discussed in Section 4.2 to some of the alternative solution procedures. The test set has been created using project generator Pro-Gen/max and contains 90 projects with 500 activities and 1, 3, or 5 resources each. For all algorithms a time limit of 100 seconds has been imposed, which refers to a Pentium personal computer with 200 MHz clock pulse. The results were communicated by Zimmermann (2001b).

Table 4.1 shows the results obtained for the **resource investment problem**, where besides the tree-based tabu search procedure ("TS") we have tested truncated versions (filtered beam search, "FBS") of the branch-and-bound algorithms of Nübel (1999) and Neumann and Zimmermann (2000). Since tight lower bounds for large resource levelling problems are not available, we give the mean deviation Δ_{best} from the objective function value of a best solution found by the three procedures. p_{best} denotes the percentage of instances for which the respective method has found a best solution (the values sum to more than 100 % because for some instances, a best solution was found by more than one procedure).

Table 4.1. Performance of algorithms for the resource investment problem

Algorithm	Δ_{best}	p_{best}
Nübel (1999) FBS	23 %	6.7 %
Neumann and Zimmermann (2000) FBS	18 %	11.1 %
Neumann et al. (2003a) TS	3 %	90.0 %

The data from Table 4.1 suggest that the tabu search heuristic provides markedly better schedules on the average than the truncated exact algorithms. For 81 out of the 90 projects, the tree-based approach yields a best solution. In addition, the mean deviation from the best solution found is considerably smaller than for the two other algorithms.

The results for the **total squared resource utilization cost problem** are given in Table 4.2. The tree-based tabu search procedure has been compared to the priority-rule ("PR") and tabu search ("TS") methods by Neumann and Zimmermann (2000). The priority-rule method has been run as a multi-pass procedure with ten priority rules. Again, we give the mean deviation Δ_{best} from the best objective function value and the percentage p_{best} of best solutions found.

Table 4.2. Performance of algorithms for the total squared utilization cost problem

Algorithm	Δ_{best}	p_{best}
Neumann and Zimmermann (2000) PR	10 %	4.4 %
Neumann and Zimmermann (2000) TS	3 %	43.3 %
Neumann et al. (2003a) TS	1 %	68.9 %

Not surprisingly, the schedule-improvement procedures outperform the priority-rule method. As for the resource investment problem, the tree-based approach again shows the best performance among the tested algorithms. Compared to the tabu search of Neumann and Zimmermann (2000), the favorable behavior is probably due to the small size of the neighborhoods to be explored and the little time needed for moving from one schedule to another.

5

Supplements

When coping with real-life resource allocation problems, some of the assumptions of our three basic project scheduling problems may be too restrictive. This chapter is dedicated to expansions of the basic models which permit us to cover some features that are frequently encountered in practice.

In Section 5.1 we deal with *break calendars*, which specify time intervals during which some renewable resources cannot be used (such as weekends or night shifts, where skilled staff is not available). In that case, it is often necessary to relax the requirement that activities must not be interrupted when being in progress. Instead, we assume that the execution of certain activities can be suspended during breaks, whereas other activities still must not be interrupted. We explain how to perform temporal scheduling computations in presence of break calendars and outline how the enumeration scheme for regular objective functions discussed in Section 3.1 can be generalized to this problem setting.

When performing projects whose activities are distributed over different locations sharing common resources like manpower, heavy machinery, or equipment, *changeover times* for tear down, transportation, and reinstallation of resource units have to be taken into account. During the changeover, those resource units are not available for processing activities. Due to the transportation of resource units, the changeover times are generally sequence-dependent, which means that the time needed for changing over a resource unit between the execution of two consecutive activities depends on both activities. In Section 5.2 we show how to adapt the relaxation-based approaches to the occurrence of sequence-dependent changeover times.

In many applications of project management, the assignment of resources to the project activities is not (completely) predetermined by technology. We may then perform certain activities in *alternative execution modes*, which differ in durations, time lags, and resource requirements. The execution modes of an activity reflect tradeoffs between the time and resource demands. For example, the duration of an activity may be shortened by increasing the number of allotted resource units (time-resource tradeoff) or some resources used may be replaced by other resources (resource-resource tradeoff). If in that case the selection of an appropriate execution mode for each activity in the project planning phase is deferred from the time and resource estimations to the resource allocation step, we obtain a multi-mode resource allocation problem. In Section 5.3 we are concerned with relaxation-based procedures for solving multi-mode resource allocation problems with finitely many execution modes.

As we have seen in Section 1.3, the concept of (discrete) cumulative resources offers a straightforward way of modelling constraints arising from discrete material flows in assembly environments. Sometimes, however, inventories of intermediate products are not depleted and replenished batchwise at the occurrence of certain events but rather continuously over the execution time of consuming and producing real activities. Such continuous material flows are, for example, typical of mass production in the process industries. Material flows may also be semicontinuous, which means that facilities may be operated in batch or continuous production modes. In Section 5.4 we develop the concept of *continuous cumulative resources* and we propose a relaxation-based approach to solving resource allocation problems with the latter type of resources and convex objective functions. Resource conflicts are stepwise resolved by introducing linear constraints which ensure that at the start or completion of some activity, the inventory level is between the safety stock and the storage capacity. For each activity we branch over the alternatives whether or not the activity contributes to settling the resource conflict in question.

In the following Sections 5.1 to 5.4 we closely follow the presentation in the book of Neumann et al. (2003b), Sects. 2.11, 2.14, 2.15, and 2.12.2.

5.1 Break Calendars

In many real-life projects, certain renewable resources are not available during breaks like weekends or scheduled maintenance times. Scheduling the activities subject to break calendars is termed *calendarization*. For what follows, we assume that some real activities may be interrupted during a break, whereas others must not be interrupted due to technical reasons. Hence, the set of all real activities V^a decomposes into the set V_{bi}^a of all (break-)interruptible activities and the set V_{ni}^a of all non-interruptible activities. The processing of interruptible activities $i \in V_{bi}^a$ can only be stopped at the beginning of a break and has to be resumed at the end of the break. This assumption distinguishes calendarization from preemptive project scheduling problems, where activities may be interrupted at any point in time (see, e.g., Demeulemeester and Herroelen 1996). Furthermore, for each interruptible activity $i \in V_{bi}^a$, a *minimum execution time* $e_i \in \mathbb{N}$ is prescribed during which i has to be in progress without being suspended, e.g., $e_i = 1$. To simplify notation, we set $e_i := p_i$ for non-interruptible activities $i \in V_{ni}^a$ and assume that for activities $i \in V_{bi}^a$, the time between any two successive breaks is not less than e_i.

In this section we first describe procedures presented by Franck et al. (2001*a*) for the temporal scheduling of projects subject to break calendars for activities and prescribed time lags. We then briefly sketch how the relaxation-based approach for regular objective functions discussed in Section 3.1 can be adapted to the presence of break calendars. Preliminary versions of the temporal scheduling methods have been devised by Zhan (1992) and Franck (1999), Sect. 3.3. An alternative approach can be found in Trautmann (2001*b*). Here, the calendar-dependent precedence relationships between activities are taken into account by distinguishing between start-to-start, start-to-completion, completion-to-start, and completion-to-completion time lags.

A *break calendar* can be regarded as a right-continuous step function b : $\mathbb{R} \to \{0, 1\}$ where $b(t) = 0$ if time $t < 0$ or if t falls into a break, and $b(t) = 1$, otherwise. $\int_t^{t'} b(\tau)d\tau$ is the *total working time* in interval $[t, t'[$. In practice, different renewable resources $k \in \mathcal{R}^\rho$ may have different calendars. We then obtain the corresponding *activity calendars* b_i for activities $i \in V^a$ by setting $b_i(t) := 0$ exactly if i requires some resource $k \in \mathcal{R}^\rho$ which is not available at time t. If $b_i(t) = 0$, we have to suspend the execution of activity $i \in V_{bi}^a$ being in progress at time t. For activities $i \in V_{ni}^a$, the time interval between the start and completion of i must not contain any time t where $b_i(t) = 0$.

The constraints arising from minimum execution times e_i can be stated as follows:

$$b_i(\tau) = 1 \quad (i \in V^a, \ S_i \leq \tau < S_i + e_i) \tag{5.1}$$

If $i \in V_{ni}^a$, (5.1) means that the execution of i must not be interrupted by a break.

Let $C_i \geq S_i + p_i$ again denote the completion time of activity $i \in V^a$. In interval $[S_i, C_i[$, activity i is in progress at time t precisely if $b_i(t) = 1$. Thus, given start time S_i, the completion time $C_i(S_i)$ of i is uniquely determined by

$$C_i(S_i) = \min\{t \geq S_i + p_i \mid \int_{S_i}^t b_i(\tau)d\tau = p_i\}$$

Clearly, minimum and maximum time lags may depend on calendars, too. For example, a precedence constraint between activities i and j refers to the completion time C_i and thus to the calendar b_i of activity i. Therefore, we introduce a *time lag calendar* b_{ij} for each arc $(i, j) \in E$ of project network N. Point in time t is taken into account when computing the total working time between the starts of activities i and j exactly if $b_{ij}(t) = 1$. That is, $\int_{S_i}^{S_j} b_{ij}(\tau)d\tau$ equals the total working time in interval $[S_i, S_j[$ if $S_i \leq S_j$ and equals the negative total working time in interval $[S_j, S_i[$, otherwise.

The actual minimum difference Δ_{ij} between start times S_i and S_j that is prescribed by arc $(i, j) \in E$ depends on start time S_i and calendar b_{ij}:

$$\Delta_{ij}(S_i) = \min\{t \geq 0 \mid \int_{S_i}^t b_{ij}(\tau) \, d\tau \geq \delta_{ij}\} - S_i \quad ((i, j) \in E)$$

$S_i + \Delta_{ij}(S_i)$ is the earliest point in time $t \geq 0$ for which the total working time in interval $[S_i, t[$ or $[t, S_i[$, respectively, is greater than or equal to $|\delta_{ij}|$.

Since $b_{ij}(t) \in \{0,1\}$ for all $t \geq 0$, it holds that $|\Delta_{ij}(S_i)| \geq |\delta_{ij}|$, and $\Delta_{ij}(S_i)$ and δ_{ij} have the same sign.

For temporal scheduling, the temporal constraints $S_j - S_i \geq \delta_{ij}$ for all $(i,j) \in E$ have to be replaced by

$$S_j - S_i \geq \Delta_{ij}(S_i) \quad ((i,j) \in E)$$

which due to $b_{ij}(t) \geq 0$ for all $t \in \mathbb{R}$ can also be written as

$$\int_{S_i}^{S_j} b_{ij}(\tau)d\tau \geq \delta_{ij} \quad ((i,j) \in E) \tag{5.2}$$

The interpretation of inequality (5.2) is as follows. If $\delta_{ij} \geq 0$, then the total working time $\int_{S_i}^{S_j} b_{ij}(\tau)d\tau$ between the starts of activity i at time S_i and the start of activity j at time S_j must be at least δ_{ij}. If $\delta_{ij} < 0$, then $\int_{S_i}^{S_j} b_{ij}(\tau)d\tau \geq \delta_{ij}$ means that the total working time $\int_{S_j}^{S_i} b_{ij}(\tau)d\tau = -\int_{S_i}^{S_j} b_{ij}(\tau)d\tau$ between S_j and S_i must not exceed $-\delta_{ij}$. Notice that for minimum time lags $d_{ij}^{min} = \delta_{ij} \geq 0$, constraint (5.2) is at least as tight as the ordinary temporal constraint $S_j - S_i \geq \delta_{ij}$, whereas maximum time lags $d_{ji}^{max} = -\delta_{ij} > 0$ are relaxed by considering breaks. Given start time S_i for activity i, the minimum start time S_j of activity j satisfying (5.2) is

$$t^* := \min\{t \geq 0 \mid \int_{S_i}^t b_{ij}(\tau) \, d\tau \geq \delta_{ij}\}$$

Constraints (5.1) and (5.2) are referred to as *calendar constraints*. A schedule S satisfying the calendar constraints is called *calendar-feasible*.

We now explain how to integrate the calendar constraints into the computation of earliest schedule ES by modifying the label-correcting method given by Algorithm 1.1. Algorithm 3.2 for the minimization of regular objective functions subject to temporal and disjunctive precedence constraints can be adapted similarly. The problem of finding the earliest calendar-feasible schedule ES can be formulated as follows:

$$\left. \begin{array}{ll} \text{Minimize} & \sum_{i \in V} S_i \\ \text{subject to} & (5.1) \text{ and } (5.2) \\ & S_i \geq 0 \quad (i \in V) \end{array} \right\} \tag{5.3}$$

We start the label-correcting algorithm with $ES = (0, -\infty, \ldots, -\infty)$ and successively delay activities until all calendar constraints are satisfied. At the beginning, queue Q only contains the project beginning event 0. At each iteration, we dequeue an activity $i \in V$ from Q. If i is a real activity, we check whether start time ES_i complies with calendar b_i by computing the earliest point in time $t^* \geq ES_i$ for which there is no break in interval $[t^*, t^* + e_i[$ (cf. constraints (5.1)). In case of $ES_i < t^*$, the start of activity i must be delayed until time t^*. Next, we check inequalities (5.2) for all arcs $(i,j) \in E$ with initial node i. To this end, we compute the earliest start time

$t^* := \min\{t \geq ES_j \mid \int_{ES_i}^{t} b_{ij}(\tau)d\tau \geq \delta_{ij}\}$ of activity j given start time ES_i for activity i. If $ES_j < t^*$, schedule ES does not satisfy the corresponding prescribed time lag, and thus we increase ES_j up to t^*. In that case or if $b_j(\tau) = 0$ for some $t^* \leq \tau < t^* + e_j$, we enqueue j to Q if $j \notin Q$. Algorithm 5.1 summarizes this procedure.

Algorithm 5.1. Earliest calendar-feasible schedule

Input: MPM project network $N = (V, E, \delta)$, partition $\{V_{bi}^a, V_{ni}^a\}$ of set V^a, activity
  calendars b_i for $i \in V^a$, time lag calendars b_{ij} for $(i,j) \in E$.
Output: Earliest schedule ES.

  set $ES_0 := 0$, $Q := \{0\}$, and $ES_i := -\infty$ for all $i \in V \setminus Q$;
  while $Q \neq \emptyset$ **do**
    dequeue i from Q;
    if $i \in V^a$ **then**
      determine $t^* := \min\{t \geq ES_i \mid b_i(\tau) = 1 \text{ for all } t \leq \tau < t + e_i\}$;
      if $t^* > \bar{d}$ **then** terminate; (∗ there is no time-feasible schedule ∗)
      else if $ES_i < t^*$ **then** set $ES_i := t^*$;
    for all $(i,j) \in E$ **do**
      determine $t^* := \min\{t \geq ES_j \mid \int_{ES_i}^{t} b_{ij}(\tau)d\tau \geq \delta_{ij}\}$;
      if $ES_j < t^*$ **then**
        set $ES_j := t^*$;
        if $j \notin Q$ **then** enqueue j to Q;
      if $j \in V^a \setminus Q$ and $b_j(\tau) = 0$ for some $t^* \leq \tau < t^* + e_j$ **then** enqueue j to Q;
  return earliest schedule ES;

Let β denote the number of breaks in all activity and time lag calendars. If some activity i is inspected more than $n(\beta+1)$ times, then there is no schedule satisfying the calendar constraints, and the algorithm can be stopped. Franck et al. (2001a) have shown that if the calendars are given as sorted lists of start and end times of breaks, Algorithm 5.1 can be implemented to run in $\mathcal{O}(mn\beta)$ time.

The latest schedule LS can be computed by using a similar label-correcting procedure again starting at node 0 and proceeding from terminal nodes j to initial nodes i of arcs $(i,j) \in E$. In difference to Algorithm 5.1, t^* is set to be the *lastest* time for which condition (5.1) or (5.2), respectively, is fulfilled (for details we refer to Neumann et al. 2003b, Sect. 2.11).

The enumeration scheme for resource allocation problems with regular objective functions (see Algorithm 3.1) can be used without almost any modification for the case of calendar constraints as well. Schedule $S = \min(\cup_{\rho \in P} \mathcal{S}_T(\rho))$ is then computed by the adaptation of Algorithm 3.2 to the case of break calendars, where the calendars b_{ij} for pairs $(i,j) \in \rho$ coincide with calendars b_i if $i \in V^a$ and are given by $b_{ij}(t) = 1$ for all $0 \leq t \leq \bar{d}$ if $i \in V^e$. $\mathcal{S}_T(\rho)$ now denotes the set of all schedules satisfying the calendar constraints (5.1) and (5.2) for relation network $N(\rho)$. Similarly to the case without calendars, it can be shown that set $\mathcal{S}_T(\rho)$, though generally being disconnected, possesses a unique minimal point (cf. Franck 1999, Sect. 3.2) and that this property still carries over to the union $\cup_{\rho \in P} \mathcal{S}_T(\rho)$ of sets $\mathcal{S}_T(\rho)$.

5.2 Sequence-Dependent Changeover Times

This section is concerned with sequence-dependent changeover times arising when several (sub-)projects using common renewable resources are performed simultaneously at different sites (*multi-site scheduling*, see e.g., Sauer et al. 1998). When a unit of resource $k \in \mathcal{R}^\rho$ passes from the execution of an activity i at a location a to an activity j to be carried out at a different location b, the unit has to be torn down after the completion of i, transported from a to b, and put into service for processing j. Thus, the changeover time of resource k between the execution of activities i and j generally depends on resource k and on both activities i and j.

There is an extensive literature dealing with sequence-dependent changeovers in shop-floor environments, where changeover times are caused by replacing tools or cleaning. The great majority of the papers considers the problem of minimizing the total cost associated with changeovers (for a literature review we refer to Aldowaisan et al. 1999). Brucker and Thiele (1996) have devised a branch-and-bound algorithm for a general-shop problem where the makespan is to be minimized subject to precedence constraints and sequence-dependent changeover times between operations. Kolisch (1995), Ch. 8, has shown how to model changeover times between activities of a project by introducing alternative execution modes for the activities (see Section 5.3). The changeover times between two activities are assumed to be equal to a sequence-independent setup time or equal to zero. Moreover, the capacity R_k of each resource $k \in \mathcal{R}^\rho$ equals one. Trautmann (2001a), Sect. 3.3, has devised a branch-and-bound algorithm for minimizing the project duration in case of arbitrary resource capacities R_k, single-unit resource requirements $r_{ik} \in \{0, 1\}$, and general sequence-dependent changeover times.

In the sequel, we drop the assumption of single-unit resource requirements and consider any regular or convexifiable objective function f. Let $V_k^a := \{i \in V^a \mid r_{ik} > 0\}$ be the set of all activities using resource $k \in \mathcal{R}^\rho$. With $\vartheta_{ij}^k \in \mathbb{Z}_{\geq 0}$ we denote the changeover time from activity an $i \in V_k^a$ to an activity $j \in V_k^a$ on resource k, where $\vartheta_{ii}^k = 0$ for all $i \in V_k^a$. We suppose that the *weak triangle inequality*

$$\vartheta_{hi}^k + p_i + \vartheta_{ij}^k \geq \vartheta_{hj}^k$$

is satisfied for all $k \in \mathcal{R}^\rho$ and all $h, i, j \in V_k^a$. This assumption is generally met in practice because otherwise it would be possible to save changeover time by processing additional activities. For notational convenience we additionally assume that there are neither changeovers from the project beginning event 0 to activities $i \in V^a$ (setups) nor changeovers from activities $i \in V^a$ to the project termination event $n + 1$ (teardowns). The latter condition can always be fulfilled by introducing the minimum time lags $d_{0i}^{min} = \max_{k \in \mathcal{R}^\rho : i \in V_k^a} \vartheta_{0i}^k$ and $d_{i,n+1}^{min} = \max_{k \in \mathcal{R}^\rho : i \in V_k^a} \vartheta_{i,n+1}^k$ and then putting $\vartheta_{0i}^k := \vartheta_{i,n+1}^k = 0$ for all $k \in \mathcal{R}^\rho$ and all $i \in V_k^a$.

The resource-constrained project scheduling problem (P) with sequence-dependent changeover times can be formulated as follows. We strive at minimizing objective function f such that all temporal and cumulative-resource constraints are observed and at any point in time, the demands for renewable resources by activities and changeovers do not exceed the respective resource capacities. More precisely, let for given resource $k \in \mathcal{R}^\rho$, $X_k : V_k^a \to \mathbb{P}(\mathbb{N})$ be a mapping providing for each activity $i \in V_k^a$ the set of units of resource k processing activity i, i.e.,

$$|X_k(i)| = r_{ik} \quad (i \in V^a) \tag{5.4}$$

We call a schedule S *changeover-feasible* if for each resource $k \in \mathcal{R}^\rho$, mapping X_k can be chosen such that

$$\left.\begin{array}{l} S_j \geq S_i + p_i + \vartheta_{ij}^k \\ \text{or } S_i \geq S_j + p_j + \vartheta_{ji}^k \end{array}\right\} \quad (i, j \in V_k^a : i \neq j, \ X_k(i) \cap X_k(j) \neq \emptyset) \tag{5.5}$$

and

$$X_k(i) \subseteq \{1, \dots, R_k\} \quad (i \in V_k^a) \tag{5.6}$$

(5.5) says that if there is a unit of resource k processing both activities i and j, then activities i and j (including the possible changeover in between) must not overlap. (5.6) limits the availability of resource k to R_k units. Since all changeover times are nonnegative, a changeover-feasible schedule always observes the renewable-resource constraints (1.7).

In the following, we develop an equivalent characterization of the changeover-feasibility of schedules, which will serve as a basis for the solution method discussed later on and which draws from a model used by Nägler and Schönherr (1989) for solving time-resource and time-cost tradeoff problems. The underlying concepts go back to a model for aircraft scheduling presented in Lawler (1976), Sect. 4.9. A similar tanker scheduling problem has already been studied in an early paper by Dantzig and Fulkerson (1954). Let S be some schedule and let $k \in \mathcal{R}^\rho$ be a renewable resource. The analogue to schedule-induced strict order $\theta(S)$ introduced in Subsection 2.1.1 is the relation

$$\theta^k(S) := \{(i, j) \in V_k^a \times V_k^a \mid S_j \geq S_i + p_i + \vartheta_{ij}^k\}$$

Owing to the weak triangle inequality and because $p_i > 0$ for all $i \in V^a$, relation $\theta^k(S)$ is transitive and asymmetric and thus represents a strict order in set V_k^a. In contrast to the case without changeover times, however, $\theta^k(S)$ does not represent an interval order in general. We illustrate the latter statement by an example.

Example 5.1. Consider the schedule S depicted in Figure 5.1a and assume that the changeover times are $\vartheta_{12} = \vartheta_{34} = 0$ and $\vartheta_{14} = \vartheta_{32} = 1$. The strict order induced by schedule S is $\theta(S) = \{(1,2),(3,4)\}$, whose precedence graph $G(\theta(S)) = 2\mathbf{P}_2$ is shown in Figure 5.1b. Since a strict order θ is an interval order if and only if its precedence graph does not contain the parallel composition $2\mathbf{P}_2$ of two arcs as induced subgraph (see, e.g., Möhring 1984 or Trotter 1992, Sect. 3.8), $\theta(S)$ is not an interval order.

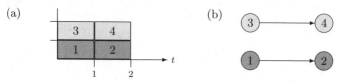

Fig. 5.1. Schedule-induced strict orders are no longer interval orders: **(a)** Gantt chart for schedule S; **(b)** precedence graph $G(\theta(S))$

Let for given schedule S and resource $k \in \mathcal{R}^\rho$, X_k be a mapping satisfying conditions (5.4) and (5.5) and let $r_k(S) := |\cup_{i \in V_k^a} X_k(i)|$ denote the number of resource units used. Clearly, S is changeover-feasible exactly if $r_k(S) \le R_k$ for all $k \in \mathcal{R}^\rho$. We consider an antichain U in schedule-induced strict order $\theta^k(S)$. It follows from the definition of $\theta^k(S)$ that $[S_i, S_i + p_i + \vartheta_{ij}^k[\cap [S_j, S_j + p_j + \vartheta_{ji}^k[\neq \emptyset$ for any two activities $i, j \in U$. (5.5) then implies that $X_k(i) \cap X_k(j) = \emptyset$ for any $i, j \in U$. This means that $|\cup_{i \in U} X_k(i)| = \sum_{i \in U} |X_k(i)| = \sum_{i \in U} r_{ik}$. On the other hand, it is obvious that for any subset $U' \subseteq V_k^a$, the number $|\cup_{i \in U'} X_k(i)|$ of resource units occupied by activities from U' is less than or equal to the joint requirements $\sum_{i \in U'} r_{ik}$ for resource k. Consequently, $r_k(S)$ equals the weight $\sum_{i \in U_k} r_{ik}$ of a maximum-weight antichain U_k in $\theta^k(S)$. Since all activities from set U_k pairwise overlap in time, U_k can be regarded as an *active set* $\mathcal{A}_k(S)$ for S. Schedule S is changeover-feasible precisely if none of the active sets $\mathcal{A}_k(S)$ with $k \in \mathcal{R}^\rho$ is forbidden.

Now recall that such a maximum-weight antichain U_k is a maximum-weight stable set in the precedence graph $G(\theta^k(S))$ equipped with node weights r_{ik} ($i \in V_k^a$). Since $G(\theta^k(S))$ is transitive, stable set U_k can be determined in $\mathcal{O}(n^3)$ time by computing a minimum (s,t)-flow u^k of value $\phi^k(u^k) = r_k(S)$ in the flow network $\overline{G}_k(\theta^k(S))$ with node set $V_k^a \cup \{s,t\}$ and arc set $\theta^k(S) \cup (\{s\} \times V_k^a) \cup (V_k^a \times \{t\})$, where nodes $i \in V_k^a$ are associated with lower capacities r_{ik} (cf. Subsection 2.1.1). Example 5.1 shows that strict order $\theta^k(S)$ generally does not represent an interval order, for which a maximum-weight stable set in the precedence graph can be found in linear time by computing a maximum-weight clique in the associated interval graph, cf. Golumbic (2004), Sects. 4.7 and 8.2.

The lower node capacities r_{ik} can be transformed into equivalent arc capacities by splitting up every node $i \in V_k^a$ into two nodes i' and i'' linked by arc (i', i'') with lower capacity $l_{i'i''} = r_{ik}$ and infinite upper capacity. The network flow methods then do not only provide a minimum (s, t)-flow u^k in $\overline{G}_k(\theta^k(S))$ but also a maximum (s, t)-cut $[U'_k, U''_k]$, whose capacity equals the minimum flow value $\phi(u^k)$ (see, e.g., Ahuja et al. 1993, Sect. 6.5). In addition, it can easily be shown that any maximum (s, t)-cut in $\overline{G}_k(\theta^k(S))$ is a uniformly directed cut containing only forward arcs. Thus, $\mathcal{A}_k(S) = \{i \in V^a_k \mid (i', i'') \in [U'_k, U''_k]\}$. As has already been noticed by Möhring (1985), Sect. 1.5, the computation of a maximum (s, t)-cut may also be performed in the transitive reduction of $\overline{G}_k(\theta^k(S))$ (i.e., in the network which arises from $\overline{G}_k(\theta^k(S))$ by replacing the arc set with its covering relation). In that case, any maximum (s, t)-cut $[U'_k, U''_k]$ contains only arcs (i', i'') obtained by splitting up some node $i \in V^a_k$, i.e., $\mathcal{A}_k(S) = \{i \in V^a_k \mid i' \in U'_k\}$.

To adapt the enumeration schemes for regular and convexifiable objective functions from Algorithms 3.1 and 3.3, respectively, to the occurrence of sequence-dependent changeover times, we make the following modifications. First, we replace the active sets $\mathcal{A}(S, t)$ at times t by active sets $\mathcal{A}_k(S)$. If for some $k \in \mathcal{R}^\rho$, $\mathcal{A}_k(S)$ is a forbidden set, we compute the set $\mathcal{B}$ of all minimal delaying alternatives B for $F = \mathcal{A}_k(S)$. In case of a regular objective function f, for given $B \in \mathcal{B}$ we then introduce the disjunctive precedence constraint

$$\min_{j \in B} S_j \geq \min_{i \in A}(S_i + p_i + \vartheta^k_{ij})$$

between sets $A = F \backslash B$ and B including the changeover times ϑ^k_{ij} on k between $i \in A$ and $j \in B$. If f is convexifiable and $\{i\} \times B$ is some minimal delaying mode with $B \in \mathcal{B}$ and $i \in A = F \backslash B$, we add ordinary precedence constraints

$$S_j \geq S_i + p_i + \vartheta^k_{ij} \quad (j \in B)$$

between activity i and all activities $j \in B$, again including the changeover times ϑ^k_{ij}.

5.3 Alternative Execution Modes for Activities

In practice an activity can often be carried out in one out of finitely many alternative execution modes with different processing times, time lags, and resource requirements. The multiple modes give rise to several types of tradeoffs permitting a more efficient use of resources. Sometimes the tradeoffs include the consumption of *nonrenewable resources* like the project budget. As for renewable resources, the availability of nonrenewable resources is limited. The availability of nonrenewable resources, however, does not refer to individual points in time but to the entire planning period. Each time an activity is carried out, the residual availability of a nonrenewable resource is decreased by the corresponding resource demand. Thus, nonrenewable resources can be viewed as special cumulative resources (cf. Section 1.3) that are depleted but never replenished. This implies that for nonrenewable resources, resource-feasibility solely depends on the selection of activity modes and not on the schedule. That is the reason why nonrenewable resources can be omitted when dealing with single-mode project scheduling problems.

Since the early 1980s, the (discrete) multi-mode project duration problem with precedence constraints among the activities instead of general temporal constraints has been treated by several authors. The case of resource-resource tradeoffs has already been considered by Elmaghraby (1977), Sect. 3.4.2. Exact algorithms have been reviewed and their performance has been tested by Hartmann and Drexl (1998). At present, the most efficient method for solving this problem is the branch-and-bound algorithm of Sprecher and Drexl (1998). Hartmann (1999*b*), Sect. 7.3, has compared several heuristic approaches. An experimental performance analysis presented in the latter reference reveals that among the tested heuristics, the best procedure is a genetic algorithm published in Hartmann (2001). A special case of the multi-mode project duration problem has been studied by Demeulemeester et al. (2000), who have developed a branch-and-bound algorithm for the discrete time-resource trade-off problem. For each real activity, a workload for a single renewable resource is specified. The alternative execution modes arise from all undominated integral duration-requirement combinations the product of which is at least equal to the given workload.

For the case of general temporal constraints, four different algorithms have been proposed in literature. The tabu search procedure by De Reyck and Herroelen (1999) performs a local search in the set of possible mode assignments to activities. For given execution modes, the resulting single-mode problem is then solved by the branch-and-bound algorithm of De Reyck and Herroelen (1998*a*). Franck (1999), Sect. 7.2, has adapted a priority-rule method by Kolisch (1995), Sect. 6.2, to the case of general temporal constraints. At each iteration, the activity to be scheduled is chosen on the basis of a first priority rule. A second priority rule provides the execution mode for the selected activity. A streamlined multi-pass version of this procedure can be found in Heilmann (2001). Dorndorf (2002), Ch. 6, has described an extension of the branch-and-bound algorithm by Dorndorf et al. (2000*c*) for the single-mode project duration problem (cf. Subsection 3.1.4) to the multi-mode case, where mode assignment and activity scheduling are iterated alternately. Brucker and Knust (2003) have presented an adaptation of their lower bound for the single-mode problem (see Subsection 3.1.3) to the presence of multiple execution modes. The corresponding linear program is again solved by column-generation techniques.

In this section we discuss the enumeration scheme of a branch-and-bound procedure proposed by Heilmann (2003) for the multi-mode project duration problem, where the selection of activity modes and the allocation of resources are performed in parallel. The basic principle of this relaxation-based enumeration scheme can be used for solving multi-mode resource-constrained project scheduling problems with arbitrary regular or convexifiable objective functions. Roughly speaking, the idea is to consider single-mode problems arising from *mode relaxations* where only the unavoidable resource requirements, core durations, and core time lags occurring in all selectable execution modes are taken into account. The mode relaxations are stepwise refined by assigning execution modes to activities and thus reducing the sets of selectable modes. For what follows, we assume that only the requirements for renewable and nonrenewable resources depend on the mode selection. The case where execution modes also differ in requirements for cumulative resources can be treated similarly (see Trautmann 2001a, Sect. 3.1).

A discrete multi-mode resource allocation problem decomposes into two subproblems: the discrete *mode assignment problem* and the (single-mode) *resource allocation problem*. Let $\mathcal{M}_i$ denote the set of alternative execution modes for activity $i \in V$, where $|\mathcal{M}_i| = 1$ if $i \in V^e$. We call a binary vector $\underline{x} = (\underline{x}_{im_i})_{i \in V, m_i \in \mathcal{M}_i}$ with $\sum_{m_i \in \mathcal{M}_i} \underline{x}_{im_i} \leq 1$ a (partial) assignment of modes $m_i \in \mathcal{M}_i$ to activities $i \in V$ (an *assignment*, for short), where $\underline{x}_{im_i} = 1$ if activity i is carried out in mode m_i and $x_{im_i} = 0$, otherwise. An assignment $x' > \underline{x}$ is called an extension of $\underline{x}$. An assignment x satisfying the *mode assignment constraints*

$$\sum_{m_i \in \mathcal{M}_i} x_{im_i} = 1 \quad (i \in V) \tag{5.7}$$

is termed a *full assignment*. Solving the mode assignment problem consists in finding a full assignment x such that x complies with the temporal and nonrenewable-resource constraints. Each assignment $\underline{x}$ defines a corresponding single-mode resource allocation problem.

Now let

$$\mathcal{M}_i(\underline{x}) := \left\{ \begin{array}{l} \mathcal{M}_i, \text{ if } \sum_{m_i \in \mathcal{M}_i} \underline{x}_{im_i} = 0 \\ \{m_i\} \text{ with } \underline{x}_{im_i} = 1, \text{ otherwise} \end{array} \right.$$

be the set of modes that can be selected for activity i in full-assignment extensions $x \geq \underline{x}$ and let $\mathcal{R}^\nu$ be the set of nonrenewable resources with availabilities $R_k \in \mathbb{N}$. By $r_{ikm_i} \in \mathbb{Z}_{\geq 0}$ we denote the requirement for resource $k \in \mathcal{R}^\rho \cup \mathcal{R}^\nu$ if real activity $i \in V^a$ is executed in mode $m_i \in \mathcal{M}_i$. Then

$$r_{ik}(\underline{x}) := \min_{m_i \in \mathcal{M}_i(\underline{x})} r_{ikm_i}$$

is the (unavoidable) requirement of activity $i \in V^a$ for resource $k \in \mathcal{R}^\rho \cup \mathcal{R}^\nu$ given assignment $\underline{x}$. Assignment $\underline{x}$ is called resource-feasible if $\underline{x}$ satisfies the nonrenewable-resource constraints

$$\sum_{i \in V^a} r_{ik}(\underline{x}) \leq R_k \quad (k \in \mathcal{R}^\nu) \tag{5.8}$$

Alternative assignments $\underline{x}$ are associated with different single-mode project networks $N(\underline{x})$. Without loss of generality, we assume that the node set V and the arc set E of $N(\underline{x})$ are the same for all assignments $\underline{x}$. For each arc

$(i, j) \in E$, the associated time lag may depend on the execution modes of both activities i and j. Hence, the weight of an arc $(i, j) \in E$ in the multi-mode project network N is a matrix $\delta_{ij} = (\delta_{im_i jm_j})_{m_i \in \mathcal{M}_i, m_j \in \mathcal{M}_j}$, where the elements $\delta_{im_i jm_j} \in \mathbb{Z}$ denote the scalar arc weights that refer to the execution of activities i and j in modes $m_i \in \mathcal{M}_i$ and $m_j \in \mathcal{M}_j$. For assignment $\underline{x}$,

$$\delta_{ij}(\underline{x}) := \min_{m_i \in \mathcal{M}_i(\underline{x})} \min_{m_j \in \mathcal{M}_j(\underline{x})} \delta_{im_i jm_j}$$

is the resulting (core) weight of arc (i, j) in network $N(\underline{x})$. An assignment $\underline{x}$ is called time-feasible if $N(\underline{x})$ does not contain any cycle of positive length. A time- and resource-feasible assignment is referred to as a feasible assignment. A schedule S is said to be time-feasible with respect to assignment $\underline{x}$ if S satisfies the temporal constraints

$$S_j - S_i \geq \delta_{ij}(\underline{x}) \quad ((i, j) \in E) \tag{5.9}$$

The set of schedules which are time-feasible with respect to assignment $\underline{x}$ are denoted by $\mathcal{S}_T(\underline{x})$

Define $p_{im_i} \in \mathbb{N}$ to be the processing time if real activity $i \in V^a$ is executed in mode $m_i \in \mathcal{M}_i$. The (core) duration of activity $i \in V$ given assignment $\underline{x}$ is

$$p_i(\underline{x}) := \min_{m_i \in \mathcal{M}_i(\underline{x})} p_{im_i}$$

For schedule S, the set of real activities being in progress at time t then equals $\mathcal{A}(S, \underline{x}, t) := \{i \in V^a \mid S_i \leq t < S_i + p_i(\underline{x})\}$ and $r_k(S, \underline{x}, t) := \sum_{i \in \mathcal{A}(S, \underline{x}, t)} r_{ik}(\underline{x})$ is the demand for resource $k \in \mathcal{R}^\rho$ at time t. A schedule S which satisfies the renewable-resource constraints

$$r_k(S, \underline{x}, t) \leq R_k \quad (k \in \mathcal{R}^\rho, \ 0 \leq t \leq \overline{d}) \tag{5.10}$$

as well as the cumulative-resource constraints (1.20) is called resource-feasible with respect to assignment $\underline{x}$. By $\mathcal{S}_R(\underline{x})$ we denote the set of all schedules satisfying (5.10). Recall that the resource-feasibility of an assignment $\underline{x}$ requires that the nonrenewable-resource constraints (5.8) are fulfilled. A schedule that is time- and resource-feasible with respect to assignment $\underline{x}$ is termed feasible with respect to $\underline{x}$. $\mathcal{S}(\underline{x}) = \mathcal{S}_T(\underline{x}) \cap \mathcal{S}_R(\underline{x}) \cap \mathcal{S}_C$ is the set of all feasible schedules with respect to $\underline{x}$. The multi-mode resource-constrained project scheduling problem can now be stated as follows:

$$
\left.
\begin{array}{ll}
\text{Minimize} & f(S) \\
\text{subject to} & \displaystyle\sum_{m_i \in \mathcal{M}_i} x_{im_i} = 1 \qquad (i \in V) \\
& x_{im_i} \in \{0, 1\} \qquad (i \in V, \ m_i \in \mathcal{M}_i) \\
& S \in \mathcal{S}_T(x) \cap \mathcal{S}_R(x) \cap \mathcal{S}_C
\end{array}
\right\} \text{(MP)}
$$

A feasible solution to problem (MP) consists in a schedule-assignment pair (S, x), where x is a feasible full assignment (i.e., a solution to the mode-assignment problem) and S is a feasible schedule with respect to x (i.e., a feasible solution to the respective single-mode project scheduling problem). An optimal solution is a feasible solution (S, x) with minimum objective function value $f(S)$.

From Theorem 1.12 it immediately follows that finding a feasible solution (S, x) is NP-hard. In addition, Kolisch (1995), Sect. 2.3, and Schwindt (1998b) have shown by transformations from KNAPSACK and PRECEDENCE-CONSTRAINED KNAPSACK, respectively, that the problems of testing whether there is a resource-feasible or a time-feasible full mode assignment x are already NP-complete. Consequently, the resource relaxation of a multi-mode resource allocation problem is NP-hard. Hence, to obtain a problem that can be solved efficiently, the mode assignment constraints (5.7) have to be relaxed as well. The *mode relaxation* for an assignment $\underline{x}$ then reads

$$\left. \begin{array}{ll} \text{Minimize} & f(S) \\ \text{subject to} & \mathcal{S}_T(\underline{x}) \cap \mathcal{S}_R(\underline{x}) \cap \mathcal{S}_C \end{array} \right\} \quad (\text{P}(\underline{x}))$$

Obviously, the single-mode resource-constrained project scheduling problem $(\text{P}(\underline{x}))$ is a relaxation of all mode relaxations $(\text{P}(\underline{x}'))$ belonging to extensions $\underline{x}'$ of $\underline{x}$, i.e.,

$$\mathcal{S}(\underline{x}') \subseteq \mathcal{S}(\underline{x}) \quad (\underline{x}' \geq \underline{x})$$

This observation is the starting point for a relaxation-based enumeration scheme for solving multi-mode problem (MP). Let ρ be some relation in node set V, and let $\mathcal{S}_T(\rho, \underline{x}) := \{S \in \mathcal{S}_T(\underline{x}) \mid S_j \geq S_i + p_i(\underline{x}) \text{ for all } (i, j) \in \rho\}$ be the relation polytope belonging to ρ and assignment $\underline{x}$. The algorithm starts with the empty assignment $\underline{x} = 0$. For the corresponding single-mode problem $(\text{P}(\underline{x}))$, schedules are enumerated as minimal points of appropriate (unions of) relation polytopes $\mathcal{S}_T(\rho, \underline{x})$, see Algorithms 3.1 and 3.3. Each time a schedule S feasible with respect to $\underline{x}$ has been obtained, the execution mode of some activity i with $\sum_{m_i \in \mathcal{M}_i} \underline{x}_{im_i} = 0$ is fixed such that the resulting assignment $\underline{x}'$ is still feasible (if there is no mode $m_i \in \mathcal{M}_i$ such that $\underline{x}'$ is feasible, we perform backtracking). Then, the time-feasibility of S with respect to the new assignment $\underline{x}'$ is restored. Due to $\mathcal{S}(\underline{x}') \subseteq \mathcal{S}(\underline{x})$, S may be not resource-feasible with respect to $\underline{x}'$. In that case, the enumeration of schedules is resumed by extending the current relation ρ until a schedule S' which is feasible with respect to $\underline{x}'$ has been found. These steps are reiterated until a feasible full assignment x has been reached or there is no feasible extension of the current assignment $\underline{x}'$.

5.4 Continuous Cumulative Resources

In this section we deal with continuous cumulative resources whose inventory is depleted and replenished at constant rates by the activities of the project. This type of resources has been considered by Schwindt (2002) and Neumann et al. (2005) in the context of scheduling problems arising in the process industries. Recently, Sourd and Rogerie (2005) have presented constraint propagation techniques for computing lower and upper approximations to the loading profiles of continuous cumulative resources.

The concept of continuous cumulative resources also covers the renewable and (discrete) cumulative resources, which we have considered until now. For the case of convex objective functions f, we show how the expanded resource-constrained project scheduling problem can be solved by using a relaxation-based approach. The basic principle is again to substitute the resource constraints into a finite disjunction of linear inequalities, which can be viewed as parameterized precedence constraints between activities.

Let $\widetilde{\mathcal{R}}^\gamma$ be the set of continuous cumulative resources with safety stocks $\underline{R}_k \in \mathbb{Z} \cup \{-\infty\}$ and storage capacities $\overline{R}_k \in \mathbb{Z} \cup \{\infty\}$, where $\overline{R}_k \geq \underline{R}_k$. Performing an activity $i \in V$ increases the inventory in resource $k \in \widetilde{\mathcal{R}}^\gamma$ by $r_{ik} \in \mathbb{Z}$ units. Analogously to the case of discrete cumulative resources, we suppose that $\underline{R}_k \leq \sum_{i \in V} r_{ik} \leq \overline{R}_k$ for all $k \in \widetilde{\mathcal{R}}^\gamma$, which ensures that the terminal inventories are within the prescribed bounds. If $r_{ik} < 0$, we again speak of a depletion of resource k, and if $r_{ik} > 0$, we say that resource k is replenished. Depletion and replenishments arise at constant rates $\dot{r}_{ik} = r_{ik}/p_i$. This means that events $i \in V^e$ deplete and replenish at infinite rates, which corresponds to the setting for discrete cumulative resources. Since renewable-resource constraints can be expressed by temporal and discrete cumulative-resource constraints, the new model also includes both types of resource constraints that have been studied previously. By V_k^- and V_k^+ we respectively denote the sets of activities depleting or replenishing resource k. $V_k := V_k^- \cup V_k^+$ is the set of all depleting and replenishing activities for resource k. The resource constraints again say that at any point in time, the inventory level of each resource must be between the safety stock and the storage capacity.

Now let S be some schedule. By

$$x_i(S,t) := \begin{cases} 0, & \text{if } t < S_i \\ 1, & \text{if } t \geq S_i + p_i \\ (t - S_i)/p_i, & \text{otherwise} \end{cases}$$

we denote the portion of activity $i \in V$ that has been processed by time t. If $i \in V^e$, then $x_i(S,t) = 0$ if $S_i < t$, and $x_i(S,t) = 1$, otherwise. The inventory in resource $k \in \widetilde{\mathcal{R}}^\gamma$ at time t is

$$\widetilde{r}_k(S,t) := \sum_{i \in V} r_{ik} x_i(S,t)$$

The corresponding loading profile $\widetilde{r}_k(S, \cdot)$ is a right-continuous, piecewise affine function. The resource constraints can be stated as

$$\underline{R}_k \leq \widetilde{r}_k(S,t) \leq \overline{R}_k \quad (k \in \widetilde{\mathcal{R}}^\gamma,\ 0 \leq t \leq \overline{d}) \tag{5.11}$$

A schedule satisfying resource constraints (5.11) is called resource-feasible. Let $\widetilde{\mathcal{S}}_C$ denote the set of resource-feasible schedules. The set of all feasible schedules is $\mathcal{S} = \mathcal{S}_T \cap \widetilde{\mathcal{S}}_C$. The resource-constrained project scheduling problem to be dealt with reads as follows:

$$\left.\begin{array}{ll} \text{Minimize} & f(S) \\ \text{subject to} & S \in \mathcal{S}_T \cap \widetilde{\mathcal{S}}_C \end{array}\right\} \quad (\widetilde{\text{P}})$$

where f is some convex objective function. An optimal schedule is a schedule S solving problem $(\widetilde{\text{P}})$.

Next, we explain the basic principle of the solution procedure. For simplicity of exposition we assume for the moment that $V_k \subseteq V^a$ for all $k \in \widetilde{\mathcal{R}}^\gamma$. Similarly to the relaxation-based algorithms from Chapter 3, we first delete the resource constraints and solve the resulting time-constrained project scheduling problem. Subsequently, resource conflicts are stepwise sorted out by refining the relaxation with new constraints. For notational convenience we suppose that all storage capacities are infinite. This can always be ensured by the following transformation (cf. Remark 1.21a). For each resource $k \in \widetilde{\mathcal{R}}^\gamma$, we set $\overline{R}_k := \infty$ and add a fictitious resource k' with requirements $r_{ik'} = -r_{ik}$ for all $i \in V_k$, safety stock $\underline{R}_{k'} = -\overline{R}_k$, and storage capacity $\overline{R}_{k'} = \infty$.

Let S be an optimal solution to the resource relaxation and assume that at time t, the inventory in some resource $k \in \widetilde{\mathcal{R}}^\gamma$ falls below the safety stock, i.e., $\widetilde{r}_k(S, t) < \underline{R}_k$. We partition V_k into two sets A and B with the following meaning. Set A contains all activities $j \in V_k^-$ to be completed by time t and all activities $j \in V_k^+$ to be started no earlier than at time t:

$$\left.\begin{array}{ll} S_j \leq t - p_j & (j \in A \cap V_k^-) \\ S_j \geq t & (j \in A \cap V_k^+) \end{array}\right\} \quad (5.12)$$

The total depletion of the inventory in resource k at time t caused by activities $j \in A$ equals $-\sum_{j \in A \cap V_k^-} r_{jk}$. The activities j from set B must be scheduled in such a way that at time t, their net replenishment of resource k is greater than or equal to the shortfall $\underline{R}_k - \sum_{j \in A \cap V_k^-} r_{jk}$ caused by the activities from set A. This can be ensured as follows. For each activity $j \in B$, we introduce a continuous decision variable x_j with

$$0 \leq x_j \leq 1 \quad (j \in B) \tag{5.13}$$

providing the portion of activity j that will be processed by time t. The requirement that the inventory in resource k at time t must not fall below $\underline{R}_k$ then reads

$$\sum_{j \in B} r_{jk} x_j \geq \underline{R}_k - \sum_{j \in A \cap V_k^-} r_{jk} \tag{5.14}$$

The coupling between decision variables x_j and S_j is achieved by the temporal constraints (parameterized in x_j)

$$\left.\begin{array}{ll} S_j \geq t - p_j x_j & (j \in B \cap V_k^-) \\ S_j \leq t - p_j x_j & (j \in B \cap V_k^+) \end{array}\right\} \tag{5.15}$$

Inequalities (5.15) ensure that for each schedule S satisfying (5.15) it holds that $x_j \geq x_j(S,t)$ if activity $j \in B$ depletes and $x_j \leq x_j(S,t)$ if activity $j \in B$ replenishes the stock of k. Adding constraints (5.12) to (5.15) to the relaxation removes the inventory shortage at time t.

The inventory in resource k attains its minimum at a point in time when some replenishing activity i is started or when some depleting activity i is completed. That is why time t can always be chosen to be equal to S_i for some $i \in V_k^+$ or equal to $S_i + p_i$ for some $i \in V_k^-$, and thus we can replace t in (5.12) and (5.15) by S_i or $S_i + p_i$. We then write A^{ik} and B^{ik} instead of A and B as well as x_j^{ik} instead of x_j. Note that without loss of generality we can assume $i \in A^{ik}$ for all $k \in \widetilde{\mathcal{R}}^\gamma$ and all $i \in V_k$ because the corresponding inequality (5.12) is always satisfied. Passing from constants t to variables S_i ensures that only a finite number of constraints have to be introduced before the resource constraints (5.11) are satisfied.

From the above reasoning it follows that $\widetilde{\mathcal{S}}_C$ again represents the union of finitely many polyhedra. The set of all minimal points of $\widetilde{\mathcal{S}}_C$, however, is generally uncountable, which implies that the set $\mathcal{AS}$ of all active schedules is infinite (and hence so are all of its supersets depicted in Figure 2.4).

The solution procedure is now as follows. We solve the convex program

$$\left.\begin{array}{ll} \text{Minimize} & f(S) \\ \text{subject to} & S \in \mathcal{S}_T \\ & \text{(5.12) to (5.15) for partitions } \{A^{ik}, B^{ik}\} \text{ selected} \end{array}\right\} \tag{5.16}$$

and add new constraints of type (5.12) to (5.15) to problem (5.16) until either the search space $\mathcal{P}$ becomes void or the resulting schedule S is feasible. Then, we return to an alternative partition $\{A^{ik}, B^{ik}\}$ and proceed until all alternatives have been investigated. Convex program (5.16) can be solved in polynomial time because its feasible region $\mathcal{P}$ represents a polytope. Of course, the objective function value of any optimal solution to (5.16) represents a lower bound on the objective function value $f(S)$ of any feasible schedule S satisfying the added constraints of type (5.12) to (5.15).

Next we discuss some implementation issues. Assume that the inventory in some resource $k \in \widetilde{\mathcal{R}}^\gamma$ falls below the safety stock at time $t = S_i$ ($i \in V_k^+$) or $t = S_i + p_i$ ($i \in V_k^-$). To enumerate the sets A^{ik} and B^{ik} we construct a binary tree as follows. Each level of the tree belongs to one activity $j \in V_k$. For each activity j we branch over the alternatives $j \in A^{ik}$ and $j \in B^{ik}$ and add the corresponding constraints (5.12) or (5.13), (5.15), as well as for both alternatives the relaxation

$$\sum_{j \in B^{ik}} r_{jk} x_j^{ik} \geq \underline{R}_k - \sum_{j \in A^{ik} \cap V_k^-} r_{jk} - \sum_{j \in V_k^+ \setminus (A^{ik} \cup B^{ik})} r_{jk}$$

of constraint (5.14) to the convex program (5.16). Each leaf of the tree corresponds to one distinct partition $\{A^{ik}, B^{ik}\}$. We can stop the enumeration for activity i as soon as the inventory shortage at time S_i or $S_i + p_i$ is settled, even if $A^{ik} \cup B^{ik} \subset V_k$. In the latter case, it may be necessary to resume the branching later on if the shortage reappears while dealing with other resource conflicts. Since for each resource $k \in \widetilde{\mathcal{R}}^\gamma$ and each activity $i \in V_k$, the construction of the corresponding sets A^{ik} and B^{ik} requires at most $|V_k|$ steps, the height of the branch-and-bound tree is of order $\mathcal{O}(|\widetilde{\mathcal{R}}^\gamma| n^2)$.

The computational effort can be reduced considerably by testing whether the search space $\mathcal{P}$ has become void before solving convex program (5.16). Let $\widetilde{d}_{ij}$ be the minimum time lag between activities i and j that is implied by the prescribed temporal constraints, inequalities (5.12), and inequalities (5.15) where x_j^{ik} is set to be equal to 1 if $j \in V_k^-$ and equal to 0, otherwise. Assume that for some activity $j \in V_k$ the addition to set A^{ik} or B^{ik} leads to a new temporal constraint $S_j - S_i \geq \delta_{ij}$. Then $\mathcal{P} = \emptyset$ if $\delta_{ij} + \widetilde{d}_{ji} > 0$. In that case, the alternative set B^{ik} or A^{ik}, respectively, can immediately be selected for activity j.

Now let (S, x) be an optimal solution to (5.16) such that schedule S is feasible. We then obtain a feasible schedule S' with $f(S') \leq f(S)$ by

(a) moving all activities $j \in V_k$ from A^{ik} to B^{ik} for which (5.12) is active,
(b) moving all activities $j \in V_k^-$ from B^{ik} to A^{ik} for which $x_j^{ik} = 1$, and
(c) moving all activities $j \in V_k^+$ from B^{ik} to A^{ik} for which $x_j^{ik} = 0$

and solving convex program (5.16) again. Based on this dominance rule, feasible solutions belonging to leaves of the enumeration tree can be improved and thus the current upper bounds can be decreased by performing the above transformations (a) to (c).

Eventually, we consider the general case including discrete depletions and replenishments at the occurrence times of events. For events $j \in B \cap V^e$ decision variable x_j can be fixed to 0 if $j \in V_k^-$ and to 1 if $j \in V_k^+$ because $p_j = 0$ (compare (5.15)). If activity i with $t = S_i$ or $t = S_i + p_i$ is chosen to be an event, then i must deplete the stock of resource k. Moreover, for an event $j \in B \cap V_k^-$ it may happen that $S_j = t$ though $x_j = 0$, i.e., $x_j < x_j(S, t)$. As a consequence, the shortage at time t may persist after having introduced constraints (5.12) to (5.15), in which case we perform backtracking. If problem $(\widetilde{P})$ is solvable, the enumeration tree contains alternative partitions removing the shortage.

6

Applications

The present chapter is concerned with applications of the concepts developed in Chapters 1 to 5 to production planning problems in the manufacturing and process industries, to the evaluation of investment projects, and to resource allocation problems that are subject to different kinds of uncertainty.

In Section 6.1 we discuss how scheduling problems arising in make-to-order assembly environments can be modelled as resource-constrained project scheduling problems. For different product structures, we consider the definition of appropriate minimum and maximum time lags ensuring a non-preemptive execution of overlapping operations.

Section 6.2 is devoted to a hierarchical three-stage approach to small-batch production planning using resource allocation methods from project management. The approach comprises the master production scheduling, multi-level lot sizing, and temporal plus capacity planning stages. At all levels, the scarcity of resources is taken into account, which differentiates this approach from most production planning and control systems used in practice. The lacking integration of capacity aspects is the essential reason for the generally poor performance of the latter systems.

When scheduling batch plants in the process industries, a variety of technological peculiarities have to be taken into account. In contrast to manufacturing, the batch processing times are mostly independent of the batch size and the intermediate products must be stocked in dedicated storage facilities. In addition, intermediate products may be perishable and to guarantee the purity of output products, the processing units have to be cleaned between the execution of certain operations. In Section 6.3 we deal with a two-phase method for production scheduling in the process industries, which decomposes the problem into a batching and a batch scheduling problem. For given primary requirements, the batching phase provides the numbers and sizes of the batches to be produced. Subsequently, the batches are scheduled on the processing units in the batch scheduling phase. The batching problem can be formulated as a mixed-integer linear program of polynomial size. By using the concepts of renewable and cumulative resources in combination with the supplements from Chapter 5, the batch scheduling problem can be modelled as a resource-constrained project scheduling problem.

In practice, it is customary to evaluate investment projects based on the net present value criterion. The maximum net present value of a time-constrained investment project can, e.g., be computed by using the steepest descent method for convexifiable objective functions discussed in Chapter 3. In literature, however, it is commonly accepted that often the discount rate to be applied (i.e., the required rate of return) cannot be determined with sufficient accuracy. Moreover, the project deadline may be subject to negotiations between the investor and his customers. In Section 6.4 we show how using the steepest descent approach, the project net present value can be represented as a function of the discount rate and project deadline. On the basis of this function, investment projects with uncertain discount rate can be evaluated for a variable project deadline.

Throughout our previous discussion we have supposed that data such as activity durations, time lags, and resource requirements are deterministic quantities. Clearly, this is a simplifying assumption, which nevertheless is justified in many cases when the project data can be forecast reliably and small deviations from schedule do not seriously affect the execution of the project. Sometimes, however, the latter conditions are not met, in particular when coping with long-term projects like in the building industry or with production scheduling problems where machines and equipment may be subject to disruption. It is then expedient to take uncertainty into account already when scheduling the project or to adapt the schedule in a suitable fashion during its implementation. In Section 6.5 we propose two deterministic strategies for coping with uncertainty in project management. The anticipative approach consists in scheduling the project in a way that the impact of perturbations is minimized. Alternatively or additionally, one may use a reactive approach, where the project is rescheduled after each disruption and the objective is to minimize the changes with respect to the previous schedule.

6.1 Make-to-Order Production Scheduling

We consider the processing of a given set of customer orders in a multi-level make-to-order manufacturing environment, where no inventories are built up for future sale. At first, we recall some basic concepts from materials requirements planning (see, e.g., Nahmias 1997, Sect. 6.1). We assume that each final product consists of several subassemblies, which in turn may contain several components from lower production levels. Let P^f be the set of all final products ordered and let P be the set of all (intermediate or final) products l under consideration. Generally speaking, the product structure of a firm can be represented as a *gozinto graph* $G = (P, A, a)$ with node set P. Arc set A contains an arc (l, l') weighted by *input coefficient* $a_{ll'} \in \mathbb{N}$ if $a_{ll'}$ units of product l are directly installed into one unit of product l'. P^f coincides with the set of all sinks of G.

Now let $x_l \in \mathbb{Z}_{\geq 0}$ denote the gross requirements for products $l \in P$. The gross requirements x_l for final products $l \in P^f$ are equal to the primary requirements d_l given by the customer orders. The gross requirements x_l for intermediate products l can easily be obtained by a *bill of materials explosion*, i.e., by solving the system of linear equations $x_l = d_l + \sum_{(l,l') \in A} a_{ll'} x_{l'}$ $(l \in P)$. Since there are no stocks available, the gross requirements x_l coincide with the amounts q_l of products l to be manufactured.

Each product $l \in P$ must be processed on machines of different types k in a prescribed order, which is given by the *process plan* of product l. Several identical machines of each type k (k-machines, for short) may be available. The processing of a batch of product l on a k-machine is referred to as an *operation*, which is denoted by kl. The execution of operation kl requires a (sequence-independent) *setup time* ϑ_{kl} during which the machine is occupied. For what follows we assume that no items of product l are needed for installing the machine. In addition, we suppose that the production is performed according to a *single-lot strategy*, i.e., all units of a product are processed in one batch of size x_l. The latter assumption is generally met in make-to-order production since each product is manufactured in response to a customer order, and splitting the batches would incur additional setup times without saving considerable holding cost. Hence, the *processing time* of operation kl is

$$p_{kl} = \vartheta_{kl} + x_l u_{kl} \tag{6.1}$$

where $u_{kl} \in \mathbb{N}$ is the unit processing time needed for producing one item of product l on a k-machine.

The make-to-order production scheduling problem consists in finding an operation schedule such that no two operations overlap in time on a machine, the operation sequences given by the process plans are observed, a sufficient amount of input products is available during the execution of each operation, and some objective function (e.g., the makespan) is minimized. In the following, we show how the production scheduling problem can be modelled as a resource-constrained project scheduling problem with renewable and cumulative resources. The model is based on the previous work by Günther (1992) and Neumann and Schwindt (1997).

For each operation kl we introduce one real activity, also denoted by kl, whose duration p_{kl} is given by (6.1). A machine type k is identified with a renewable resource $k \in \mathcal{R}^\rho$. Resource capacity R_k equals the number of k-machines available. Each activity kl requires one unit of resource k.

Project network N is obtained by exploding each node $l \in P$ of gozinto graph G into the respective (directed) path from the initial operation kl to the terminal operation $k'l$ in the process plan of product l (see Figure 6.1). The arcs $(l, l') \in A$ are then replaced by arcs $(k'l, k''l')$ linking the terminal operation $k'l$ of l with the initial operation $k''l'$ of l'. Moreover, all initial operations of products at the lowest production level are connected with the project beginning event 0, and the terminal operations of the final products are connected with the project termination event $n+1$. Finally, backward arc $(n+1, 0)$ is added.

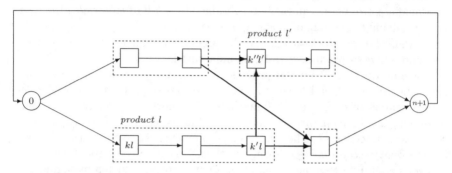

Fig. 6.1. Project network without arc weights arising from gozinto graph

We proceed by assigning weights $\delta_{kl,k'l'}$ to the arcs $(kl, k'l')$ of N. The arcs emanating from node 0 are weighted with 0 and the arcs terminating at node $n+1$ are weighted with the duration of the respective initial node. The weight $\delta_{n+1,0} = -\overline{d}$ is chosen to be the negative maximum makespan allowed. Now let kl and $k'l$ be two consecutive operations in the process plan of product l. At first, we consider the case where $u_{kl} \leq u_{k'l}$, which is depicted in Figure 6.2. Clearly, we may start the execution of operation $k'l$ when the preceding operation kl has been completed. From Figure 6.2 it can be seen, however, that much time can be saved if we allow for *overlapping operations*. The processing of the first item of product l on the k'-machine can then be started as soon as the first item on the k-machine has been completed without causing any idle time on the k'-machine. Hence, instead of adding a precedence constraint between kl and $k'l$, we introduce a time lag of $\delta_{kl,k'l} = \vartheta_{kl} + u_{kl} - \vartheta_{k'l} < p_{kl}$ units of time between the starts of operations kl and $k'l$. The time lag ensures that at any point in time where $k'l$ is in progress, a sufficient amount of product l has already been processed on the k-machine. Note that, as shown in Figure 6.2, time lag $\delta_{kl,k'l}$ may even become negative, in which case we have a maximum time lag of $-\delta_{kl,k'l}$ units of time between operations $k'l$ and kl.

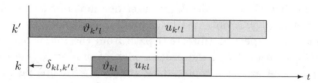

Fig. 6.2. Overlapping operations kl and $k'l$ with $u_{kl} \leq u_{k'l}$

The case where $u_{kl} > u_{k'l}$ is illustrated in Figure 6.3. Here, starting operation $k'l$ at the completion of the first item of product l on the k-machine would mean that after the processing of the first item on the k'-machine, the required second item from the k-machine is not finished. Thus, we synchronize both operations in a way that the *last* item on the k'-machine is processed after the completion of operation kl, i.e., $\delta_{kl,k'l} = \vartheta_{kl} + x_l u_{kl} - (x_l - 1)u_{k'l} - \vartheta_{k'l}$.

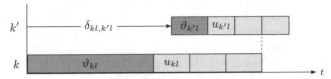

Fig. 6.3. Overlapping operations kl and $k'l$ with $u_{kl} > u_{k'l}$

In sum, between two consecutive operations kl and $k'l$ belonging to one and the same product $l \in P$, we introduce the time lag

$$\delta_{kl,k'l} = \begin{cases} \vartheta_{kl} + u_{kl} - \vartheta_{k'l}, & \text{if } u_{kl} \leq u_{k'l} \\ \vartheta_{kl} + x_l u_{kl} - (x_l - 1)u_{k'l} - \vartheta_{k'l}, & \text{otherwise} \end{cases} \qquad (6.2)$$

which is the smallest lapse of time that guarantees that operation $k'l$ need not be interrupted because no items are available.

In practice, it is often expedient to transfer items in batches from one machine to another. The *transportation lot size* $y_l \in \mathbb{N}$ for product $l \in P$ is then specified by the size of pallets or containers used for the transport of l. In addition, we suppose all machines of a given type k to be grouped in a k-shop, where $t_{kk'} \in \mathbb{Z}_{\geq 0}$ denotes the *transfer time* from the k- to the k'-shop (implicitly, we have supposed until now that $y_l = 1$ and $t_{kk'} = 0$ for all products l and all machine types k, k'). Formula (6.2) can easily be adapted to the case of general transportation lot sizes and transfer times by noting that the items now arrive at the k'-shop in transfer batches of size y_l. If $u_{kl} \leq u_{k'l}$, this means that the first batch is conveyed $\vartheta_{kl} + y_l u_{kl}$ units of time after the start of kl, whereas for $u_{kl} > u_{k'l}$, y_l items of product l remain to be processed on the k'-machine after the completion of kl. In both cases, the respective transfer time $t_{kk'}$ must be included. We then obtain the following formula for the time lag $\delta_{kl,k'l}$ between consecutive operations:

$$\delta_{kl,k'l} = \begin{cases} \vartheta_{kl} + y_l u_{kl} - \vartheta_{k'l} + t_{kk'}, & \text{if } u_{kl} \leq u_{k'l} \\ \vartheta_{kl} + x_l u_{kl} - (x_l - y_l)u_{k'l} - \vartheta_{k'l} + t_{kk'}, & \text{otherwise} \end{cases} \qquad (6.3)$$

Note that $y_l = x_l$ corresponds to nonoverlapping product processing, where (6.3) provides the same value for both cases $u_{kl} \leq u_{k'l}$ and $u_{kl} > u_{k'l}$.

Next, we consider the transition from the terminal operation kl in the process plan of a product l to the initial operation $k'l'$ in the process plan of a succeeding product l' with $(l, l') \in A$. We assume that l' is the only product containing items of product l. In particular, the latter assumption is always fulfilled if the product structure is linear or convergent, i.e., if the gozinto graph G is an intree. The case of *common parts*, which are installed into different products l', is studied below. To simplify writing, we establish the convention that $y_l / a_{ll'}$ is integral, which means that all items of product l needed for the production of one unit of product l' are transferred at the same time. The first item of product l' cannot be processed before $a_{ll'}$ items of product l have been completed on the k-machine. If the time $a_{ll'} u_{kl}$ needed for producing $a_{ll'}$ items of l is less than or equal to unit processing time $u_{k'l'}$, we can start the processing of l' as soon as the first transfer batch of product l has been conveyed from the k- to the k'-shop. Otherwise, we start the processing of the last $y_l / a_{ll'}$ items of product l' on machine k' after the last transfer of y_l items of product l from the k- to the k'-shop. Hence, the time lag $\delta_{kl,k'l'}$ between terminal operation kl and initial operation $k'l'$ is chosen to be

$$
\delta_{kl,k'l'} = \begin{cases} \vartheta_{kl} + y_l u_{kl} - \vartheta_{k'l'} + t_{kk'}, & \text{if } a_{ll'} u_{kl} \leq u_{k'l} \\ \vartheta_{kl} + a_{ll'} x_{l'} u_{kl} - (x_{l'} - \frac{y_l}{a_{ll'}}) u_{k'l'} - \vartheta_{k'l'} + t_{kk'}, & \text{otherwise} \end{cases} \quad (6.4)
$$

Note that formula (6.3) may be interpreted as the special case where $l' = l$ and $a_{ll'} := 1$.

We now turn to general product structures containing common parts $l \in P$. The presence of common parts leads to an *assignment sequence problem*, where we have to decide on the order in which completed items of product l are allotted to succeeding products l'. For a given assignment sequence, appropriate time lags may then be computed in analogy to the case of a convergent product structure. For details we refer to Neumann and Schwindt (1997). In the latter reference, a procedure for finding a suitable *block-structured* assignment sequence has been devised, where all items allotted to one and the same product l' are processed consecutively. For that case, time lags $\delta_{kl,k'l'}$ can again be written in closed form.

Alternatively, common parts can be dealt with by introducing cumulative resources. This approach, which has not been considered by Neumann and Schwindt (1997), offers the prospect of being independent of an assignment sequence to be specified in advance. Let $l \in P$ be some common part. We again consider the case where all items of l being assigned to some product are processed one after another, and for simplicity we assume that l is installed into two products, say, l' and l''. At first, we identify product l with a cumulative resource $l \in \mathcal{R}^\gamma$ with zero safety stock $\underline{R}_l$ and infinite storage capacity $\overline{R}_l$. We then decompose a copy of operation kl into two auxiliary operations kl' and kl'' with durations $p_{kl'} = a_{ll'} x_{l'} u_{kl}$ and $p_{kl''} = a_{ll''} x_{l''} u_{kl}$ to be executed on the same fictitious k-machine (which must be represented by a separate renewable resource $\hat{k}$ with capacity $R_{\hat{k}} = 1$). To ensure that after the setup of the k-machine, operations kl' and kl'' are processed in parallel with operation kl, we add the time lags $\delta_{kl,kl'} = \delta_{kl,kl''} = \vartheta_{kl}$, $\delta_{kl',kl} = p_{kl'} - p_{kl}$, and $\delta_{kl'',kl} = p_{kl''} - p_{kl}$. Because kl' and kl'' cannot overlap, they must be processed consecutively without any delay in between. The *start* events of both operations kl' and kl'' replenish the cumulative resource by $a_{ll'}x_{l'}$ and $a_{ll''}x_{l''}$ units, and the start events of initial operations $k'l'$ and $k''l''$ in the process plans of products l' and l'' deplete the inventory of l by $a_{ll'}x_{l'}$ and $a_{ll''}x_{l''}$ units. Eventually, we introduce time lags $\delta_{kl',k'l'}$ and $\delta_{kl'',k''l''}$ of type (6.4) between the auxiliary operations kl' and kl'' and the respective initial operations $k'l'$ and $k''l''$, which guarantee that a sufficient amount of product l is available when starting operations $k'l'$ and $k''l''$.

6.2 Small-Batch Production Planning in Manufacturing Industries

In this section we review a capacity-oriented hierarchical planning method for small-batch multi-level production planning in manufacturing industries, which has been proposed by Neumann and Schwindt (1998). An earlier version of this approach is described in Franck et al. (1997). We consider the three planning stages *capacitated master production scheduling*, *multi-level lot sizing*, and *temporal plus capacity planning* (in the original paper, an additional *fine planning* stage has been included). The optimization problems arising at the capacitated master production scheduling and temporal plus capacity planning stages can be formulated as resource-constrained project scheduling problems. Alternative approaches to hierarchical production planning have, e.g., been devised by Carravilla and de Sousa (1995), Schneeweiß (1995), Drexl and Kolisch (1996), Schneeweiß (2003), Ch. 6, and Kolisch (2001b), Ch. 4. Elements of capacity-oriented production planning and control systems have been discussed in Drexl et al. (1994).

At the stage of **capacitated master production scheduling**, a *master production schedule* (MPS) has to be determined, which translates the primary requirements for final products into monthly production orders for final products and main components such that the workload of work centers is as smooth as possible over time. An even utilization of the work centers helps to avoid expensive capacity adjustment measures and facilitates the determination of feasible solutions at subsequent planning stages, where explicit resource constraints have to be taken into account. The planning horizon of this first stage is usually about one year comprising twelve periods of one month each.

For the final products the amounts to be produced and corresponding month-precise delivery dates are given by the customer orders. We assume that all customer orders must be met on time. From the order quantities of final products and the product structure of the company, the gross requirements for main components at lower production levels can be computed by a bill of materials explosion. To obtain the net requirements, we subtract the corresponding available stocks.

To schedule the production of the final products and main components (referred to as *main products* in what follows), we model the problem of determining an appropriate MPS as a *resource levelling problem* with, e.g., the total squared utilization cost as objective function. To this end, we first define a project with renewable resources for each individual customer order. The production of the net requirement for each main product i of such a customer order is regarded as an activity i of the project. The duration p_i of activity i results from summing up the setup and processing times for product i and the components of product i at lower production levels. To obtain the minimum time lag d_{ij}^{min} between the start of activity i and the start of any subsequent activity j in the product structure, some buffer for waiting times arising when scheduling the components of all production levels has to be added to p_i. This time buffer can be estimated by using concepts from queueing theory (see Söhner 1995, Ch. 3). The renewable resources required for carrying out the activities of the project coincide with the respective work centers involved. The resource requirements of product i are assumed to be distributed uniformly over the execution time p_i of activity i.

The project networks for all customer orders are then joined together to make a *multi-project network* by adding the project beginning and termination nodes 0 and $n+1$ and connecting nodes 0 and $n+1$ with all initial and terminal activities, respectively, of the individual project networks. The backward arc $(n+1,0)$ corresponding to the project deadline $\overline{d}$ is weighted by $-\overline{d} = -\Delta$, where Δ denotes the planning horizon (typically about one year). A delivery date $\overline{d}_i$ for some product i can be modelled by a maximum time lag $d_{0i}^{max} = \overline{d}_i - p_i$ between the project start and the start of activity i.

The objective function of the resource levelling problem can be chosen to be any of the objective functions dealt with in Subsection 2.3.2. A solution S to the resource levelling problem provides month-precise milestones for the production of the gross requirements for the main products.

At the stage of **multi-level lot sizing**, the main products are decomposed into intermediate products for which weekly production quantities (also called *lots* or *batches*) are computed. In the lot sizing model, the planning horizon of roughly three months is divided into periods of one week each. The production orders for the main products, which define the primary requirements of the lot sizing model, are given by the MPS.

The production of the intermediate products requires several resources. Each resource corresponds to a group of machines. The processing of a product on a resource necessitates a setup of the resource, which takes a setup time and incurs a setup cost. Additional costs arise from stocking products. Setup and processing times are given in time units (for example, hours). For a given resource, the *aggregate* per-period availability corresponds to the workload in time units which can be executed by the machines of the corresponding group within one period. The objective is to determine lots for the intermediate products such that no backlogging occurs, the per-period availabilities of all resources are observed in all periods, and the sum of setup and inventory holding costs is minimized. This problem represents a *multi-level capacitated lot sizing problem*, for which Tempelmeier and Derstroff (1996) have developed the following Lagrangean-based heuristic. By relaxing the inventory balance and capacity constraints, a decomposition of the original problem into several single-level uncapacitated lot sizing problems of the classical Wagner-Whitin type is obtained, which can be solved efficiently by dynamic programming (cf. Wagelmans et al. 1992). Violations of the relaxed constraints are taken into consideration via a Lagrangean penalty function, whose multipliers are iteratively updated in the course of a subgradient optimization procedure.

Intermediate products may be further broken down into individual components. At the stage of **temporal plus capacity planning**, the production of those components has to be scheduled on groups of identical machines for each week (period of the lot sizing stage). The weekly gross requirements for the individual components can be found by a bill of materials explosion from the lots for intermediate products computed at the lot sizing stage. Since all lots have to be processed within one week, we aim at minimizing the maximum completion time of all operations, i.e., the makespan. As has been shown in Section 6.1, the latter production scheduling problem can be modelled as a project duration problem with renewable and cumulative resources.

Since at the lot sizing stage, only aggregate per-period capacities of resources have been taken into account, it may happen that the makespan found at the temporal plus capacity planning stage exceeds the deadline of one week. In that case, we have to re-perform lot sizing such that the size of at least one lot is reduced. This can be achieved by decreasing the aggregate capacity of resources whose capacity has been violated, which corresponds to a feedback mechanism originally proposed by Lambrecht and Vanderveken (1979) for the special case of a job shop environment.

6.3 Production Scheduling in the Process Industries

In this section we are concerned with production scheduling in the process industries, where similarly to the case of manufacturing dealt with in Section 6.1, final products arise from several successive transformations of intermediate products. In contrast to manufacturing, however, where a limited number of piece goods are processed on machines, in the process industries the transformations are performed by chemical reactions of bulk goods, liquids, or gases on *processing units* such as reactors, heaters, or filters. The transformation of input products into output products on a dedicated processing unit is called a *task*. Each task may consume several input products and may produce several output products, whose amounts may be chosen within prescribed bounds. Perishable products must be consumed in the space of a given shelf life time, which may be equal to zero. In the latter case, the intermediate product cannot be stocked. In addition, the storable intermediate products must be stocked in dedicated *storage facilities* like tanks or silos.

That is why storage problems play an important role in the process industries (see, e.g., Schwindt and Trautmann 2002). Further peculiarities encountered in the process industries are cyclic product structures, sequence-dependent cleaning times on processing units, and large processing times, which may necessitate the explicit consideration of breaks like night-shifts or weekends.

Throughout this section we assume that the production is operated in *batch mode*, which means that at the beginning of a task, the input products are loaded into the processing unit, and the output becomes available at the termination of the task. The case of continuous production mode can be dealt with by using the concept of continuous cumulative resources introduced in Section 5.4. As a rule, the production is organized according to batch mode if small amounts of a large number of final products are required (whereas the continuous production mode is typical of basic materials industry such as oil or dyestuff industries). The combination of a task and the corresponding quantity produced is called a *batch*. An *operation* corresponds to the processing of a batch. Since the batch sizes are limited by the capacity of the processing units, a task may be performed more than once, resulting in several corresponding operations. In contrast to manufacturing, the processing times of operations are generally independent of the respective batch sizes.

The production scheduling problem to be dealt with consists in allocating processing units and storage facilities over time to the production of given primary requirements such that all operations are completed within a minimum *makespan*. This objective is particularly important in batch production, where often a large number of different products are processed on multi-purpose equipment (cf. Blömer and Günther 1998). In this case, the production plant is configured according to the set of production orders released. Before processing the next set of production orders, the plant has generally to be rearranged, which requires the completion of all operations.

There is an extensive literature dealing with production scheduling in the process industries. Most of the solution approaches discussed are based on time-indexed or continuous-time mixed-integer programming formulations of the problem, cf. e.g., Kondili et al. (1993), Pinto and Grossmann (1995), Blömer and Günther (1998, 2000), or Burkard et al. (1998). For a detailed review of literature, we refer to Blömer (1999), Sect. 4.2, and Schwindt and Trautmann (2000).

The special feature of the approach by Neumann et al. (2001), which we shall discuss in what follows, is the decomposition of the production scheduling problem into a *batching* and a *batch scheduling* problem. A similar technique has been used by Brucker and Hurink (2000) for solving a related production scheduling planning problem. This decomposition offers the prospect of markedly decreasing the severe computational requirements incurred by solving the entire production scheduling problem at once. The batching phase generates appropriate batches, which in the course of the batch scheduling phase are subsequently scheduled on the processing units subject to inventory constraints. The batching problem can be formulated as a mixed-integer linear program. The batch scheduling problem can be viewed as a multi-mode resource-constrained project scheduling problem with renewable and cumulative resources, sequence-dependent changeover times, and calendars.

We first deal with the **batching problem**. Batching converts the given primary requirements for final products into individual batches for tasks, where the objective is to minimize the workload, i.e., the total amount of work to be performed on the processing units. For each task we determine a collection of batches such that all primary requirements can be satisfied, there is sufficient capacity for stocking the residual inventories after the completion of all operations, the prescribed bounds on the batch sizes are observed, and the workload to be processed is minimum.

We are going to formulate the batching problem as a mixed-integer linear program (see Schwindt 2001 and Neumann et al. 2002). Let T be the set of all tasks s, and let U be the set of all processing units k. $U_s \subseteq U$ is the set of all processing units on which task s can be executed. By p_{ks} we designate the processing time of task s on processing unit $k \in U_s$. The mean processing time of task s on any processing unit $k \in U_s$ is $\bar{p}_s = \sum_{k \in U_s} p_{ks}/|U_s|$, and $\nu_s = \lceil \sum_{k \in U_s} \bar{d}/p_{ks} \rceil$ is an upper bound on the number of batches for task s which can be executed in the planning period $[0, \bar{d}]$. For each task $s \in T$, a lower bound $\underline{q}_s$ and an upper bound $\bar{q}_s$ on the batch size are given. The lower bound generally arises from technological or economical requirements, whereas the upper bound equals the capacity of the respective processing units.

By P we again denote the set of all products l to be produced, and d_l is the primary requirement for product l. Each storable product $l \in P$ is stocked in a dedicated storage facility of capacity c_l. For simplicity we assume that there are no initial stocks of products l, that a sufficient amount of raw materials is available, and that no safety stocks have to be taken into account. Each product $l \in P$ arises as output of some tasks $s \in T$, and each intermediate product $l \in P$ is also input to some other tasks $s' \in T$. The analogue to the input coefficients in manufacturing are the input and output proportions $-1 \leq a_{ls} \leq 1$, which provide the proportions of products l in the input or output, respectively, of task s. We have $a_{ls} < 0$ if l is an input product of s and $a_{ls} > 0$ if l is an output product of task s. For products l that are neither consumed nor produced by task s, we set $a_{ls} := 0$. For what follows we assume that the proportions a_{ls} cannot be varied (Neumann et al. 2002 have considered the general case of flexible input and output proportions).

The batching problem can now be formulated by introducing, for each task $s \in T$, ν_s continuous variables $q_s^\mu \geq 0$ ($\mu = 1, \ldots, \nu_s$) with the following meaning. If the number of batches for task s is greater than or equal to μ, q_s^μ provides the size of the μ-th batch and $q_s^\mu = 0$, otherwise. In addition, we need binary variables x_s^μ with $x_s^{\mu+1} \leq x_s^\mu$ ($\mu = 1, \ldots, \nu_s - 1$), where $x_s^\mu = 1$ indicates that there exists a μ-th batch for task s and $x_s^\mu = 0$, otherwise. The total workload to be processed then equals $\sum_{s \in T} \bar{p}_s \sum_{\mu=1}^{\nu_s} x_s^\mu$ (recall that the processing time of a batch is independent of the batch size). The linking between variables q_s^μ and x_s^μ can be achieved by the inequalities $q_s^\mu/\overline{q}_s \leq x_s^\mu \leq q_s^\mu/\underline{q}_s$, which at the same time ensure that the batch sizes are between the lower and upper bounds $\underline{q}_s$ and $\overline{q}_s$.

$a_{ls}q_s^\mu$ is the increase in the inventory of product l after one execution of task s (which is negative if l is an input product of s). The quantity of product l remaining on stock after the execution of all batches equals $\sum_{s\in T} a_{ls} \sum_{\mu=1}^{\nu_s} q_s^\mu$, which must not be less than the primary requirements d_l for product l. On the other hand, the residual amount of product l after the delivery of the demands must not exceed the storage capacity c_l for product l.

In sum, the batching problem can be stated as the following mixed-integer linear program:

$$
\left.
\begin{aligned}
\text{Minimize} \quad & \sum_{s\in T} \overline{p}_s \sum_{\mu=1}^{\nu_s} x_s^\mu \\
\text{subject to} \quad & d_l \leq \sum_{s\in T} a_{ls} \sum_{\mu=1}^{\nu_s} q_s^\mu \leq d_l + c_l \quad (l \in P) \\
& q_s^\mu/\overline{q}_s \leq x_s^\mu \leq q_s^\mu/\underline{q}_s \quad (s \in T, \ \mu = 1, \ldots, \nu_s) \\
& x_s^{\mu+1} \leq x_s^\mu \quad (s \in T, \ \mu = 1, \ldots, \nu_s - 1) \\
& x_s^\mu \in \{0, 1\} \quad (s \in T, \ \mu = 1, \ldots, \nu_s) \\
& q_s^\mu \geq 0 \quad (s \in T, \ \mu = 1, \ldots, \nu_s)
\end{aligned}
\right\} \quad (6.5)
$$

A feasible solution (q, x) to batching problem (6.5) provides a set of operations to be scheduled on the processing units. For each task $s \in T$, we have $\sum_{\mu=1}^{\nu_s} x_s^\mu$ corresponding operations.

We now turn to the **batch scheduling problem**, which consists in allocating the resources to the operations over time such that the processing of all batches is completed within a minimum amount of time, i.e., the makespan is minimized. A variety of technological and organizational constraints have to be taken into account. A task generally requires different types of resources: processing units with sequence-dependent cleaning times, input products, and storage facilities for output products. The availability of these resources is limited by capacities and inventories. Break calendars specify time intervals during which specific tasks cannot be processed. Certain tasks can be suspended during a break (e.g., packaging), whereas other tasks (e.g., chemical reactions) cannot be interrupted at all. Some tasks may be executed on alternative processing units differing in speed and cleaning times. Finally, there may be perishable intermediate products, which cannot be stored. In what follows we develop a resource-constrained project scheduling model for the batch scheduling problem, which has been discussed in Neumann et al. (2003b), Sect. 2.16 (see also Schwindt and Trautmann 2000 and Neumann et al. 2002, who have proposed similar models for batch scheduling).

Analogously to the case of make-to-order production dealt with in Section 6.1, the execution of all operations can be viewed as a project, where the makespan to be minimized corresponds to the project duration S_{n+1}. For each operation we introduce one real activity $i \in V^a$. The activity durations p_i are equal to the processing times of the corresponding tasks. In addition, we introduce two events $g, h \in V^e$ for each operation i, representing the start and the completion of i. Minimum and maximum time lags $d_{ig}^{min} = d_{ig}^{max} = 0$ and $d_{ih}^{min} = d_{ih}^{max} = p_i$ ensure that g occurs at the start and h at the completion of i.

Each operation is executed on a processing unit. We combine identical processing units to form a pool. Each pool is modelled as a renewable resource $k \in \mathcal{R}^\rho$. Processing units are identical if they can operate the same tasks with the same processing and cleaning times. The requirement r_{ik} of activity i for resource k equals 1 if operation i is carried out on a processing unit of pool k and 0, otherwise. The resource capacity R_k is equal to the number of processing units in the corresponding pool.

The cleaning times between consecutive operations on a processing unit can be modelled by introducing sequence-dependent changeover times between the activities (cf. Section 5.2). The changeover time ϑ_{ij}^k between two activities i and j on renewable resource $k \in \mathcal{R}^\rho$ equals the cleaning time after operation i if j requires a cleaning of resource k. When checking the changeover-feasibility of some schedule S, the lower capacities of all arcs in the flow network equal 0 or 1 because $r_{ik} = 1$ holds for all activities i requiring resource k. Hence, the corresponding minimum-flow problem can be solved in $\mathcal{O}(n|\theta^k(S)|)$ time by augmenting path algorithms (cf. Ahuja et al. 1993, Sect. 6.5).

Certain operations cannot be in progress during breaks. We model breaks by introducing an activity calendar b_i for each real activity $i \in V^a$ (cf. Section 5.1). If operation i cannot be processed during breaks, $b_i(t) = 0$ exactly if time t falls into a break. For the remaining activities $i \in V^a$, we have $b_i(t) = 1$ for all $t \in [0, \overline{d}]$.

Some tasks $s \in T$ can be executed on alternative processing units $k \in U_s$ belonging to different pools. For each corresponding activity i, we introduce one execution mode m_i for each alternative processing unit operation i can be executed on (cf. Section 5.3). The requirements for renewable resources as well as the durations and changeover times then refer to individual execution modes instead of activities.

Intermediate storage facilities can be modelled as (discrete) cumulative resources. We identify each intermediate product l to be stocked with one cumulative resource $l \in \mathcal{R}^\gamma$ with safety stock $\underline{R}_l = 0$ and storage capacity $\overline{R}_l = c_l$. The requirements of start and completion events $g, h \in V^e$ of operations i for resource l can be determined as follows. Assume that operation i corresponds to the μ-th execution of task s. If l is an input product of task s, i.e., $a_{ls} < 0$, then $r_{gl} = a_{ls}q_s^\mu$. If l is an output product of s, i.e., $a_{ls} > 0$, we have $r_{hl} = a_{ls}q_s^\mu$. Note that the integrality of resource requirements $r_{gl}, r_{hl} \in \mathbb{Z}$ may necessitate a subsequent scaling of all requirements and storage capacities by some factor $c \in \mathbb{Q}$, which does not affect the time complexities of the solution algorithms discussed.

Finally, we turn to perishable intermediate products. We only consider the case where a perishable product must be consumed immediately. The case of general shelf life times can be modelled by introducing auxiliary events and cumulative resources (see Schwindt and Trautmann 2002). Let l be a perishable output product produced by some operation i. Then there must exist some operation j that immediately consumes the amount of l arising at the completion of operation i. This can be ensured by introducing a minimum and a maximum time lag $d_{ij}^{min} = d_{ij}^{max} = p_i$ pulling the start of j to the completion of i, provided that there is a one-to-one correspondence between operations producing and consuming perishable products. The latter requirement can easily be integrated into the batching problem and is generally met in practice because otherwise small deviations of the realized from the predicted processing times would most often imply the loss of perishable substances. If the condition is not met, the immediate consumption of a perishable intermediate product can be enforced by introducing a corresponding cumulative resource l with $\underline{R}_l = \overline{R}_l = 0$.

Table 6.1, which is taken from Neumann et al. (2003b), Sect. 2.16, summarizes the input data of a batch scheduling problem and their respective counterparts in the resource-constrained project scheduling model.

Table 6.1. Batch scheduling vs. project scheduling

Batch scheduling	Project scheduling
Operations	Activities
Makespan	Project duration
Pools of identical processing units	Renewable resources
Cleaning times	Sequence-dependent changeover times
Breaks	Activity calendars
Alternative processing units	Multiple execution modes
Intermediate storage facilities	Cumulative resources
Perishable intermediate products	Minimum and maximum time lags, cumulative resources

Based on the above decomposition of the production scheduling problem into batching and batch scheduling, Schwindt and Trautmann (2000) have been able to provide a feasible solution to a benchmark problem from industry submitted by Westenberger and Kallrath (1995) for the first time (see also Kallrath 2002). The latter case study covers most of the features occurring in the production scheduling problem of batch plants. Neumann et al. (2002) have shown that the decomposition approach also compares favorably with monolithic time-indexed mixed-integer linear programming formulations of the problem.

6.4 Evaluation of Investment Projects

In this section we discuss a parametric optimization procedure, which has been proposed by Schwindt and Zimmermann (2002) for evaluating investment projects with respect to different project deadline and discount rate scenarios (see also Zimmermann and Schwindt 2002). Project managers are frequently confronted with the problem to decide whether some given investment project should be performed or to select one out of several mutually exclusive investment projects from a given portfolio. For the assessment of investments, the net present value criterion is well-established in research and practice (see, e.g., Brealey and Myers 2002, Ch. 5). In classical preinvestment analysis, investments are specified by a stream of payments, i.e., a series of payments with associated payment times. Given a stream of payments and a proper discount rate, the net present value of the project is obtained by summing up all payments discounted to the project beginning (case (a) in Figure 6.4, where exogenous parameters are written in italics).

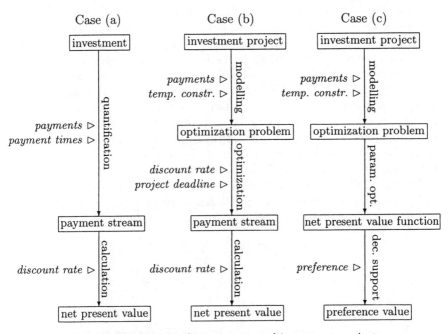

Fig. 6.4. Evaluation of investments and investment projects

In case of *investment projects*, the payment times are no longer given in advance but are subject to optimization. An investment project consists of a set of events each of which is associated with a payment. Moreover, there are prescribed minimum and maximum time lags between the occurrence of events. Thus, the stream of payments results from maximizing the net present value of the project subject to the temporal constraints that are given by the minimum and maximum time lags (case (b) in Figure 6.4).

The formulation of the latter optimization problem presupposes the knowledge of the *required rate of return* (i.e., the discount rate) for discounting the payments and the specification of a *maximum project duration* (i.e., the project deadline). When dealing with real investments in material goods like in the building industry, however, often neither is the proper discount rate to be applied known with sufficient accuracy nor is the project deadline fixed when the investment project must be evaluated. The required rate of return is a theoretical quantity and can only be estimated (see Brealey and Myers 2002, Ch. 23). The project deadline generally arises from negotiations between the investor performing the project and his customers. The *parametric optimization approach* by Schwindt and Zimmermann (2002) provides the maximum project net present value as a function of the discount rate and project deadline chosen. The resulting net present value curve can then serve as a basis for the decision of the investor, which depends on his individual risk preference (case (c) in Figure 6.4).

Let V^e be the set of project events, including the project beginning 0 and the project termination $n + 1$, the start events of project activities, and milestones at the completion of subprojects. The project events and the corresponding prescribed time lags among them can be represented by an *event-on-node network* $N = (V^e, E, \delta)$ with node set V^e, arc set E, and arc weights δ_{ij} for $(i, j) \in E$ (see Subsection 1.1.2). Each event $i \in V^e$ belonging to an activity start is associated with a (negative) disbursement $c_i^f < 0$ for bought-in supplies or outside services. Progress payments $c_j^f > 0$ arise when subprojects with milestones $j \in V^e$ have been finished. Progress payments generally refer to the direct cost which is incurred by the activities of the corresponding subproject (cf. Daynand and Padman 1997).

Given a discount rate $\alpha > 0$ and a project deadline $\overline{d}$, the *time-constrained net present value problem* reads as follows, where the project deadline $\overline{d}$ is specified by arc $(n + 1, 0) \in E$ with weight $\delta_{n+1,0} = -\overline{d}$:

$$\left. \begin{aligned} \text{Maximize} \quad & C^\alpha(S) := \sum_{i \in V^e} c_i^f e^{-\alpha S_i} \\ \text{subject to} \quad & S_j - S_i \geq \delta_{ij} \quad ((i, j) \in E) \\ & S_0 = 0 \end{aligned} \right\} \tag{6.6}$$

Let $\mathcal{S}_T^{\overline{d}}$ denote the feasible region of problem (6.6) for project deadline $\overline{d}$ and let C^* be the corresponding optimal objective function value. A time-feasible schedule S with maximum net present value $C^\alpha(S) = C^*$ can be determined by the steepest descent method from Subsection 3.2.2, where $f(S) = -C^\alpha(S)$.

Until now we have assumed that discount rate α and project deadline $\overline{d}$ are exogenous parameters. As we have mentioned above, however, the proper discount rate α can only be estimated and the project deadline $\overline{d}$ may be subject to negotiations. Thus, for an adequate evaluation of the investment project it is necessary to know the project net present value for a range of relevant values of α and $\overline{d}$. In the sequel, we describe a parametric optimization procedure that determines the maximum project net present value C^* as a function of discount rate α and project deadline $\overline{d}$. This algorithm extends a method by Grinold (1972), who has studied the dependency between C^* and the project deadline $\overline{d}$. Clearly, since $\mathcal{S}_T^{\overline{d}'} \supseteq \mathcal{S}_T^{\overline{d}}$ if $\overline{d}' \geq \overline{d}$, C^* is nondecreasing in $\overline{d}$.

The following considerations are based on two basic observations that derive from the study of schedule sets and objective functions in Sections 2.2 and 2.3. First, since the net present value objective function is linearizable, there always exists an optimal solution S to the time-constrained net present value problem (6.6) that is a vertex of the feasible region $\mathcal{S}_T^{\overline{d}}$ of (6.6). Second, each vertex S of $\mathcal{S}_T^{\overline{d}}$ can be represented by a spanning tree $G = (V^e, E_G)$ of project network N.

The basic idea for computing *net present value function*

$$C^* : [0, \infty[\times [ES_{n+1}, \infty[\to \mathbb{R}$$

with $C^*(\alpha, \overline{d}) = \max\{C^{\alpha}(S) \mid S \in \mathcal{S}_T^{\overline{d}}\}$ is to cover its domain by a finite number of sets $\mathcal{M}$ such that on each of those sets, function C^* can be specified in closed form. Clearly, C^* is a closed-form function on subsets $\mathcal{M}$ of its domain where the active constraints for optimal schedules S are the same for all $(\alpha, \overline{d}) \in \mathcal{M}$ (and thus optimal schedules S can be represented by one and the same spanning tree G of N). For given spanning tree G, we call an $\subseteq$-maximal connected set $\mathcal{M}$ with the latter property a *validity domain* of G. Now let U_{ij} be the node set of the subtree which results from G by deleting arc (i, j) and does not contain node 0. Recall that arc $(i, j) \in E_G$ is called a forward arc if it is oriented in direction of the unique path from node 0 to node j in G, and a backward arc, otherwise (see Section 4.1). In addition, let $C_{ij}^{\alpha}(S)$ be the net present value of the events from set U_{ij} given schedule S. The following four remarks indicate how to compute the validity domains $\mathcal{M}$ of spanning trees G belonging to optimal schedules.

Remarks 6.1.

(a) Given α and $\overline{d}$, vertex S of $\mathcal{S}_T^{\overline{d}}$ is optimal if and only if there exists a spanning tree G representing S such that for each arc $(i, j) \in E_G$, it holds that $C_{ij}^{\alpha}(S) \geq 0$ if arc (i, j) is a forward arc and $C_{ij}^{\alpha}(S) \leq 0$ if (i, j) is a backward arc. The latter condition is equivalent to the requirement that there does not exist a feasible ascent direction z at S (see Subsection 3.2.2). Hence, the set U of all events that are shifted in time when modifying project deadline $\overline{d}$ coincides with set $U_{n+1,0}$ if backward arc $(n+1, 0) \in E_G$ and is empty, otherwise.

(b) Given discount rate $\alpha > 0$, a spanning tree G belonging to an optimal vertex S of $\mathcal{S}_T^{\overline{d}}$ does not change when modifying project deadline $\overline{d}$, until a temporal constraint $S_j - S_i \geq \delta_{ij}$ with $(i, j) \notin E_G$ becomes active.

This property is immediate from the binary monotonicity of objective function C^α (see Subsection 2.3.1).

(c) Given deadline $\overline{d}$, a spanning tree G belonging to an optimal vertex S of $S_T^{\overline{d}}$ does not change when modifying discount rate α, until for some arc $(i,j) \in E_G$, net present value $C_{ij}^\alpha(S)$ changes in sign. This property is a consequence of (a).

(d) When modifying deadline $\overline{d}$ for fixed spanning tree G, it follows from (b) that the deadline for which a new temporal constraint becomes active is independent of discount rate α. Symmetrically, when modifying discount rate α for fixed G, the discount rate for which $C_{ij}^\alpha(S) = 0$ for some $(i,j) \in E_G$ does not depend on deadline $\overline{d}$. This can be seen as follows. Let S' be an optimal vertex belonging to spanning tree G and deadline $\overline{d}'$. Then for given arc $(i,j) \in E_G$,

$$
\begin{aligned}
C_{ij}^\alpha(S') &= \sum_{h \in U_{ij}} c_h e^{-\alpha S_h'} \\
&= \sum_{h \in U_{ij} \setminus U} c_h e^{-\alpha S_h} + \sum_{h \in U_{ij} \cap U} c_h e^{-\alpha(S_h + \overline{d}' - \overline{d})} \\
&= \sum_{h \in U_{ij} \setminus U} c_h e^{-\alpha S_h} + e^{-\alpha(\overline{d}' - \overline{d})} \sum_{h \in U_{ij} \cap U} c_h e^{-\alpha S_h} \quad (6.7)
\end{aligned}
$$

Now recall that set U either coincides with set $U_{n+1,0}$ or is void. As a consequence, nodes i and j necessarily belong to the same set U or $V \setminus U$ unless $(i,j) = (n+1,0)$. For $U = U_{n+1,0}$ we have $U_{ij} = U$ if $(i,j) = (n+1,0)$, $U_{ij} \subset U$ if $i,j \in U$, and $U_{ij} \cap U = \emptyset$ if $i,j \notin U$. This means that independently of set U and arc (i,j) we have (1) $U_{ij} \cap U = \emptyset$ or (2) $U_{ij} \setminus U = \emptyset$. In case (1), it follows from (6.7) that $C_{ij}^\alpha(S') = C_{ij}^\alpha(S)$ and in case (2), equation (6.7) provides $C_{ij}^\alpha(S') = e^{-\alpha(\overline{d}' - \overline{d})} C_{ij}^\alpha(S)$. In sum, for each $(i,j) \in E_G$ it holds that $C_{ij}^\alpha(S') = 0$ precisely if $C_{ij}^\alpha(S) = 0$.

For a given spanning tree G, the net present value function C^* takes the form

$$
\begin{aligned}
C^*(\alpha, \overline{d}) &= \sum_{i \in V^e \setminus U} c_i^f e^{-\alpha S_i} + \sum_{i \in U} c_i^f e^{-\alpha(S_i + \overline{d} - S_{n+1})} \\
&= \sum_{i \in V^e \setminus U} c_i^f e^{-\alpha S_i} + e^{-\alpha(\overline{d} - S_{n+1})} \sum_{i \in U} c_i^f e^{-\alpha S_i} \quad (6.8)
\end{aligned}
$$

where schedule S is any optimal schedule that is specified by spanning tree G and U is the set of all events shifted when modifying $\overline{d}$. If $(n+1,0) \notin E_G$ and thus $U = \emptyset$, function C^* is constant in project deadline $\overline{d}$.

The amount by which $\overline{d}$ can be increased until a temporal constraint becomes binding is

$$
\sigma^+(G) = \min\{S_j - S_i - \delta_{ij} \mid (i,j) \in E \setminus \{(n+1,0)\} : i \in U, \ j \in V^e \setminus U\}
$$

Analogously, for the amount by which $\bar{d}$ can be decreased, we obtain

$$\sigma^-(G) = \min\{S_j - S_i - \delta_{ij} \mid (i,j) \in E : i \in V^e \setminus U, \ j \in U\}$$

The spanning tree G' for an optimal schedule S' to project deadline $\bar{d}' = \bar{d} + \sigma^+(G)$ or $\bar{d}' = \bar{d} - \sigma^-(G)$ can be constructed without re-performing any optimization by first, adding the arc (i,j) for the new active temporal constraint to G and second, deleting an oppositely directed arc (g,h) with minimum absolute net present value $|C_{gh}^\alpha(S')|$ in the resulting (undirected) cycle in G.

We now turn to the problem of finding the smallest discount rate $\alpha' > \alpha$ where some $C_{ij}^{\alpha'}(S)$ with $(i,j) \in E_G$ changes in sign. Let $\alpha_{ij}^1 < \alpha_{ij}^2 < \cdots < \alpha_{ij}^\nu$ denote all discount rates $\alpha_{ij} > \alpha$ such that for given optimal schedule S,

$$C_{ij}^{\alpha_{ij}}(S) = \sum_{h \in U_{ij}} c_h^f e^{-\alpha_{ij} S_i} = 0 \tag{6.9}$$

Each of those discount rates α_{ij} corresponds to an internal rate of return for the payment stream given by payments c_h^f for $h \in U_{ij}$ and schedule S. Thus, discount rates α_{ij} can be determined by one of the standard algorithms for the calculation of internal rates of return (see, e.g., Zheng and Sun 1999). The following condition is necessary and sufficient for a change in sign of $C_{ij}^{\alpha'}(S)$ at $\alpha' = \alpha_{ij}$, where $\Delta\alpha := \min\{\alpha_{ij}^1 - \alpha, \alpha_{ij}^2 - \alpha_{ij}^1, \ldots, \alpha_{ij}^\nu - \alpha_{ij}^{\nu-1}\}$:

$$\text{sign} \sum_{h \in U_{ij}} c_h^f e^{-(\alpha_{ij} - \Delta\alpha/2)S_i} \neq \text{sign} \sum_{h \in U_{ij}} c_h^f e^{-(\alpha_{ij} + \Delta\alpha/2)S_i} \tag{6.10}$$

For each set U_{ij}, we calculate the smallest discount rate $\alpha_{ij} > \alpha$ for which (6.9) and (6.10) are satisfied. An optimal schedule S' for discount rate $\alpha' := \min_{(i,j) \in E_G} \alpha_{ij}$ then results from delaying events $h \in U_{ij}$ by $\sigma^+(G)$ time units if (i,j) is a forward arc of G or from putting events $h \in U_{ij}$ forward by $\sigma^-(G)$ time units if (i,j) is a backward arc of G. The corresponding spanning tree G' can be determined analogously to the case where deadline $\bar{d}$ is varied.

In summary, each spanning tree G is valid for a rectangular set $\mathcal{M}$ which can be specified by the bottom left corner $(\alpha, \bar{d})$ and the top right corner $(\alpha', \bar{d}')$ (see Figure 6.5). For given α and $\bar{d}$, the values of α' and $\bar{d}'$ can be computed as described above. On the validity domain $\mathcal{M}$ for G, the net present value function can be written in the closed form (6.8).

Algorithm 6.1 provides a procedure for computing all bottom-left corners $(\alpha, \bar{d})$ of sets $\mathcal{M}$ along with the corresponding spanning trees G that uniquely define function C^* on sets $\mathcal{M}$. Q is a list of triples $(\alpha, \bar{d}, G)$ sorted according to nondecreasing discount rates α, ties being broken on the basis of increasing deadlines $\bar{d}$. For convenience we again put $\min \emptyset := \infty$. How to find an appropriate initial discount rate $\alpha^0 > 0$ is described in Schwindt and Zimmermann (2002).

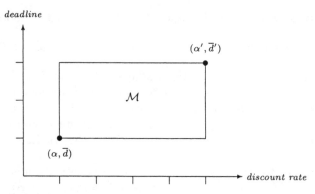

Fig. 6.5. Validity domain $\mathcal{M}$ for spanning tree G

Algorithm 6.1. Computation of net present value function

Input: Event-on-node network $N = (V^e, E, \delta)$, cash flows c_i^f for all events $i \in V^e$, initial discount rate $\alpha^0 > 0$.
Output: Set $\mathcal{C}$ of triples $(\alpha, \overline{d}, G)$.

  compute spanning tree G belonging to optimal schedule for $\overline{d} = ES_{n+1}$ and $\alpha = \alpha^0$;
  initialize list $Q := \{(0, ES_{n+1}, G)\}$ and set of triples $\mathcal{C} := \{(0, ES_{n+1}, G)\}$;
  while $Q \neq \emptyset$ **do**
    delete first element $(\alpha, \overline{d}, G)$ and all other elements $(\alpha, \cdot, G)$ from list Q;
    repeat
      determine $\alpha' := \min\{\alpha_{ij} \mid (i,j) \in E_G, \ \alpha_{ij} \text{ satisfies (6.9) and (6.10)}\}$;
      if $\alpha' < \infty$ **then**
        construct the spanning tree G' belonging to α' and $\overline{d}$;
        add triple $(\alpha', \overline{d}, G')$ to Q and $\mathcal{C}$;
      if $\sigma^+(G) < \infty$ **then**
        set $\overline{d}' := \overline{d} + \sigma^+(G)$;
        construct the spanning tree G' belonging to α and $\overline{d}'$;
        if there is no triple $(\cdot, \overline{d}', G')$ in list Q **then** add triple $(\alpha, \overline{d}', G')$ to $\mathcal{C}$;
        set $\overline{d} := \overline{d}'$ and $G := G'$;
      else put $\overline{d}' := \infty$;
    until $\overline{d}' = \infty$;
  return $\mathcal{C}$;

6.5 Coping with Uncertainty

In this section we propose two deterministic strategies for coping with uncertainty in resource allocation problems. When executing a project, unforeseen downtimes of resources, staff time off, reworking time, late delivery of raw materials or bought-in parts, or imprecise time and resource estimations may cause considerable deviations from the schedule determined. Basically, there are two ways of taking uncertainty into account when performing the resource allocation. First, we may *anticipate* deviations from predictive data by including the knowledge of uncertainty into the scheduling decisions. Second, when implementing the schedule, we may also *react* on disruptions in a way minimizing the impact of the required adaptations. An overview of different approaches to project scheduling under uncertainty is given by Demeulemeester and Herroelen (2002), Chs. 9 and 10, and Herroelen and Leus (2005), including stochastic, fuzzy, robust, and reactive project scheduling. Robust and reactive methods for project or production scheduling are reviewed in Herroelen and Leus (2004*b*) and Aytug et al. (2005), respectively.

Substantial work has been done in the area of (anticipative) *stochastic project scheduling problem*, where activity durations are modelled as stochastic variables and one attempts to minimize the expected value of a *regular* or *locally regular* objective function (see Möhring 2000 and Uetz 2003 for overviews and Stork 2001 for an in-depth treatment of the project duration problem). Algorithms for stochastic project scheduling are based on the concept of scheduling policies, which may be regarded as a specific application of the theory of stochastic dynamic programming to scheduling problems. Various classes of policies have been developed, which show a different behavior with respect to robustness and computational requirements. In principle, the policies studied define (ordinary or disjunctive) precedence relationships inducing feasible strict orders in the set of real activities. During the project execution, an activity is started as soon as all of its predecessors in that strict order have been completed. If we deal with arbitrary nonregular objective functions, those policies cannot be applied because it is generally no longer optimal to start activities at their earliest time- and resource-feasible start times.

An alternative **anticipative approach** to coping with uncertainty in planning problems refers to the concept of *robust plans* (see Scholl 2001, Ch. 4). We say that a plan is robust if it tends to require only minor revisions during its implementation. In project scheduling, a robust schedule may be defined on the basis of the *free floats* of activities as follows. For the moment we assume that only temporal constraints have to be observed. How to integrate resource constraints into this approach will be explained below. In Subsection 1.1.3 we have defined the concepts of early and late free floats with respect to the earliest and latest schedules. When implementing a schedule S, we may regard the activities as being "frozen", i.e., $ES_i = LS_i = S_i$ for all $i \in V$. In that case, the *early free float* EFF_i of an activity $i \in V$ with respect to schedule S is the maximum amount of time by which the start of activity i can be delayed given that any other activity j can be begun at its previous start time S_j. Symmetrically, the *late free float* LFF_i with respect to schedule S is the maximum amount of time by which the start of activity i can be advanced given that any other activity j can be begun at its previous start times S_j. Hence, a schedule that maximizes the (weighted) sum of all early and late free floats contains the maximum (weighted) temporal buffers for shifting activities in time without affecting the start times of any other activity. Such a schedule can be computed by minimizing the convex objective function f of the *total weighted free float problem* (see Subsection 2.3.1) with

$$f(S) = \sum_{i \in V} w_i^f \left(\max_{(j,i) \in E} [S_j + \delta_{ji}] - \min_{(i,j) \in E} [S_j - \delta_{ij}] \right)$$

where weights $w_i^f \in \mathbb{N}$ can be chosen to reflect the degree of uncertainty with respect to start time S_i. The time-constrained total weighted free float problem can be transformed into a time-constrained project scheduling problem with a linear objective function $\tilde{f}$ by introducing, for each $i \in V$, two auxiliary activities i' and i'' where (1) $S_{i'} \geq S_j + \delta_{ji}$ for all $(j, i) \in E$ and (2) $S_{i''} \leq S_j - \delta_{ij}$ for all $(i, j) \in E$. Conditions (1) and (2) can be expressed via additional arcs (j, i') with weights $\delta_{ji'} = \delta_{ji}$ for all $(j, i) \in E$ and arcs (i'', j) with weights $\delta_{i'',j} = \delta_{ij}$ for all $(i, j) \in E$. Linear objective function $\tilde{f}$ is then given by $\tilde{f}(S) = \sum_{i \in V} w_i^f (S_{i'} - S_{i''})$. A similar model for time-constrained robust project scheduling under a probabilistic scenario has been studied by Herroelen and Leus (2004a). The objective function considered in the latter paper is the expected weighted deviation in start times between the realized schedule and baseline schedule S, where it is assumed that no activity i is started before its predictive start time S_i.

We now drop our assumption of infinite resource availability. In the presence of resource constraints, the free floats depend on the way in which resource conflicts are resolved. Similarly to stochastic project scheduling, the conflict resolution strategy can be specified as a feasible relation ρ in the set V of all activities (cf. Subsections 2.1.1 and 2.1.2). The feasibility of ρ implies that in combination with the temporal constraints, the precedence constraints among real activities and among events given by pairs $(i, j) \in \rho$ guarantee that the resource constraints are satisfied. Thus, by substituting project network N into relation network $N(\rho)$ and minimizing f on relation polytope $\mathcal{S}_T(\rho)$, we obtain a feasible robust schedule that maximizes the total weighted free float for the given set of precedence constraints. It remains to show how to determine a feasible relation ρ such that the minimizer S of f on $\mathcal{S}_T(\rho)$ also minimizes f on the set $\mathcal{S}$ of all feasible schedules, i.e., such that S is a feasible schedule with maximum total weighted free float. First, we notice that when replacing project network N with relation network $N(\rho)$, the objective function to be minimized turns into $f^\rho : \mathcal{S}_T \rightarrow \mathbb{R}$ with

$$f^\rho(S) = \sum_{i \in V} w_i^f \left(\max_{(j,i) \in E \cup \rho} [S_j + \delta_{ji}^\rho] - \min_{(i,j) \in E \cup \rho} [S_j - \delta_{ij}^\rho] \right)$$

where δ_{ji}^ρ and δ_{ij}^ρ denote the weights of arcs (j, i) and (i, j) in relation network $N(\rho)$. Thus, the objective function to be minimized explicitly depends on ρ. From the definition of f^ρ it follows that $f^\rho(S) \leq f^{\rho'}(S)$ for all $S \in \mathcal{S}_T$ if ρ' is an extension of ρ. In addition, it obviously holds that $\mathcal{S}_T(\rho') \subseteq \mathcal{S}_T(\rho)$ if $\rho' \supset \rho$. That is why the feasible relation ρ sought can be chosen among the $\subseteq$-minimal feasible relations. The latter relations can be generated by using a modification of the relaxation-based enumeration scheme given by Algorithm 3.3. At each iteration it is checked whether or not the relation ρ we branch from is feasible by finding minimum (s,t)-flows in specific relation-induced flow networks belonging to the induced preorder $\theta = \Theta(D(\rho))$ (cf. Subsections 2.1.1 and 2.1.2). Instead of breaking up forbidden active sets $\mathcal{A}(S,t)$ we then break up maximum (s,t)-cuts U in the respective flow networks (for details see Sections 4.1 and 5.2, where we have applied similar techniques).

The problem where for given schedule S the resource allocation (i.e., an appropriate (s,t)-flow) is to be determined in such a way that the expected weighted deviation between the realized schedule and schedule S is minimized has been investigated by Leus and Herroelen (2004).

The **reactive approach** is as follows. Assume that we want to minimize some regular or convexifiable objective function like the project duration, the total tardiness cost, the total inventory holding cost, or the net present value of the project. At first, we determine an optimal schedule S for objective function f by using the relaxation-based enumeration scheme. We then start performing the project according to schedule S. Each time the schedule becomes infeasible due to the breakdown of resources or overrun on activity durations, we determine a new schedule S' that first, complies with the updated constraints and second, resembles as much as possible previous schedule S. The reason is that we want to avoid disruptions in the project execution that may arise from substantial modifications of the schedule. The resemblance between schedules S and S' may, e.g., be measured by the (weighted Manhattan) distance

$$\Delta(S',S) = \|S' - S\| := \sum_{i \in V} w_i |S'_i - S_i|$$

where $w_i \in \mathbb{N}$ are integers specifying the cost for shifting the start of activity $i \in V$ by one unit of time. $\Delta(S',S)$ coincides with the objective function value $\widetilde{f}(S')$ of schedule S' if $\widetilde{f}$ is chosen to be the *total earliness-tardiness cost* function with due dates d_i being equal to completion times $S_i + p_i$ and $w_i^e = w_i^t = w_i$ for all $i \in V$. Thus, we may determine a new feasible schedule S' by minimizing the total earliness-tardiness cost with respect to previous schedule S and put $S := S'$. In case of frequent schedule revisions, the computational effort for rescheduling the project can be markedly decreased by providing, in addition to schedule S, a feasible relation ρ in set V. We then minimize the total earliness-tardiness cost $\widetilde{f}$ on the intersection of relation polytope $\mathcal{S}_T(\rho)$ with the updated feasible region S'. An appropriate $\subseteq$-minimal feasible relation ρ can be determined in the same way as for the anticipative approach.

Conclusions

Summary. In this book we have been concerned with models, algorithms, and applications of deterministic resource allocation problems in project management. A special emphasis has been placed on developing a unifying framework within which a variety of project scheduling problems can be treated. Those problems involve *general temporal constraints* given by prescribed minimum and maximum time lags, different types of *scarce resources*, and a broad class of *regular and nonregular objective functions*. The diversity of the models proposed allows to cover many features arising in applications beyond the proper field of project management like short-term production planning in the manufacturing or process industries.

The main contributions of this monograph are

- an in-depth analysis of temporal constraints and different kinds of resource constraints (Chapter 1),
- the formulation of resource constraints in terms of specific relations in the activity set, which permits a classification of schedules and objective functions (Chapter 2),
- the development of efficient solution procedures for time-constrained project scheduling and resource allocation, which are based on the results of the previous structural analysis (Chapters 3 and 4),
- the expansion of the basic resource allocation models to problems with break calendars, sequence-dependent changeover times in distributed projects, alternative execution modes for activities, and consumption and renewal of resources at constant rates (Chapter 5), and
- the application of concepts from resource allocation in project management to first, production scheduling in the manufacturing and process industries, second, the evaluation of investment projects with respect to variable project deadline and discount rate, and third, deterministic strategies for coping with uncertainty in project planning (Chapter 6).

In particular, we have generalized order-based approaches for project scheduling with renewable resources to resource allocation problems including *cumulative resources* that are depleted and replenished over time. The concept of cumulative resources offers a natural way of studying several resource types that have been dealt with in literature (renewable, nonrenewable, and recyclable resources). In addition, cumulative resources have many immediate applications in their own right such as scarce budgets, material flows, or limited storage capacities.

Suggestions for future research. When planning real-life projects, managers usually have to deal with problems that are much less well-structured than the models treated in this book. However, to make resource allocation amenable to methods of Operations Research, it is generally necessary to make simplifying assumptions on the objectives pursued and constraints included. Thus, bridging the gap between theoretical concepts and practical requirements remains a challenging field of further research. The following topics may be directions of future developments.

- In certain applications it is more expedient to specify, for each activity, a *workload* rather than a fixed duration and fixed resource requirements because there is no need for keeping a constant amount of resource units allocated to the activities over their execution time. It is then necessary to define lower and upper bounds on the time-dependent resource requirements of activities and to relate the prescribed temporal constraints to the activity progress.

- The *scheduling policies* developed for project scheduling with stochastic activity durations assume a locally regular objective function. For this type of objective functions, the precedence relationships among activities can readily be translated into optimal start times during the project execution. When dealing with nonregular objective functions important in practice such as the project net present value or inventory holding cost, new concepts need to be developed for coping with stochastic activity durations.

- In literature, the concept of *partially renewable resources* has been devised for modelling resources whose availability is defined on unions of time intervals. Partially renewable resources allow for modelling timetabling and working-shift scheduling aspects like maximum working times during weekends or flexible break intervals (see Böttcher et al. 1999). The capacity of such a partially renewable resource can be regarded as being continuously consumed over the execution time of activities. It may thus be interesting to study the relationship between the concepts of continuous cumulative and partially renewable resources.

- Our computational experience with algorithms for resource allocation problems indicates that effective *consistency tests* have a large impact on the efficiency of exact solution methods. Until now, those consistence tests have primarily been devised for renewable-resource constraints. Hence, the development of new consistency tests referring to the scarcity of cumulative resources is an issue of future research.

References

1. Aarts E, Lenstra JK (2003a) Introduction. In: Aarts E, Lenstra JK (eds) Local Search in Combinatorial Optimization. Princeton University Press, Princeton, pp 1–17
2. Aarts E, Lenstra JK, eds (2003b) Local Search in Combinatorial Optimization. Princeton University Press, Princeton
3. Ahuja RK, Magnanti TL, Orlin JB (1993) Network Flows. Prentice Hall, Englewood Cliffs
4. Aldowaisan T, Allahverdi A, Gupta JN (1999) A review of scheduling research involving setup considerations. Omega 27:219–239
5. Ausiello G, d'Atri A, Saccà D (1983) Graph algorithms for functional dependency manipulation. Journal of the ACM 30:752–766
6. Avriel M, Diewert WE, Schaible S, Zang I (1988) Generalized Concavity. Plenum Press, New York
7. Aytug H, Lawley MA, McKay K, Mohan S, Uzsoy R (2005) Executing production schedules in the face of uncertainties: A review and some future directions. European Journal of Operational Research 161:86–110
8. Baker KR (1974) Introduction to Sequencing and Scheduling. John Wiley, New York
9. Bang-Jensen J, Gutin G (2002) Digraphs: Theory, Algorithms and Applications. Springer, Berlin
10. Baptiste P, Le Pape C, Nuijten W (1999) Satisfiability tests and time-bound adjustments for cumulative scheduling problems. Annals of Operations Research 92:305–333
11. Bartusch M, Möhring RH, Radermacher FJ (1988) Scheduling project networks with resource constraints and time windows. Annals of Operations Research 16:201–240
12. Beck JC (2002) Heuristics for scheduling with inventory: Dynamic focus via constraint criticality. Journal of Scheduling 5:43–69
13. Bell CE, Park K (1990) Solving resource-constrained project scheduling problems by A* search. Naval Research Logistics 37:61–84
14. Bellman R (1958) On a routing problem. Quarterly of Applied Mathematics 16:87–90
15. Berge C (1970) Graphes et Hypergraphes. Dunod, Paris

16. Blömer F (1999) Produktionsplanung und -steuerung in der chemischen Industrie: Ressourceneinsatzplanung von Batchprozessen auf Mehrzweckanlagen. Gabler, Wiesbaden

17. Blömer F, Günther HO (1998) Scheduling of a multi-product batch process in the chemical industry. Computers in Industry 36:245–259

18. Blömer F, Günther HO (2000) LP-based heuristics for scheduling chemical batch processes. International Journal of Production Research 35:1029–1052

19. Böttcher J, Drexl A, Kolisch R, Salewski F (1999) Project scheduling under partially renewable resource constraints. Management Science 45:543–559

20. Brealey RA, Myers SC (2002) Principles of Corporate Finance. McGraw-Hill, Irwin

21. Brinkmann K, Neumann K (1996) Heuristic procedures for resource-constrained project scheduling with minimal and maximal time lags: The resource-levelling and minimum project-duration problems. Journal of Decision Systems 5:129–156

22. Brucker P (1973) Die Erstellung von CPM-Netzplänen. In: Gessner P, Henn R, Steinecke V, Todt H (eds) Proceedings in Operations Research 3. Physica, Würzburg, pp 122–130

23. Brucker P, Hurink J (2000) Solving a chemical batch scheduling problem by local search. Annals of Operations Research 96:17–38

24. Brucker P, Knust S (2003) Lower bounds for resource-constrained project scheduling problems. European Journal of Operational Research 149:302–313

25. Brucker P, Thiele O (1996) A branch & bound method for the general-shop problem with sequence dependent setup-times. OR Spektrum 18:145–161

26. Brucker P, Drexl A, Möhring RH, Neumann K, Pesch E (1999) Resource-constrained project scheduling: Notation, classification, models, and methods. European Journal of Operational Research 112:3–41

27. Brucker P, Knust S, Schoo A, Thiele O (1998) A branch and bound algorithm for the resource-constrained project scheduling problem. European Journal of Operational Research 107:272–288

28. Burgess AR, Killebrew JB (1962) Variation in activity level on a cyclic arrow diagram. The Journal of Industrial Engineering 13:76–83

29. Burkard RE, Kocher M, Rudolf R (1998) Rounding strategies for mixed integer programs arising from chemical production planning. Yugoslav Journal of Operations Research 8:9–23

30. Carlier J (1989) Scheduling under financial constraints. In: Słowiński R, Węglarz J (eds) Advances in Project Scheduling. Elsevier, Amsterdam, pp 187–224

31. Carlier J, Pinson E (1989) An algorithm for solving the job-shop problem. Management Science 35:164–176

32. Carlier J, Rinnooy Kan AHG (1982) Scheduling subject to nonrenewable resource constraints. Operations Research Letters 1:52–55

33. Carravilla MA, de Sousa JP (1995) Hierarchical production planning in a make-to-order company: A case study. European Journal of Operational Research 86:43–56

34. Cesta A, Oddi A, Smith SF (2002) A constraint-based method for project scheduling with time windows. Journal of Heuristics 8:109–136

35. Chauvet F, Proth JM (1999) The PERT problem with alternatives: Modelisation and optimization. Publication interne no. 3651, INRIA

36. Christofides N, Alvarez-Valdes R, Tamarit JM (1987) Project scheduling with resource constraints: A branch and bound approach. European Journal of Operational Research 29:262–273
37. Dantzig GB, Fulkerson DR (1954) Minimizing the number of tankers to meet a fixed schedule. Naval Research Logistics Quarterly 1:217–222
38. Davis EW (1966) Resource allocation in project network models: A survey. The Journal of Industrial Engineering 17:177–188
39. Davis EW (1973) Project scheduling under resource constraints: Historical review and categorization of procedures. AIIE Transactions 5:297–313
40. Daynand N, Padman R (1997) On modelling payments in projects. Journal of the Operational Research Society 48:906–918
41. De Reyck B (1998) Scheduling Projects with Generalized Precedence Relations: Exact and Heuristic Procedures. PhD thesis, University of Leuven, Leuven
42. De Reyck B, Herroelen WS (1998a) A branch-and-bound procedure for the resource-constrained project scheduling problem with generalized precedence relations. European Journal of Operational Research 111:152–174
43. De Reyck B, Herroelen WS (1998b) An optimal procedure for the resource-constrained project scheduling problem with discounted cash flows and generalized precedence relations. Computers and Operations Research 25:1–17
44. De Reyck B, Herroelen WS (1999) The multi-mode resource-constrained project scheduling problem with generalized precedence relations. European Journal of Operational Research 119:538–556
45. De Reyck B, Demeulemeester EL, Herroelen WS (1999) Algorithms for scheduling project with generalized precedence constraints. In: Węglarz J (ed) Project Scheduling: Recent Models, Algorithms and Applications. Kluwer, Boston, pp 77–105
46. Demeulemeester EL, Herroelen WS (1992) A branch-and-bound procedure for the multiple resource-constrained project scheduling problem. Management Science 38:1803–1818
47. Demeulemeester EL, Herroelen WS (1996) An efficient optimal solution procedure for the preemptive resource-constrained project scheduling problem. European Journal of Operational Research 90:334–348
48. Demeulemeester EL, Herroelen WS (1997) Benchmark results for the resource-constrained project scheduling problem. Management Science 43:1485–1492
49. Demeulemeester EL, Herroelen WS (2002) Project Scheduling: A Research Handbook. Kluwer, Boston
50. Demeulemeester EL, De Reyck B, Herroelen WS (2000) The discrete time/resource tradeoff problem in project networks: A branch-and-bound approach. IIE Transactions 32:1059–1069
51. Doersch RH, Patterson JH (1977) Scheduling a project to maximize its net present value: A zero-one programming approach. Management Science 23:882–889
52. Domschke W, Drexl A (1991) Kapazitätsplanung in Netzwerken. OR Spektrum 13:63–76
53. Dorndorf U (2002) Project Scheduling with Time Windows. Physica, Heidelberg
54. Dorndorf U, Pesch E, Phan-Huy T (2000a) A branch-and-bound algorithm for the resource-constrained project scheduling problem. Mathematical Methods of Operations Research 52:413–439

55. Dorndorf U, Pesch E, Phan-Huy T (2000b) Constraint propagation techniques for the disjunctive scheduling problem. Artificial Intelligence 122:189–240

56. Dorndorf U, Pesch E, Phan-Huy T (2000c) A time-oriented branch-and-bound algorithm for resource-constrained project scheduling with generalised precedence constraints. Management Science 46:1365–1384

57. Dorndorf U, Phan Huy T, Pesch E (1999) A survey of interval capacity consistency tests for time- and resource-constrained scheduling. In: Węglarz J (ed) Project Scheduling: Recent Models, Algorithms and Applications. Kluwer, Boston, pp 213–238

58. Drexl A, Kolisch R (1996) Assembly management in machine tool manufacturing and the PRISMA-Leitstand. Production and Inventory Management Journal 37:55–57

59. Drexl A, Fleischmann B, Günther HO, Stadtler H, Tempelmeier H (1994) Konzeptionelle Grundlagen kapazitätsorientierter PPS–Systeme. Zeitschrift für betriebswirtschaftliche Forschung 46:1022–1045

60. Elmaghraby SE (1977) Activity Networks: Project Planning and Control by Network Models. John Wiley, New York

61. Elmaghraby SE (1995) Activity nets: A guided tour through some recent developments. European Journal of Operational Research 82:383–408

62. Elmaghraby SE, Kamburowki J (1992) The analysis of activity networks under generalized precedence relations. Management Science 38:1245–1263

63. Fest A, Möhring RH, Stork F, Uetz M (1999) Resource-constrained project scheduling with time windows: A branching scheme based on dynamic release dates. Technical Report 596, Technical University of Berlin

64. Fisher H, Thompson GL (1963) Probabilistic learning combinations of local job-shop scheduling rules. In: Muth JF, Thompson GL (eds) Industrial Scheduling. Prentice Hall, Englewood Cliffs, pp 225–251

65. Floyd RW (1962) Algorithm 97: Shortest path. Communications of the ACM 5:345

66. Franck B (1999) Prioritätsregelverfahren für die ressourcenbeschränkte Projektplanung mit und ohne Kalender. Shaker, Aachen

67. Franck B, Neumann K, Schwindt C (1997) A capacity-oriented hierarchical approach to single-item and small-batch production planning using project-scheduling methods. OR Spektrum 19:77–85

68. Franck B, Neumann K, Schwindt C (2001a) Project scheduling with calendars. OR Spektrum 23:325–334

69. Franck B, Neumann K, Schwindt C (2001b) Truncated branch-and-bound, schedule-construction, and schedule-improvement procedures for resource-constrained project scheduling. OR Spektrum 23:297–324

70. Garey MR, Johnson DS (1979) Computers and Intractability: A Guide to the Theory of NP-Completeness. Freeman, New York

71. Giffler B, Thompson GL (1960) Algorithms for solving production-scheduling problems. Operations Research 8:487–503

72. Glover F, Laguna F (1997) Tabu Search. Kluwer, Dordrecht

73. Goldfarb T, Todd MJ (1989) Linear programming. In: Nemhauser GL, Rinnooy Kan AHG, Todd MJ (eds) Optimization, Handbooks in Operations Research and Management Science Vol 1. North Holland, Amsterdam, pp 73–170

74. Goldwasser MH, Motwani R (1999) Complexity measures for assembly sequences. International Journal of Computational Geometry and Application 9:371–418

75. Golumbic MC (2004) Algorithmic Graph Theory and Perfect Graphs, Annals of Discrete Mathematics Vol 57. Elsevier, Amsterdam

76. Grinold RC (1972) The payment scheduling problem. Naval Research Logistics 19:123–136

77. Grötschel M, Lovász L, Schrijver A (1998) Geometric Algorithms and Combinatorial Optimization. Springer, Berlin

78. Günther HO (1992) Netzplanorientierte Auftragsterminierung bei offener Fertigung. OR Spektrum 14:229–240

79. Hajdu M (1997) Network Scheduling Techniques for Construction Project Management, Nonconvex Optimizations and Its Applications Vol 16. Kluwer, Dordrecht

80. Hartmann S (1998) A competitive genetic algorithm for resource-constrained project scheduling. Naval Research Logistics 45:733–750

81. Hartmann S (1999a) Project Scheduling under Limited Resources: Models, Methods, and Applications, Lecture Notes in Economics and Mathematical Systems Vol 478. Springer, Berlin

82. Hartmann S (1999b) Project scheduling with multiple modes: A genetic algorithm. Annals of Operations Research 102:111–136

83. Hartmann S (2001) Project scheduling with multiple modes: A genetic algorithm. Annals of Operations Research 102:111–136

84. Hartmann S, Drexl A (1998) Project scheduling with multiple modes: A comparison of exact algorithms. Networks 32:283–298

85. Hartmann S, Kolisch R (2000) Experimental evaluation of state-of-the-art heuristics for the resource-constrained project scheduling problem. European Journal of Operational Research 127:394–407

86. Heilmann R (2001) Resource-constrained project scheduling: A heuristic for the multi-mode case. OR Spektrum 23:335–357

87. Heilmann R (2003) A branch-and-bound procedure for the multi-mode resource-constrained project scheduling problem with minimum and maximum time lags. European Journal of Operational Research 144:348–365

88. Heilmann R, Schwindt C (1997) Lower bounds for RCPSP/max. Report WIOR-511, University of Karlsruhe

89. Held M, Wolfe P, Crowder HP (1974) Validation of subgradient optimization. Mathematical Programming 6:62–88

90. Herroelen WS (1972) Resource-constrained project scheduling: The state of the art. Operational Research Quarterly 23:261–275

91. Herroelen WS, Leus R (2004a) The construction of stable project baseline schedules. European Journal of Operational Research 156:550–565

92. Herroelen WS, Leus R (2004b) Robust and reactive project scheduling: A review and classification of procedures. International Journal of Production Research 42:1599–1620

93. Herroelen WS, Leus R (2005) Project scheduling under uncertainty: Survey and research potentials. European Journal of Operational Research 165:289–306

94. Herroelen WS, De Reyck B, Demeulemeester EL (1998) Resource-constrained project scheduling: A survey of recent developments. Computers and Operations Research 25:279–302

95. Herroelen WS, Demeulemeester EL, Van Dommelen P (1996) An optimal recursive search procedure for the deterministic unconstrained max-NPV project scheduling problem. Research Report 9603, University of Leuven

96. Herroelen WS, Van Dommelen P, Demeulemeester EL (1997) Project network models with discounted cash flows: A guided tour through recent developments. European Journal of Operational Research 100:97–121

97. Hertz A, Taillard E, De Werra D (2003) Tabu search. In: Aarts E, Lenstra JK (eds) Local Search in Combinatorial Optimization. Princeton University Press, Princeton, pp 121–136

98. Hiriart-Urruty JB, Lemaréchal C (1993) Convex Analysis and Minimization Algorithms I. Springer, Berlin

99. Horst R, Tuy H (1996) Global Optimization: Deterministic Approaches. Springer, Berlin

100. Icmeli O, Erengüç SS (1996) A branch and bound procedure for the resource-constrained project scheduling problem with discounted cash flows. Management Science 42:1395–1408

101. Icmeli O, Erengüç SS, Zappe CJ (1993) Project scheduling problems: A survey. International Journal of Operations and Production Management 13:80–91

102. Igelmund G, Radermacher FJ (1983) Preselective strategies for the optimization of stochastic project networks under resource constraints. Networks 13:1–28

103. Jacoby SLS, Kowalik JS, Pizzo JT (1972) Iterative Methods for Nonlinear Optimization Problems. Prentice Hall, Englewood Cliffs

104. Kaerkes R, Leipholz B (1977) Generalized network functions in flow networks. Operations Research Verfahren 27:225–273

105. Kallrath J (2002) Planning and scheduling in the process industry. OR Spectrum 24:219–250

106. Kamburowski J (1990) Maximizing the project net present value in activity networks under generalized precedence relations. In: Proceedings of 21st DSI Annual Meeting, San Diego, pp 748–750

107. Keeling R (2000) Project Management: An International Perspective. Macmillan, Basingstoke

108. Kelley JE (1961) Critical path planning and scheduling: Mathematical basis. Operations Research 9:296–320

109. Kelley JE (1963) The critical-path method: Resource planning and scheduling. In: Muth JF, Thompson GL (eds) Industrial Scheduling. Prentice Hall, Englewood Cliffs, pp 347–365

110. Kerzner H (2003) Project Management: A Systems Approach to Planning, Scheduling, and Controlling. Holt, Rinehart, and Winston, New York

111. Kimms A (2001a) Mathematical Programming and Financial Objectives for Scheduling Projects. Kluwer, Boston

112. Kimms A (2001b) Maximizing the net present value of a project under resource constraints using a Lagrangian relaxation based heuristic with tight upper bounds. Annals of Operations Research 102:221–236

113. Kiwiel KC (1986) A linearization method for minimizing certain quasidifferentiable functions. In: Demyanov VF, Dixon LCW (eds) Quasidifferential Calculus. North-Holland, Amsterdam, pp 85–94

114. Klein R (2000) Scheduling of Resource-Constrained Projects. Kluwer, Boston

115. Klein R, Scholl A (1998) Computing lower bounds by destructive improvement: An application to resource-constrained project scheduling. European Journal of Operational Research 112:322–346

116. Klein R, Scholl A (2000) Scattered branch and bound. Central European Journal of Operational Research 7:177–201

117. Knuth DE (1998) Sorting and Searching, The Art of Computer Programming Vol 3. Addison-Wesley, Reading

118. Kolisch R (1995) Project Scheduling under Resource Constraints: Efficient Heuristics for Several Problem Classes. Physica, Heidelberg

119. Kolisch R (1996) Serial and parallel resource-constrained project scheduling methods revisited: Theory and computation. European Journal of Operational Research 90:320–333

120. Kolisch R (1997) Investitionsplanung in Netzwerken. Zeitschrift für Betriebswirtschaft 67:1057–1072

121. Kolisch R (2000) Integrated scheduling, assembly area-, and part-assignment for large scale make-to-order assemblies. International Journal of Production Economics 64:127–141

122. Kolisch R (2001a) Entwicklungen und Anwendungen in der Projektplanung: Ein Überblick. Betriebswirtschaftliche Forschung und Praxis 2001:212–226

123. Kolisch R (2001b) Make-to-Order Assembly Management. Springer, Berlin

124. Kolisch R, Hartmann S (1999) Heuristic algorithms for the resource-constrained project scheduling problem: Classification and computational analysis. In: Węglarz J (ed) Project Scheduling: Recent Models, Algorithms and Applications. Kluwer, Boston, pp 147–178

125. Kolisch R, Heß K (2000) Efficient methods for scheduling make-to-order assemblies under resource, assembly area, and part availability constraints. International Journal of Production Research 38:207–228

126. Kolisch R, Padman R (2001) An integrated survey of project scheduling. Omega 29:249–272

127. Kolisch R, Schwindt C, Sprecher A (1999) Benchmark instances for project scheduling problems. In: Węglarz J (ed) Project Scheduling: Recent Models, Algorithms and Applications. Kluwer, Boston, pp 197–212

128. Kondili E, Pantelides CC, Sargent RWH (1993) A general algorithm for short-term scheduling of batch operations: I. MILP formulation. Computers and Chemical Engineering 17:211–227

129. Laborie P (2003) Algorithms for propagating resource constraints in AI planning and scheduling: Existing approaches and new results. Artificial Intelligence 143:151–188

130. Lambrecht MR, Vanderveken H (1979) Production scheduling and sequencing for multi-stage production systems. OR Spektrum 1:103–114

131. Laue HJ (1968) Efficient methods for the allocation of resources in project networks. Unternehmensforschung 12:133–143

132. Lawler EL (1976) Combinatorial Optimization: Networks and Matroids. Holt, Rinehart, and Winston, New York

133. Leus R, Herroelen WS (2004) Stability and resource allocation in project scheduling. IIE Transactions 36:667–682

134. Levy FK, Thompson GL, Wiest JD (1963) Multi-ship multi-shop workload smoothing program. Naval Research Logistics Quarterly 9:37–44

135. Lewis JP (1998) Mastering Project Management: Applying Advanced Concepts of Systems Thinking, Control and Evaluation, Resource Allocation. McGraw-Hill, New York

136. Lopez P, Erschler J, Esquirol P (1992) Ordonnancement de tâches sous contraintes: Une approche énergétique. RAIRO Automatique, Productique, Informatique Industrielle 26:453–481

137. Meredith JR, Mantel SJ (2002) Project Management: A Managerial Approach. John Wiley and Sons, New York

138. Moder JJ, Phillips CR (1964) Project Management with CPM and PERT. Van Nostrand Reinhold Company, New York

139. Möhring RH (1984) Minimizing costs of resource requirements in project networks subject to a fixed completion time. Operations Research 32:89–120

140. Möhring RH (1985) Algorithmic aspects of comparability graphs and interval graphs. In: Rival I (ed) Graphs and Orders. D. Reidel Publishing Company, Dordrecht, pp 41–101

141. Möhring RH (1989) Computationally tractable classes of ordered sets. In: Rival I (ed) Algorithms and Order. Kluwer, Dordrecht, pp 105–193

142. Möhring RH (2000) Scheduling under uncertainty: Optimizing against a randomizing adversary. In: Jansen K, Khuller S (eds) Approximation Algorithms for Combinatorial Optimization: Third International Workshop (APPROX 2000), Lecture Notes in Computer Science Vol 1913. Springer, Berlin, pp 15–26

143. Möhring RH, Schulz AS, Stork F, Uetz M (2001) On project scheduling with irregular starting time costs. Operations Research Letters 28:149–154

144. Möhring RH, Schulz AS, Stork F, Uetz M (2003) Solving project scheduling problems by minimum cut computations. Management Science 49:330–350

145. Möhring RH, Skutella M, Stork F (2004) Scheduling with AND/OR precedence constraints. SIAM Journal on Discrete Mathematics 33:393–415

146. Nägler G, Schönherr S (1989) Resource allocation in a network model: The LEINET system. In: Słowiński R, Węglarz J (eds) Advances in Project Scheduling. Elsevier, Amsterdam, pp 327–354

147. Nahmias S (1997) Production and Operations Analysis. Irwin, Homewood

148. Nesterov Y, Nemirovskii A (1994) Interior-Point Polynomial Algorithms in Convex Programming. Society for Industrial and Applied Mathematics, Philadelphia

149. Neumann K (1999a) A heuristic procedure for constructing an activity-on-arc project network. In: Gaul W, Schader M (eds) Mathematische Methoden der Wirtschaftswissenschaften. Physica, Heidelberg, pp 328–336

150. Neumann K (1999b) Scheduling of projects with stochastic evolution structure. In: Węglarz J (ed) Project Scheduling: Recent Models, Algorithms and Applications. Kluwer, Boston, pp 309–332

151. Neumann K, Schwindt C (1997) Activity-on-node networks with minimal and maximal time lags and their application to make-to-order production. OR Spektrum 19:205–217

152. Neumann K, Schwindt C (1998) A capacitated hierarchical approach to make-to-order production. European Journal of Automation 32:397–413

153. Neumann K, Schwindt C (2002) Project scheduling with inventory constraints. Mathematical Methods of Operations Research 56:513–533

154. Neumann K, Zhan J (1995) Heuristics for the minimum project-duration problem with minimal and maximal time lags under fixed resource constraints. Journal of Intelligent Manufacturing 6:145–154

155. Neumann K, Zimmermann J (1999a) Methods for resource-constrained project scheduling with regular and nonregular objective functions and schedule-dependent time windows. In: Węglarz J (ed) Project Scheduling: Recent Models, Algorithms and Applications. Kluwer, Boston, pp 261–287

156. Neumann K, Zimmermann J (1999b) Resource levelling for projects with schedule-dependent time windows. European Journal of Operational Research 117:591–605

157. Neumann K, Zimmermann J (2000) Procedures for resource levelling and net present value problems in project scheduling with general temporal and resource constraints. European Journal of Operational Research 127:425–443

158. Neumann K, Zimmermann J (2002) Exact and truncated branch-and-bound procedures for resource-constrained project scheduling with discounted cash flows and general temporal constraints. Central European Journal of Operations Research 10:357–380

159. Neumann K, Nübel H, Schwindt C (2000) Active and stable project scheduling. Mathematical Methods of Operations Research 52:441–465

160. Neumann K, Schwindt C, Trautmann N (2001) Short-term planning of batch plants in process industries. In: Kischka P, Leopold-Wildburger U, Möhring RH, Radermacher FJ (eds) Models, Methods and Decision Support in Management. Physica, Heidelberg, pp 211–226

161. Neumann K, Schwindt C, Trautmann N (2002) Advanced production scheduling for batch plants in process industries. OR Spectrum 24:251–279

162. Neumann K, Schwindt C, Trautmann N (2005) Scheduling of continuous and discontinuous material flows with intermediate storage restrictions. European Journal of Operational Research 165:495–509

163. Neumann K, Schwindt C, Zimmermann J (2003a) Order-based neighborhoods for project scheduling with nonregular objective functions. European Journal of Operational Research 149:325–343

164. Neumann K, Schwindt C, Zimmermann J (2003b) Project Scheduling with Time Windows and Scarce Resources. Springer, Berlin

165. Nübel H (1999) A branch-and-bound procedure for the resource investment problem subject to temporal constraints. Report WIOR-574, University of Karlsruhe

166. Özdamar L, Ulusoy G (1995) A survey on the resource-constrained project scheduling problem. IIE Transactions 27:574–586

167. Papadimitriou CH, Steiglitz K (1998) Combinatorial Optimization: Algorithms and Complexity. Dover, Mineola

168. Patterson JH, Słowiński R, Talbot FB, Węglarz J (1989) An algorithm for a general class of precedence and resource constrained project scheduling problems. In: Słowiński R, Węglarz J (eds) Advances in Project Scheduling. Elsevier, Amsterdam, pp 3–28

169. Pinto JK, ed (1998) Project Management Handbook. Jossey-Bass Publishers, San Francisco

170. Pinto M, Grossmann IE (1995) A continuous time mixed integer linear programming model for short term scheduling of multistage batch plants. Industrial Engineering Chemistry Research 34:3037–3051

171. Pritsker AAB, Watters LJ, Wolfe PM (1969) Multi-project scheduling with limited resources. Management Science 16:93–108

172. Radermacher FJ (1978) Kapazitätsoptimierung in Netzplänen, Mathematical Systems in Economics Vol 40. Anton Hain, Meisenheim am Glan

173. Radermacher FJ (1985) Scheduling of project networks. Annals of Operations Research 4:227–252

174. Rockafellar RT (1998) Network Flows and Monotropic Optimization. Athena Scientific, Belmont

175. Roy B (1962) Graphes et ordonnancement In: Algan M, Eddison RT, Gillis PP, Castañe Ortega JM, Roy B, Viggiani S (eds) metra No. 1, Série spéciale. METRA Paris pp 83–125

176. Roy B (1964) Physionomie et traitement des problèmes d'ordonnancement In: Carré D, Darnaut P, Guitard P, Nghiem P, Pacaud P, de Rosinski J, Roy B, Sandier G (eds) Les Problèmes d'Ordonnancement. Dunod Paris pp 1–18

177. Russell AH (1970) Cash flows in networks. Management Science 16:357–373

178. Sauer J, Suelmann G, Appelrath HJ (1998) Multi-site scheduling with fuzzy concepts. International Journal of Approximate Reasoning 19:145–160

179. Schirmer A (1998) Project Scheduling with Scarce Resources: Models, Methods and Applications. Dr. Kovač, Hamburg

180. Schneeweiß C (1995) Hierarchical structures in organisations: A conceptual framework. European Journal of Operational Research 86:4–31

181. Schneeweiß C (2003) Distributed Decision Making. Springer, Berlin

182. Scholl A (2001) Robuste Planung und Optimierung. Physica, Heidelberg

183. Scholtes S (1990) On Convex Bodies and Some Applications to Optimization. Anton Hain Meisenheim, Frankfurt

184. Schwiegelshohn U, Thiele L (1999) Dynamic min-max problems. Discrete Event Dynamic Systems 9:111–134

185. Schwindt C (1998a) A branch-and-bound algorithm for the resource-constrained project duration problem subject to temporal constraints. Report WIOR-544, University of Karlsruhe

186. Schwindt C (1998b) Generation of resource-constrained project scheduling problems subject to temporal constraints. Report WIOR-543, University of Karlsruhe

187. Schwindt C (1998c) Verfahren zur Lösung des ressourcenbeschränkten Projektdauerminimierungsproblems mit planungsabhängigen Zeitfenstern. Shaker, Aachen

188. Schwindt C (1999) A branch-and-bound algorithm for the project duration problem subject to temporal and cumulative resource constraints. In: Proceedings of the International Conference on Industrial Engineering and Production Management (IEPM '99), Glasgow, pp 515–522

189. Schwindt C (2000a) A branch-and-bound algorithm for the capital-rationed net present value problem. In: Abstracts of the 17th European Conference on Operational Research (EURO XVII), Budapest, p 89

190. Schwindt C (2000b) Local search for project scheduling with convex objective functions. In: The Seventh International Workshop on Project Management and Scheduling (PMS 2000), Osnabrück, pp 239–241

191. Schwindt C (2000c) Minimizing earliness-tardiness costs of resource-constrained projects. In: Inderfurth K, Schwödiauer G, Domschke W, Juhnke F, Klein-

schmidt P, Wäscher G (eds) Operations Research Proceedings 1999. Springer, Berlin, pp 402–407

192. Schwindt C (2001) Solution procedures for production planning and detailed scheduling in process industries. In: Proceedings of the International Conference on Industrial Engineering and Production Management (IEPM '01), Québec, pp 271–280

193. Schwindt C (2002) Scheduling of continuous production in process industries. In: The Eighth International Workshop on Project Management and Scheduling (PMS 2002), Valencia, pp 314–317

194. Schwindt C, Trautmann N (2000) Batch scheduling in process industries: An application of resource-constrained project scheduling. OR Spektrum 22:501–524

195. Schwindt C, Trautmann N (2002) Storage problems in batch scheduling. In: Chamoni P, Leisten R, Martin A, Minnemann J, Stadtler H (eds) Operations Research Proceedings 2001. Springer, Berlin, pp 213–218

196. Schwindt C, Zimmermann J (2001) A steepest ascent approach to maximizing the net present value of projects. Mathematical Methods of Operations Research 53:435–450

197. Schwindt C, Zimmermann J (2002) Parametrische Optimierung als Instrument zur Bewertung von Investitionsprojekten. Zeitschrift für Betriebswirtschaft 72:593–617

198. Selle T (1999) Lower bounds for project scheduling problems with renewable and cumulative resources. Report WIOR-573, University of Karlsruhe

199. Selle T, Zimmermann J (2003) A bidirectional heuristic for maximizing the net present value of large-scale projects subject to limited resources. Naval Research Logistics 50:130–148

200. Serafini P, Speranza MG (1994a) A decomposition approach for a resource-constrained project scheduling problem. European Journal of Operational Research 75:112–135

201. Serafini P, Speranza MG (1994b) A decomposition approach in a DSS for a resource-constrained project scheduling problem. European Journal of Operational Research 79:208–219

202. Shapiro A (1990) On concepts of directional differentiability. Journal of Optimization Theory and Applications 66:477–487

203. Shewchuk JP, Chang TC (1995) Resource-constrained job scheduling with recyclable resources. European Journal of Operational Research 81:364–375

204. Shor NZ (1998) Nondifferentiable Optimization and Polynomial Problems. Kluwer, Boston

205. Simmons DM (1975) Nonlinear Programming for Operations Research. Prentice Hall, Englewood Cliffs

206. Słowiński R (1981) Multiobjective network scheduling with efficient use of renewable and nonrenewable resources. European Journal of Operational Research 7:265–273

207. Smith-Daniels DE, Padman R, Smith-Daniels VL (1996) Heuristic scheduling of capital constrained projects. Journal of Operations Management 14:241–254

208. Söhner V (1995) Hierarchisch integrierte Produktionsplanung und -steuerung. Physica, Heidelberg

209. Sourd F, Rogerie J (2005) Continuous filling and emptying of storage systems in constraint-based scheduling. European Journal of Operational Research 165:510–524

210. Sprecher A, Drexl A (1998) Multi-mode resource-constrained project scheduling by a simple, general and powerful sequencing algorithm. European Journal of Operational Research 107:431–450

211. Sprecher A, Kolisch R, Drexl A (1995) Semi-active, active, and nondelay schedules for the resource-constrained project scheduling problem. European Journal of Operational Research 80:94–102

212. Stork F (2001) Stochastic Resource-Constrained Project Scheduling. PhD Thesis, Technical University of Berlin
http://edocs.tu-berlin.de/diss/2001/stork_frederik.htm

213. Stork F, Uetz M (2005) On the generation of circuits and minimal forbidden sets. Mathematical Programming, Series A, to appear

214. Sydsæter K, Strøm A, Berck P (1999) Economist's Mathematical Manual. Springer, Berlin

215. Tavares LV (1995) A review on the contributions of Operational Research to project management. In: Proceedings of the 14th European Conference on Operational Research, Jerusalem, pp 67–82

216. Tempelmeier H, Derstroff M (1996) A Lagrangean-based heuristic for dynamic multilevel multiitem constrained lotsizing with setup times. Management Science 42:738–757

217. Trautmann N (2001a) Anlagenbelegungsplanung in der Prozessindustrie. Gabler, Wiesbaden

218. Trautmann N (2001b) Calenders in project scheduling. In: Fleischmann B, Lasch R, Derigs U, Domschke W, Rieder U (eds) Operations Research Proceedings 2000. Springer, Berlin, pp 388–392

219. Trotter WT (1992) Combinatorics and Partially Ordered Sets: Dimension Theory. Johns Hopkins University Press, Baltimore

220. Turner JR (1999) The Handbook of Project-Based Management. McGraw-Hill, London

221. Tuy H (1995) D.C. optimization: Theory, methods and algorithms. In: Horst R, Pardalos PM (eds) Handbook of Global Optimization. Kluwer, Dordrecht, pp 149–216

222. Uetz M (2002) Algorithms for Deterministic and Stochastic Scheduling. Cuvillier, Göttingen

223. Uetz M (2003) When greediness fails: Examples from stochastic scheduling. Operations Research Letters 31:413–419

224. Vanhoucke M, Demeulemeester EL, Herroelen WS (2001) An exact procedure for the resource-constrained weighted earliness-tardiness project scheduling problem. Annals of Operations Research 102:179–196

225. Verhines DR (1963) Optimum scheduling of limited resources. Chemical Engineering Progress 59:65–67

226. Wagelmans A, van Hoesel S, Kolen A (1992) Economic lot sizing: An $\mathcal{O}(n \log n)$ algorithm that runs in linear time in the Wagner-Whitin case. Operations Research 40:145–156

227. Węglarz J (1980) On certain models of resource allocation problems. Kybernetes 9:61–65

228. Westenberger H, Kallrath J (1995) Formulation of a job shop problem in process industry. Unpublished working paper, Bayer AG, Leverkusen and BASF AG, Ludwigshafen
229. Wiest JD (1963) The Scheduling of Large Projects with Limited Resources. Unpublished PhD Thesis, Carnegie Institute of Technology, Pittsburgh
230. Younis MA, Saad B (1996) Optimal resource leveling of multi-resource projects. Computers and Industrial Engineering 31:1–4
231. Zhan J (1992) Calendarization of time-planning in MPM networks. ZOR – Methods and Models of Operational Research 36:423–438
232. Zheng S, Sun F (1999) Some simultaneous iterations for finding all zeros of a polynomial with high order convergence. Applied Mathematics and Computation 99:233–240
233. Zimmermann J (2001a) Ablauforientiertes Projektmanagement: Modelle, Verfahren und Anwendungen. Gabler, Wiesbaden
234. Zimmermann J (2001b) Personal communication
235. Zimmermann J, Schwindt C (2002) Parametric optimization for the evaluation of investment projects. In: The Eighth International Workshop on Project Management and Scheduling (PMS 2002), Valencia, pp 378–382
236. Zoutendijk G (1960) Methods of Feasible Directions. Elsevier, Amsterdam
237. Zwick U, Paterson M (1996) The complexity of mean payoff games on graphs. Theoretical Computer Science 158:343–359

List of Symbols

Miscellany

$:=$	Equal by definition
$\square$	End of proof
$\lceil x \rceil$	Smallest integer greater than or equal to x
$(x)^+$	Maximum of 0 and x

Sets

$\emptyset$	Empty set
$[a, b[$	Half open interval $\{x \in \mathbb{R} \mid a \leq x < b\}$
$|X|$	Cardinality of finite set X
$B_\varepsilon(S)$	Ball of radius ε around S in $\mathbb{R}^{n+2}$
ℓ	Line segment in $\mathbb{R}^{n+2}$
$\mathbb{N}$	Set of all positive integers
$\mathcal{O}$	Landau's symbol
$\mathbb{P}(X)$	Power set of set X
$\mathbb{R}$	Set of all real numbers
$\mathbb{R}^n$	Set of all n-tuples of real numbers
$\mathbb{R}_{\geq 0}$	Set of all nonnegative real numbers
$X \subset Y$	X is proper subset of Y
$X \subseteq Y$	X is subset of Y
$X \setminus Y$	Difference of sets X and Y
$X \cap Y$	Intersection of sets X and Y
$X \cup Y$	Union of sets X and Y
$\mathbb{Z}$	Set of all integers
$\mathbb{Z}_{\geq 0}$	Set of all nonnegative integers

Projects and project activities

b_i	Activity calendar for activity i
b_{ij}	Time lag calendar for arc (i, j)
d_{ij}^{max}	Maximum time lag between the starts of activities i and j
d_{ij}^{min}	Minimum time lag between the starts of activities i and j
$\bar{d}$	Prescribed maximum project duration

m_i	Execution mode for activity i
$\mathcal{M}_i$	Set of alternative execution modes for activity i
p_i	Duration (processing time) of activity i
p_{im_i}	Duration of activity i in execution mode m_i
ϑ_{ij}^k	Sequence-dependent changeover time from activity i to activity j on resource k
V	Set of all activities
$V^a \subset V$	Set of all real activities
$V^e \subseteq V$	Set of all fictitious activities (events)
V_k^a	Set of all real activities using renewable resource k
V_k^{e-}	Set of all events depleting cumulative resource k
V_k^{e+}	Set of all events replenishing cumulative resource k

Directed graphs and networks

D	Distance matrix for project network N
d_{ij}	Length of a longest directed path (distance) from node i to node j in project network N
δ_{ij}	Weight of arc (i,j)
$\delta_{im_ijm_j}$	Weight of arc (i,j) for mode combination (m_i, m_j)
E	Arc set of project network N
$G = (V, E)$	Directed graph with node set V and arc set E
$G = (V, E, \delta)$	Weighted directed graph (network) with node set V, arc set E, and vector δ of arc weights
(i, j)	Arc with initial node i and terminal node j
$m = |E|$	Number of arcs in project network N
$n + 2 = |V|$	Number of nodes in project network N
N	Project network
$Pred(i)$	Set of all direct predecessors of node $i \in V$
$Succ(i)$	Set of all direct successors of node $i \in V$
V	Node set of project network N

Resources

F	Forbidden set of activities
$\mathcal{F}$	Set of all minimal forbidden sets
$\mathcal{F}_k^+$	Set of all minimal k-surplus sets
$\mathcal{F}_k^-$	Set of all minimal k-shortage sets
r_{ik}	Requirement of activity i for resource k
r_{ikm_i}	Requirement of activity i for resource k in execution mode m_i
$r_k(S, \cdot)$	Loading profile for resource k given schedule S
R_k	Capacity of renewable resource k or availability of nonrenewable resource k
$\underline{R}_k$	Safety stock of cumulative resource k
$\overline{R}_k$	Storage capacity of cumulative resource k
$\mathcal{R}^\gamma$	Set of all (discrete) cumulative resources
$\widetilde{\mathcal{R}}^\gamma$	Set of all continuous cumulative resources
$\mathcal{R}^\nu$	Set of all nonrenewable resources
$\mathcal{R}^\rho$	Set of all renewable resources

Objective functions

α	Continuous interest rate
c_i^f	Cash flow associated with the start of activity i
c_k	Per unit cost for resource k
$\partial^-\bar{f}/\partial S_i(S)$	Left-hand S_i-derivative of $\bar{f}$ at S
$\partial^+\bar{f}/\partial S_i(S)$	Right-hand S_i-derivative of $\bar{f}$ at S
$f : S_T \to \mathbb{R}$	Objective function to be minimized
$\bar{f} : C \to \mathbb{R}$	Continuation of objective function f
$\varphi : S_T \to X$	C^1-diffeomorphism
$\nabla \bar{f}(S)$	Derivative of $\bar{f}$ at S
$\nabla^-\bar{f}(S)$	Left-hand derivative of $\bar{f}$ at S
$\nabla^+\bar{f}(S)$	Right-hand derivative of $\bar{f}$ at S
$d\bar{f}|_S(z)$	Directional derivative of $\bar{f}$ at S in direction z
w_i	Weight of activity i
w_i^e, w_i^t	Earliness and tardiness costs for activity i per unit time
w_i^f	Weight of free floats for activity i

Relations and preorders

$cr(\theta)$	Covering relation of strict order θ
$D(\rho)$	Distance matrix for relation network $N(\rho)$
d_{ij}^ρ	Distance from node i to node j in relation network $N(\rho)$
δ_{ij}^ρ	Weight of arc (i,j) in relation network $N(\rho)$
$G(\theta)$	Precedence graph of strict order θ
$\mathcal{MFR}$	Set of all $\subseteq$-minimal feasible relations
$\min \mathcal{M}$	Minimal point of ordered set $(\mathcal{M}, \le)$ with $\mathcal{M} \subseteq \mathbb{R}^{n+2}$
$N(\rho)$	Relation network belonging to relation ρ
$Pred^\theta(i)$	Set of all predecessors of i in preorder θ
ρ, ϱ	Relation in set V
$\mathcal{SIO}$	Set of all schedule-induced strict orders in set V^a
$\mathcal{SIP}$	Set of all schedule-induced reflexive preorders in set V^e
$S_T(\rho)$	Relation polytope of relation ρ
$S_T^=(\theta)$	Equal-preorder set of preorder θ
$tr(\rho)$	Transitive hull of relation ρ
θ	Strict order in set V^a or reflexive preorder in set V^e
$\theta(S)$	Schedule-induced preorder
$\Theta(D)$	Strict order in set V^a or reflexive preorder in set V^e induced by distance matrix D

Schedules

$\mathcal{AS}$	Set of active schedules
ES	Earliest schedule
LS	Latest schedule
$\mathcal{PSS}$	Set of all pseudostable schedules
$\mathcal{QAS}$	Set of all quasiactive schedules
$\mathcal{QSS}$	Set of all quasistable schedules
S	Schedule
$\mathcal{S}$	Set of all feasible schedules

$\mathcal{S}_C$	Set of all resource-feasible schedules with respect to cumulative resources
$\mathcal{S}_R$	Set of all resource-feasible schedules with respect to renewable resources
$\mathcal{S}_T$	Set of all time-feasible schedules
$\mathcal{SS}$	Set of all stable schedules

Temporal scheduling

C_i	Completion time of activity i
d_{ij}	Induced minimum time lag between the starts of activities i and j
EC_i	Earliest completion time of activity i
EFF_i	Early free float of activity i
ES_i	Earliest start time of activity i
LC_i	Latest completion time of activity i
LFF_i	Late free float of activity i
LS_i	Latest start time of activity i
S_i	Start time of activity i
TF_i	Total float of activity i

Resource allocation

A	Maximal feasible set
$\mathcal{A}(S,t)$	Active set at time t given schedule S
B	Minimal delaying alternative
$\mathcal{B}$	Set of all minimal delaying alternatives
C	Set of all activities scheduled
C'	Set of all activities shifted
$\mathcal{C}$	Set of candidate schedules
$\mathcal{D}_j$	Set of all tentative start times for activity j (decision set)
G	Spanning forest of project network N with arc set E_G
$g(z)$	Directional derivative of $\bar{f}$ at iterate S in direction z
lb	Lower bound on minimum objective function
$\mathcal{P}$	Search space
σ	Stepsize
u, v	Enumeration nodes
$w_k(a,b)$	Workload for renewable resource k in time interval $[a, b[$
x	Full mode assignment
$\underline{x}$	Partial mode assignment
z	Steepest descent direction

Index

Printing and Binding: Strauss GmbH, Mörlenbach